Pärttyli Rinne
Kant on Love

# Kantstudien-Ergänzungshefte

Im Auftrag der Kant-Gesellschaft
herausgegeben von
Manfred Baum, Bernd Dörflinger
und Heiner F. Klemme

Band 196

Pärttyli Rinne

Kant on Love

DE GRUYTER

ISBN 978-3-11-068521-3
e-ISBN (PDF) 978-3-11-054497-8
e-ISBN (EPUB) 978-3-11-054389-6
ISSN 0340-6059

Library of Congress Cataloging-in-Publication Data
A CIP catalog record for this book has been applied for at the Library of Congress.

Bibliographic information published by the Deutsche Nationalbibliothek
The Deutsche Nationalbibliothek lists this publication in the Deutsche Nationalbibliografie;
detailed bibliographic data are available in the Internet at http://dnb.dnb.de.

© 2019 Walter de Gruyter GmbH, Berlin/Boston
This volume is text- and page-identical with the hardback published in 2018.
Printing and binding: CPI books GmbH, Leck
♾ Printed on acid-free paper
Printed in Germany

www.degruyter.com

Acknowledgments

This book is based on the PhD thesis I wrote at the University of St Andrews between 2013 and 2016. These years were among the best of my life, and not only because of my research topic. Never before had I experienced such a sense of community and intellectual belonging as I did at the St Andrews Philosophy Department.

I am grateful to my supervisor, Professor Jens Timmermann, for all his advice. He provided me with the torch I held onto in seeking my way through the beautiful labyrinth of love in Kant. Because of Professor Timmermann, I was never completely in the dark. I am thankful for our discussions, for his careful criticism, and for his kindness and benevolence. I also wish to thank my second supervisors, Professors Marcia Baron and Sarah Broadie. Professor Baron's early feedback significantly improved my writing, and it makes me happy to think of all I've learned from Professor Broadie about love in ancient philosophy, and tacitly about wisdom in general.

I want to thank my Kantian peers in St Andrews for all their practical help, and for our endless informal exchanges, which are so important when one is formulating and trying out one's ideas: Stefano Lo Re, Leonard Randall, and Martin Sticker. I cherish our friendships. I also thank all my other fellow graduate students, as well as St Andrews Philosophy staff, for together creating a small, vibrant haven with a unique atmosphere so conducive to profound thought. I will not be wistful, but I will always carry St Andrews Philosophy in my heart.

I spent the spring of 2016 at the Humboldt University of Berlin, finalising my thesis, and I am grateful to my host, Professor Thomas Schmidt, for his hospitality and helpful comments on my research. I have also had the opportunity to discuss topics related to my work at various seminars, workshops and international conferences, and at the annual review sessions and the final oral examination at St Andrews. I thank the following people, who have clearly had an influence on this study: Martin Brecher, Alix Cohen, Rowan Cruft, Li Fan, John Haldane, Rae Langton (external examiner), Kate Moran, Barbara Sattler (internal examiner), Dieter Schönecker, Leslie Stevenson, Michael Walschots, and Günter Zöller.

I am grateful to the St Andrews & Stirling Graduate Programme in Philosophy for its financial support. I also wish to thank Johanna Wange, Project Editor at De Gruyter, Carolyn Benson (language polishing), and Florian Ruppenstein (Production Editor) for kindly helping to prepare the manuscript for publication.

Finally, I thank my family: my lovely wife Nora and our amazing twin sons Aarni and Aale. It is difficult for me to enumerate my gratitude to Nora. She is the spring of most of what is good in my life. I am grateful for her tireless support during the time it took me to write the book, for her sheer existence, and for the fact that we are together. The love I receive from her and the twins is beyond measure.

Contents

Introduction —— 1

1 Self-Love —— 18
1.1   Animal Mechanical Self-Love —— 20
1.2   The Middle Level of Self-Love —— 33
1.3   Self-Love and the Highest Good —— 48
1.4   Self-Love Persists on Three Levels —— 55

2 Sexual Love —— 57
2.1   Sexual Love and Love of Beauty —— 60
2.2   Narrow and Broad Sexual Love —— 68
2.2.1 Narrow Sexual Love —— 69
2.2.2 Broad Sexual Love —— 71
2.2.3 The Teleology of Sexual Love —— 77

3 Love of God —— 84
3.1   Love for God —— 86
3.2   God's Love —— 95
3.2.1 The End Account —— 96
3.2.2 The Ground Account —— 100
3.3   Is Love of God Self-Love? —— 105
3.4   The Ascent of Love of God —— 108

4 Love of Neighbour —— 110
4.1   The General Division Prior to *The Metaphysics of Morals* —— 112
4.2   Love of Neighbour in *The Metaphysics of Morals* —— 123
4.2.1 On the Feeling of Love —— 124
4.2.2 On Practical Love —— 130
4.3   The Feeling-Action-Cultivation Account —— 141

5 Love in Friendship —— 145
5.1   Love in Friendship Prior to *The Metaphysics of Morals* —— 146
5.2   Love in Friendship in *The Metaphysics of Morals* —— 153
5.2.1 Identifying the Love at Issue —— 154
5.2.2 Can We Bracket Love from Friendship? —— 158
5.3   Cosmopolitan Friendship: Love's Ascent Toward the Ideal Moral Community —— 162

Conclusion —— 167

Appendix: Explanatory Note on Fig. 8 —— 174

Bibliography —— 176

Index of Persons —— 183

Subject Index —— 185

Introduction

I

This work presents the first systematic, exegetical, and comprehensive study of the concept of love in the philosophy of Immanuel Kant. Love is often considered to be among the most important yet perplexing of all human phenomena, and Kant is generally thought to be among the greatest philosophers in the Western tradition. I thus find it remarkable that Kant's views on love have not previously been investigated in much depth, or with an outlook on the way the concept of love figures and operates within his philosophy as a whole.

My research will show that love is actually important to Kant's philosophy, at any rate a lot more important than commonly assumed. It may come as a surprise to see how often Kant thinks about love, how much he writes about it, and that he holds various philosophical views about it. In particular, an understanding of how the concept of love functions in Kant's practical philosophy is necessary for an overall understanding of his ethical project. Even though we might think otherwise at first glance, love plays an integral role in Kant's conception of human life.

Love is a complex and multifaceted concept, and Kant's philosophical ideas on love yield no exception to this fact. Not only are these ideas important for understanding Kant, I also think that *his views on love are interesting as such*. What the views are and how they fit together is the topic of the present volume. If one is generally open to learning from Kant, this book will hopefully show that it is also possible to learn from what he thought about love. The nature of my work is mostly interpretative, and in particular I will formulate two exegetical claims, which mark the core of the study. First, I hold that in Kant we can detect *a general division of love*, according to which love in general divides into love of benevolence [*Liebe des Wohlwollens*] and love of delight [*Liebe des Wohlgefallens*]. The general division of love in Kant is a key for understanding love in Kant. Second, I hold that by identifying various aspects of love in Kant, such as self-love, sexual love, love of God, love of neighbour, and love in friendship, and by studying the various things he says about the different aspects of love, we can detect *an ascent of love* from the strongest impulses of human nature to the highest ideals of morally deserved happiness. It is these two claims that will be clarified and defended during the course of the work.

II

There are of course reasons for the lacuna in previous research. In general, the study of Kant's moral philosophy or ethics, broadly construed, has tended to emphasise the foundations of moral philosophy as articulated in the *Groundwork of the Metaphysics of Morals* and the *Critique of Practical Reason*. Traditionally, fewer resources have been directed to research on Kant's last major contribution to moral philosophy, *The Metaphysics of Morals*, where love figures much more prominently than in the *Groundwork* or the *Critique of Practical Reason*. In the anglophone research community, the tendency to give less weight to *The Metaphysics of Morals* can also be at least partially explained by the fact that a reliable, complete translation of the entire work has only been made available in recent decades. The emphasis on the *Groundwork* in relation to *The Metaphysics of Morals* has tended to yield a picture of a 'cold' Kant, a picture of a philosopher who emphasises duty over everything else and is wary of, if not outright hostile towards, emotions or affective dispositions as part of the moral life.

When I have discussed my project with non-Kantian academic philosophers, I have often been met with surprise: '*Love* in Kant? Oh, I didn't know that Kant said anything at all about love! If he did, surely it must have been some kind of antithesis of love that he was really after…' And so on. Within the community of academic philosophers in general, Kant's views on love are clearly not well known. Within the circle of scholars working on Kant's ethics, however, this kind of picture no longer obtains, and as more attention has been given to the 'Doctrine of Virtue' in *The Metaphysics of Morals* and to Kant's anthropological works, we now have a much fuller, more balanced, and more comprehensive picture of the emotional life of the Kantian moral agent. We now know that the role of the 'natural', sensory-aesthetic part of the human cognitive apparatus as related to 'pure practical reason' or 'freedom' (to use Kant's own dualism) is much more complex and nuanced than commonly assumed by those not all that familiar with Kant's ethics. Thanks to the work of Kantian ethicists emphasising or defending the importance of emotive elements in Kant's moral philosophy, what we have been witnessing in the last thirty years or so is the emergence of a 'nicer' Kant, whose overall take on moral philosophy is 'kinder', 'warmer', or more humane than what reading merely the *Groundwork* might imply.

My work represents this 'warmer' school of Kantian ethics. However, even my kind of approach might appear too 'cold' for those who wish to ground ethics or moral norms in emotive dispositions, pain and pleasure, empathy or 'warm-heartedness', instinctive benevolence, or the feeling of love. The account of love in Kant that I seek is meant to be true to the foundations of Kant's moral thought and to the letter of his text, so that the picture I provide will be not only defensible but also exegetically balanced and accurate. For instance, even in the context of the 'nice' Kant presented here, the feeling of love can never be the objective foundation of morality. The foundation is pure practical reason and respect for the moral law.

I won't be talking much about what Kant could or should have thought about the problem of love; rather, I will systematically reconstruct the positions he did hold. My aim is to arrive at a general outline of the concept of love as it figures in my chosen target system, or in other words, in the propositional natural language 'data set' I wish to analyse. That is, I will be investigating how the word 'love' [*Liebe*] takes on different functions and meanings when it appears in various contexts within the philosophical writings of Kant.

This kind of approach has its limitations, to be sure, and I am not out to claim that Kant's conceptions of love simply sprang from pure reason in a historical vacuum. In the tradition of Western philosophy, investigations into love date back to the Presocratic Empedocles. In particular, the notion of *Eros* in Plato's *Symposium* has had an immense effect on subsequent European philosophy and culture. The connection between the concept of love and the notion of the *highest good*, which we will continue to see in Kant, originates from Plato. Besides Plato, another decisive factor contributing to how it was possible for someone to conceptualise love in 18th-century Prussia is the Christian religion, and especially the teachings of Jesus as they were preserved in the New Testament. It is not much of an exaggeration to assert that from a decidedly historical perspective, one cannot understand the context in which Kant writes about love without acknowledging the existence of at least two historical documents: the *Symposium* and the *Sermon on the Mount*.

It would be possible, and highly interesting, I think, to trace the historical genealogy of the concept of love from Plato to Kant, to consider the parallels and continuities between, for instance, the way love figures in Aristotle's and Kant's conceptions of friendship, to analyse the extent to which Kant's conceptualisations of love are indebted to, say, Augustine or Aquinas, or to his more immediate predecessors like the British moralists, or Leibniz, Wolff, or Baumgarten, or indeed to his Pietist upbringing. I would be especially inclined to point out (and this may be obvious to some) that the link between love and the highest good is common to both Platonism and Christianity, that this link is sustained through the Middle Ages in the Scholastic fusion of Plato, Aristotle, and Jesus, that it remains clearly visible in the British sentimentalists like Hutcheson, and that it influences Kant's construction of the regulative ideality of his ethical system as a whole. But this kind of historical, cultural and comparative approach is beyond the scope of my study.

The concept of love is scattered throughout Kant's massive corpus, and I will have enough work on my hands in just getting the exegesis right. Likewise, I will not enter the 'post-Kantian' domain and interpret my results in the light of later strands of German idealism; nor will I use my findings to engage with contemporary discussions in the philosophy of love. Although I believe that the approach and the general framework developed in this book can later be reworked and used to formulate a contemporary, post-Kantian philosophy of love, this is not my aim here. This study is very much Kant immanent.

As I mentioned above, Kant's conception of love has not been investigated comprehensively or in detail in the literature to date. This is not to say that there aren't any discussions of this topic, however. Since a key component of my argument concerns the novelty of my claims, I feel obliged to say at least something about how love has previously been analysed and discussed in the study of Kant. Therefore, I will now offer some general reflections on the state of previous research, and in doing this, I will refer to individual accounts only insofar as they are particularly representative of the points I wish to make.

The *Kant-Bibliographie 1945 – 1990* (Malter/Ruffing 1999), which aims to present a comprehensive bibliography of Kant-related academic writings from the period between the aforementioned years, lists some 9000 titles, 5 titles of which contain the word 'love' or '*Liebe*'. From this one can plausibly generalise that from 1945 to 1990 the 'love ratio' in Kant scholarship was approximately 1/1800. Things have changed in this regard, and in the last couple of decades in particular, research on love in Kant has grown to the point where at least one or two new papers on the topic are published each year. However, the total number of research articles in the field still only amounts to a good handful. There is no danger of drowning in the secondary literature.

I think it is possible to divide the existing research roughly into three categories. First, there are those accounts that engage with a specific aspect of love or discuss love within a particular work by Kant. These accounts yield partial knowledge, and when the discussions are sufficiently detailed and well argued, they greatly promote our understanding of love in Kant. Most of the research on love in Kant belongs more or less to this category. Examples of the first kind of approach include works by Marcia Baron (2009; 2013), Melissa Fahmy (2009; 2010), and Dieter Schönecker (2010; 2013), where the focus is the 'Doctrine of Virtue' of *The Metaphysics of Morals* or neighbourly love more generally. Second, there are accounts that mention 'love' in the title but do not actually provide an interpretation (in any significant detail) of what Kant had to say about the issues the title refers to (e.g. Miller 1985; Vanden Auweele 2014). Third, there are accounts that at least ostensibly aim to provide a more general outlook on the concept of love in Kant, or somehow claim or attempt to articulate general propositions about love in Kant (e.g. Streich 1924; Moors 2007; Schönecker 2010; Grenberg 2014). It is this third category that is actually the most interesting for the purposes of my work, since what I am after here is precisely a more general account of this kind. However, none of these previous discussions is anything close to a book-length monograph (the closest is Streich (1924)). They are not even articles dedicated solely to this issue, but rather propositions within papers, which pursue various general aims. I do not wish to come across as blaming these authors, nor am I suggesting that they should have done otherwise. What I am saying is that regarding the concept of love in Kant, the lacuna in the research is real.

III

Besides being generally exegetical in the sense that I interpret rather than evaluate, my approach has some other features that are worth highlighting. When I analyse the concept of love by investigating how the word 'love' appears in various propositional structures within a given text or set of texts, I analytically divide the concept of love into different aspects, according to how the word 'love' appears in different contexts. For example, a particularly high number of references to 'love' occur in contexts where Kant is speaking about the 'self' or 'one's own happiness', 'sexuality', 'God', 'neighbours' or 'other human beings', and 'friendship'. Analysed in these terms, the concept of love will consist at least of the aspects of 'self-love', 'sexual love', 'love of God', 'love of neighbour', and 'love in friendship'. Naturally, the interrelationships between the aspects are also very important. The aspects must be organised into a whole as rationally as possible. Just how this is to be accomplished, however, is impossible to say without first becoming well acquainted with the object of study. It is by comparing the aspects with each other that a general structure of the target concept can be approached. In this way, the concept is marked out by the instances of the word in the light of the aspects that have been identified, but in contrast with the mere word, the concept comprises a more comprehensive *propositional domain*, which includes all the aspects (or the proposition sets the aspects consist of). The comparative arrangement of the aspects should reveal the possible regularities or invariances between aspects, so that these invariances can then be said to belong generically to the concept. As such, dividing the concept of love into different sorts of love is of course nothing new (cf. e.g. Fromm 1957; Lewis 1963), but the divisions are not self-evident, and the particular way I make these divisions is novel in the study of Kant.

To clarify my approach further, I think my investigation into the concept of love in Kant must be called *quasi-inductive*. I do not claim to be analysing every possible aspect of love, let alone every single instance of the word 'love' in Kant's corpus. I am after a relatively robust yet manageable account of the concept of love, and I therefore limit the construction of the framework to those aspects that figure most prominently in Kant's philosophy. While the method is inductive in the sense that I gather textual data and make generalisations based on sample populations of the word 'love', my results are neither certain nor absolutely necessary. What I will say is merely that my division of the concept of love in Kant is one possible, plausible, or viable way of setting up a framework of analysis, and that while my results remain incomplete and hopefully subject to criticism, this study is nevertheless the first comprehensive *approximation* of what the concept of love in Kant's philosophy might look like.

To return to the basic claims made at the beginning of this introduction: what is the general division of love in Kant? As noted above, I identify five (or six) particularly important aspects of love to be discussed in the study: self-love, sexual love (and love of beauty), love of God, love of neighbour, and love in friendship. This list is not exhaustive and could be constructed otherwise, but these aspects do exist in Kant's writings, and within this framework of aspects Kant consistently uses or implies a division between two generic kinds of love: love of benevolence [*Liebe des Wohlwollens*] and love of delight [*Liebe des Wohlgefallens*]. These two loves appear *regularly*. In general, love of benevolence in Kant is *goodwill that is directed to the well-being of its object*. It can be weak or active, but the wishful or actively sought end of all instances of love of benevolence is that things go well for the object, no matter how minimal one's interest in the well-being of the object actually is. Love of delight, on the other hand, is *a pleasure taken in the physical or moral perfections, or even the sheer existence, of the object*. It does not carry an aim or an interest in the same way that love of benevolence does. Rather, it is a reaction or a response to an encounter with the object of love and its qualities. It is primarily a feeling aroused by the object in conjunction with the cognitive faculties or capacities of the agent.

In different contexts, love of benevolence and love of delight will vary according to their objects and the aspects of love to which they relate, so that they acquire somewhat different meanings and different functions depending on the aspect in question. However, I have found only one direct reference to a general division of love in Kant's published works, and the existence of the division must be shown and systematically reconstructed with various sources for each of the individual aspects. The direct remark is contained in the first part of *Religion within the Bounds of mere Reason*, where Kant discusses the origin of evil and, more precisely, its relation to self-love. Kant refers to a general division of love in a lengthy footnote: 'Like *love* in general, *self-love* too can be divided into love of *benevolence* and love of *delight* (BENEVOLENTIAE ET COMPLACENTIAE), and both (as is self-evident) must be rational.' (R, 6:45.22–25)[1] In the specific context of self-love, the general division of love basically means that we want things to go well for ourselves (love of benevolence), and that we are pleased (love of delight) when things do work out well for us (overall self-love is more complicated than this, and I discuss the complexity of the general division of self-love in ch. 1.2). The remark in the *Religion* also asserts that both love of benevolence and love of delight 'must be rational'. It is not entirely clear what this means, and whether the 'must' [*müssen*] should be understood as normative or as part of the description of the loves in question. It is also not clear whether the rationality that Kant is talking about here is meant to apply to love of benevolence and love of delight generally or merely (or specifically) *in the context of self-love*. We know from the passage itself and from several places elsewhere that Kant allows for the existence of inclination-based love of benevolence and pathological love of delight (see e.g. ch. 4.1). It is therefore clear that the phrase 'must be rational' cannot be taken to mean 'must be based on reason'. In the specific context of self-love, the rationality of love of benevolence for one-

---

[1] 'Wie *Liebe* überhaupt, so kann auch *Selbstliebe* in die des *Wohlwollens* und des *Wohlgefallens* (BENEVOLENTIAE ET COMPLACENTIAE) eingetheilt werden, und beide müssen (wie sich von selbst versteht) vernünftig sein.' It is difficult to find a satisfying translation that captures the parallelism, apparent in the German language, of the two basic forms of love. The love that is benevolence is, at its basis, willing well. It is commonly translated as 'good will', 'benevolence', or 'well-wishing'. Only the last, I believe, is implausible as a general strategy, since Kant often explicitly distinguishes between practical love of benevolence and mere wishing [*wünschen*]. The translation of *Liebe des Wohlgefallens* is trickier. *Wohlgefallen* consists of the adverbial conjunction *Wohl* ('well'), the prefix *ge*, which implies conjoining or linking together, and the verb *fallen*. So literally, it signifies something like 'fall together well'. The verb *gefallen* as such means to please or to delight, and *Wohlgefallen* is indeed sometimes translated as 'well-pleasedness'. This is quite possible as a translation, but it suggests satisfaction in an outcome, and while Kant sometimes uses *Wohlgefallen* this way, there is also in Kant an underlying sense of *Wohlgefallen*-love as an immediate sensory impulse of positive attraction, better captured by the English word 'delight' than 'well-pleased'. The English term 'good pleasure' has a biblical background and is also plausible, but like 'well-pleased' it perhaps obscures some of the immediateness and the attractive pull of *Wohlgefallen*. The English 'well-liking' (which is also used by some translators) is unwarranted, I think, for it actually means something like 'good physical condition'. *Wohlgefallen* is sometimes translated as 'satisfaction', sometimes as 'liking', and other times as 'approbation'. In the interest of remaining technically consistent, I use 'love of benevolence' and 'love of delight' in this study because I think that overall they best capture what Kant is talking about, even at the expense of the linguistic parallelism. My solution is naturally open to criticism.

self means that the inclination-based love of benevolence for oneself includes the successful long-term use of instrumental reasoning, i. e. it is rational as *prudence*. Rational love of delight for oneself, on the other hand, means either taking pleasure in one's own prudence or a kind of self-contentment that is based on one's respect for the moral law (in the last case the love of delight for oneself would be based on reason) (R, 6:45fn.; see ch. 1.2). However, if we interpret the words 'must be rational' as referring to love of benevolence and love of delight more generally, beyond the context of self-love, we may note that Kant never talks of mere non-rational animality in terms of the general division of love, and his usage of the terms seems to be limited to the context of rational beings. In this sense, love of benevolence and love of delight always *imply reason*, even when a token of benevolence or delight is pathological or based on inclination (ch. 1). This means that for Kant, love of benevolence and love of delight appear in rational creatures, entangled in their rational capacities. Some loves are derived from pure practical reason, like practical love of neighbour as the duty to be benevolent and beneficent to others (ch. 4). Similarly, love of God is an idea derived from moral reason (ch. 3). It is also the case that Kant's ethical writings involve a demand for *cultivation*, which ethically means the conscious striving to make one's cognitive apparatus more fit for what morality demands. This includes making use of one's feelings of love in the service of moral reason, and in this general sense the 'must be rational' can be interpreted as involving a demand to cultivate natural feelings of love of benevolence and love of delight in order to improve oneself morally (see esp. ch. 4.2; ch. 5).

Even though Kant's published works contain only one direct reference to love's being 'generally', 'as such', or 'all-in-all' [*überhaupt*] divided into love of benevolence and love of delight, his usage of the terms of the division runs from the early Herder lectures on ethics (1762–64) up to the late *Metaphysics of Morals* (1797) (see ch. 4). The first time the general division of love comes up explicitly in Kant's corpus is in the Collins notes on ethics, where 'all love' [*alle Liebe*] is divided into love of benevolence and love of delight (LE, 27:417.19–30).[2] There, the specific context is love of neighbour. With respect to neighbourly love, in the 1780s Kant also uses the distinction between *pathological* and *practical* love, which is especially familiar to readers of the *Groundwork*

---

[2] Because the manuscript of these notes is dated 1784/85, it is often thought that they are roughly contemporaneous with the *Groundwork of the Metaphysics of Morals*. However, as the notes are nearly identical to earlier ones ascribed to Kaehler, it has been established that the Collins notes in fact stem from the mid-1770s, which explains some of their features (like their emphasis on inclinations) compared to Kant's mature moral theory (see Denis/Sensen 2015, pp. 3–4; Naragon 2006, entry on 'Collins 2' in 'Moral Philosophy').

and the second *Critique*. The division of love of neighbour into love of benevolence and love of delight resurfaces in *The Metaphysics of Morals*, and in ch. 4 I investigate how the general division of love of neighbour can be mapped onto the more familiar pathological-practical distinction. If all the evidence is taken into account, including what Kant says about love in friendship (ch. 5), we can see that love for other human beings is generally divided into love of benevolence and love of delight, so that it is possible to love others benevolently 1) from inclination or 2) from reason, and to take delight in others 3) pathologically or 4) intellectually (see ch. 4.1; 4.3; 5.2.2; Appendix). From a religious perspective, God's love of benevolence is the ground of creation and moral duties, and his love of delight is (hopefully) an eventual favourable response to the sincere moral striving of the human being (ch. 3). How exactly the general division of love in Kant operates is to a great extent the main problem of the whole study, and my exegetical work is largely meant to corroborate the existence of the general division of love in Kant. The investigation of the general division of love reveals that the aspects of love are not isolated from each other but overlap to some extent and, taken together, form a dynamic and highly complex network of closely intertwined concepts. It should also be noted that *Kant's conception of love cannot be entirely reduced to the general division:* under the broad and complex rubric of self-love, we find the strongest, rudimental, non-rational impulses of human nature, namely those of self-preservation (love of life) and sexuality (sexual love in the narrow sense), which are discussed in terms of love but not grasped by the general division (ch. 1.1; 2.2.1).[3]

The second major claim of the study is that if we look at the different aspects of love alongside each other, we see an *ascent of love* from the natural, animal

---

[3] The distinction between love of benevolence and love of delight has its historical roots, of course, but as I already mentioned, in this work I cannot offer detailed historical comparisons or a proper account of the genealogy of this pair of concepts prior to Kant. A similar distinction appears, for instance, in Hutcheson's *An Inquiry into the Original of our Ideas of Beauty and Virtue*. There, Hutcheson divides love toward other rational agents into love of complacency and love of benevolence (see Hutcheson 1990 [1725], pp. 127 ff., Treatise II.2 – 5), which were translated into German as *Liebe aus Wohlgefallen* and *Liebe aus Wohlwollen*. Apparently, Kant owned the German translation of Hutcheson's work (I thank Michael Walschots for providing me with this information regarding the link between Hutcheson's and Kant's conceptions of love). More generally, *amor benevolentiae* and *amor complacentiae* belonged to standard Scholasticism and were discussed at length by Aquinas in the *Summa Theologiae*. In his highly intricate conceptual network of love, Aquinas includes a third general notion: *amor concupiscientiae*, or love as desire. Through Aquinas, the origin of the general division of love can be traced to Christian theology and Aristotle's concept of benevolence, especially in his discussions of *philia* in the *Nicomachean Ethics*.

impulses toward the highest moral-physical good in the form of cosmopolitan friendship – or so I will argue. Through the aspects of self-love, sexual love (and love of beauty), love of God, love of neighbour, and love in friendship, love is seen to condition important focal points in humanity's ascent from crude animality to morally deserved happiness. This picture of an ascent of love in Kant is obviously an interpretative reconstruction. Kant never systematised his discussions of love into a single whole, but the reconstruction I offer is nevertheless based firmly on what he said. It is made from the pieces Kant laid out, even though he himself never put all the pieces together. The picture contains both descriptive elements, which Kant uses to portray human nature, and prescriptive elements, which explicate notions of duty as they relate to love. The ascent concerns both the subjective level of an agent's character development and the communal level of the species. It also contains the regulative ideal of the highest good as the perfection that we humans ought to strive for. Overall, this view of an ascent of love is a conceptual classification or a hierarchy of the different kinds of love as they relate to creation, nature, and the highest moral-physical well-being. I call this picture *the ascent model of love in Kant*. The model consists generally of the various notions of love spelled out by Kant in his works, the interrelations between these notions, and the way in which the general division of love brings a relative unity to Kant's concept of love as a whole. The ascent model of love ultimately provides a panoptic view of the aspects of love discussed in this book. To make the claim more precisely, *the ascent model of love is a viable general model of love in Kant*.

For readers familiar with Plato's *Symposium* and the famous 'ladder of love' discussed in that work, the notion of an ascent model might ring a bell. Isn't Diotima's and Socrates' account of *Eros* in the latter half of the *Symposium* precisely an ascent model? Am I trying to argue that Kant is actually some kind of Platonist when it comes to love? The answer to the first question is: yes, the first ascent model of love in Western philosophy was formulated by Plato. To the second question, I'm inclined to answer *no*, but this must be carefully qualified to avoid misunderstandings. Naturally, if I am generally arguing that an ascent of love can be detected in Kant, there are going to be at least some structural similarities with Plato's (or Diotima's) account in the *Symposium*. With Plato, one begins by erotically loving the physical beauty of an individual young man, and the impulses of self-preservation and the sexual instinct likewise lie at the natural basis of Kant's conception of love. Echoing Plato's 'ladder metaphor', Kant often associates love with the notions of 'higher' and 'lower', and he continually talks about love in relation to our striving for perfection, or in relation to the cultivation of our faculties – where the ultimate end is obviously the complete highest good. What is clearly different, however, is that for Plato, the 'peak' of love's ascent is a kind of quasi-mystical vision, where the lover suddenly grasps the fundamental oneness of the idea of beauty, as if in a single, sweeping intuition. Now this is not a comparative study of love and the highest good in Plato and Kant; it is not even a study of the highest good in Kant, and I will not go into much detail in my comparison. Using Plato's ladder casually as a heuristic point of departure through which to elaborate on Kant's notion of love, I believe we can say that for Kant, the 'peak' we strive to reach is a more communal notion of love (conditioned by respect) in cosmopolitan friendship. Subjectively, it consists in *love for the moral law*, the full attainment of which signifies the absence of all contra-moral inclinations in the agent. Communally, or on the species level, it consists in the prevalence of benevolence (*Liebe des Wohlwollens*) and intellectual delight (*Liebe des Wohlgefallens*) in equal, reciprocal, and respectful human relationships that ultimately obtain throughout the planet. For Kant, the attainment of these highest modes of love is a gradual, laborious, and never-ending project of moral development. The Kantian agent is never 'rewarded' with the actualised, sweeping vision of the beautiful, radiant oneness described by Plato. For Kant, the ascent of love is less about subjectively coming to 'see' something and more about making moral progress in terms of love in one's interactions with other human beings. I am not saying that Plato's account cannot also be construed along these lines, but on the face of it at least, there are clear differences between the two. Plato's ladder of love emphasises the vision of the one as the highest good, whereas my ascent model of love in Kant emphasises the duty of moral progress.

IV

If I now briefly compare my perspective with the previous, more general propositions made on Kant and love, I believe the benefits and originality of my approach can be brought to light. First of all there is an older doctoral dissertation (55 pages) from Germany with the title *The Concept of Love According to Kant* [*Der Begriff der Liebe bei Kant*] (Streich 1924). Detlev Streich's main claim is that love can never be a moral motive for Kant. While this is strictly speaking true, Streich's coarse-grained position reduces love to a feeling, and he does not problematise his conception in the light of Section XII of the Introduction to the 'Doctrine of Virtue' (see Streich 1924, p. 38), where the feeling of love is described as a subjectively necessary predisposition for receptivity to duty. Streich does not discuss love of God or analyse the varieties of self-love; he only mentions sexual love in passing (Streich 1924, p. 46) and has a particularly one-sided view of love in friendship (he thinks it's merely burdensome [*lästig*])

(Streich 1924, pp. 42, 44). More recently, in an article on Kant and the biblical commandment of love, Martin Moors claims to 'formulate a general evaluation of Kant's philosophy of love' (Moors 2007, p. 266). However, Moors does not exactly provide this, and instead identifies six aspects 'with regard to Kant's *practical* concept of love' (Moors 2007, p. 266; emphasis added). Included in Moors's account are 'religious', 'theological', 'theonomical', 'ethical', 'voluntaristic', and 'anthropological' varieties of love. From my perspective, the first three would seem to come close to love of God, the fourth and fifth to love of neighbour, and the sixth to the notion of passion. (Moors 2007, p. 266) Moors does not discuss the varieties of self-love in significant detail; he says nothing about sexual love (and love of beauty), nor does he mention love in friendship. For Moors, Kant's notion of love as duty 'evaporates completely' (Moors 2007, p. 267), but he does not notice that an end of the duty of love is the happiness of others. From a more charitable perspective, Jeanine Grenberg has defended 'a Kantian understanding of the role of love in a well-lived human life', a love the conception of which is 'entirely moral' (Grenberg 2014, p. 211). Grenberg seems to effectively reduce 'Kant's notion of love' (Grenberg 2014, p. 220) to *love for the moral law* (see Grenberg 2014, pp. 218–219; cf. ch. 3.1 below). But I think a Kantian comprehension of love's role can hardly be reduced in this way, and besides love for the law, Grenberg provides no account of the many things Kant has to say about love.[4] The most interesting, detailed, and modest general proposal is that provided by Schönecker (2010) in the Introduction to his paper on love in Section XII of Kant's Introduction to the 'Doctrine of Virtue'. First of all, Schönecker makes clear that his list is not perfect, and the aim is only to demonstrate the complexity of the concept of love (Schönecker 2010, p. 135). Schönecker divides love in Kant into at least four contexts and twelve different meanings. The first context is *biological* and includes 1) sexual love, 2) self-love, and 3) love of life (self-preservation). The second context is the *duties of love*, where Schönecker identifies 4) *amor benevolentiae*, 5) heartfelt benevolence, 6) love for all human beings, 7) love as an aptitude to the inclination of beneficence, and 8) practical love. Schönecker's third context is *love in friendship*, where he distinguishes between 9) love as friendship with humanity, 10) the duty of benevolence as a friend of human beings, and 11) benevolence in wishes. The last context is love as a moral predisposition of *amor complacentiae*, which is 12) love of delight [*Liebe des Wohlgefallens*]. Without going into de-

---

4 Perhaps it would be more charitable to view Grenberg's account as a work in progress, because elsewhere she also discusses love in the Herder and Collins notes on ethics (see Grenberg 2015).

tail, Schönecker's analysis is very helpful, and from my perspective the only main contexts that are omitted from his account are love of God and love of beauty. As Schönecker does not ground his tentative analysis on the general division of love into love of benevolence and love of delight, it is understandable that he is not so sensitive to the operation of the division within the contexts he distinguishes. I think Schönecker's loves 4–11 can actually be viewed in terms of varying kinds or degrees of love of benevolence. Love of delight, on the other hand, is a broader notion than Schönecker acknowledges in his list; it also figures in self-love, love of God, and, arguably, in love in friendship. The context of biological or natural love can also be construed such that the non-rational impulses of love of life and sexual love (the latter of which, in the broad sense, involves more than just biology) belong to an umbrella concept of self-love, which further includes the general division of love on an actually rational level (see ch. 1).

V

This study is divided into 5 chapters according to the aspects of love on which I will focus. In these chapters, I analyse the operation of the general division of love in the relevant contexts and carve out the various building blocks that, taken together, form the ascent model of love in Kant. Kant's discussions of love take place mainly within moral philosophy, philosophy of religion, anthropology, and teleology, while he does not really talk about love in the framework of theoretical philosophy ('love' is not mentioned in the *Critique of Pure Reason*). Apart from the first *Critique*, my readings emphasise the main published works from the mature period, and I only use the lecture notes and minor writings as auxiliary tools of interpretation when helpful. My reading strategy is fairly consistent from chapter to chapter; while I tend to organise my discussions thematically around the problems related to the general division of love, I normally read Kant's works chronologically to appreciate the transformations his thoughts on love undergo over time. I believe that, like any great system or project of human thought, Kant's philosophy must be understood as a dynamic and cumulative endeavour, where more stable positions are found on which details are then built, while some positions change, wane, or become redefined, and the thought itself remains constantly at work, constantly in flux. Following the methodological advice of Ernst Cassirer, mine is not so much a study of 'puzzles' or 'apparent contradictions' in the 29 volumes of Kant's collected works but rather a study of the dynamic structure of a particular philosophical concept – a concept which a philosopher can only form gradually over the course of several decades of conceptual labour (see Cassirer 1981, pp. 1–2, cf. 137–138). Such a concept of love, while certainly not the only possible such concept, can nevertheless be very beautiful, and can perhaps help us more generally to understand what love is, how it arises, what it feels like, and what it requires from us rationally. *To understand love better* is the deeper, underlying aim that has resulted in this book.

In the first chapter, I offer a three-level interpretation of self-love in Kant. I argue that the concept of self-love can be divided according to ascending levels of rationality. I show that there is a low, arational, ground-level form of self-love that consists of the strongest animal impulses of human nature: love of life (self-preservation), sexual love and parenting (species preservation in the narrow sense), and instinctive sociality. I call this level 'animal mechanical self-love'. My analysis then turns to an actually rational level that I call the 'middle level' of self-love, where self-love is divided (in a very complex way) according to the general division of love into love of benevolence and love of delight. Lastly, I analyse self-love hypothetically, on an ideally rational level of infinite approximation towards the highest good. I argue that even in this infinite ascent an element of self-love persists. Overall, I thus argue for the *persistence of self-love* on three levels.

The second chapter has two exegetical tasks. I begin by analysing the relationship between sexual love and love of beauty, which relationship figures prominently in Kant's earlier philosophy but wanes towards the 1790s. I then formulate a distinction between *narrow and broad sexual love*, where narrow sexual love consists merely of the natural impulse of procreation, whereas broad sexual love is the natural impulse united with the moral love of benevolence in the context of heterosexual marriage. In comparison with the other chapters in this study, the chapter on sexual love also contains an evaluative element, which reflects the fact that most of the previous research in this area is feminist and therefore evaluative in orientation (as far as I know, my study is the first to analyse sexual love in Kant from an exegetical point of view). From this perspective, I show how broad sexual love supports a less misogynistic picture of Kant than is often presented, even though problems and internal tensions remain in Kant's discussions on the issue of sex.

The third chapter formulates an ascent model of love of God. I begin with the observation that love of God comprises two 'directions': a movement upwards, from human beings to God, and a movement downwards, from God to human beings. I call this starting point the *two-directionality thesis of love of God*. I proceed by analysing human beings' love for God and then God's love for human beings. For Kant, morality leads to religion, and love for God is the foundation of all inner religion. It is close to the regulative ideal of loving the moral law, which involves fulfilling one's duties *gladly* [*gern*] (thus implying the absence of contra-moral inclinations in the perfect agent). I show how God's love can be analysed in terms of its role as both an *end* and a *ground:* God's love of benevolence toward humans is (from a religious perspective) the ground of creation and duties, and God's love of delight is a moral delight God in the end hopefully takes in the sincere moral striving of the human being.

The fourth chapter proposes a novel 'feeling-action-cultivation' account of love of neighbour. I track down Kant's discussions of neighbourly love from the early Herder notes onwards, focusing on *The Metaphysics of Morals*. I propose that love of neighbour consists of both moral-rational and sensory-emotive elements and that it includes the cultivation of a moral disposition. Love of neighbour divides into love of benevolence and love of delight, so that love of benevolence towards others is either 1) benevolent or beneficent inclination or 2) active rational benevolence (practical love). Practical love is further divided into beneficence, gratitude, and sympathy. Love of delight is either a pathological or an intellectual delight taken in the perfections (or even the sheer humanity) of another. It is not merely an actual feeling but also a predisposition of sensibility to be subjectively receptive to duty.

The final chapter reconstructs Kant's mature philosophy of friendship from the perspective of love. I show the existence of the general division of love in this context and analyse the way its components function. Love in friendship is at least love of benevolence, but if the lecture notes on ethics are included as evidence, it is both love of benevolence and love of delight. In general I argue that in the context of friendship, love (conditioned by respect) marks the path towards the highest good in equal and reciprocal human relationships. Friendships as such are intimate, but the notion of a 'friend of human beings' [*Menschenfreund*; *Freund der Menschen*] brings with it a broader cosmopolitan outlook that indirectly aims at the ideal moral community in terms of friendship. I call this overall account the 'ascent view of love in Kantian friendship'. Taken together with the previous chapters of this study, this account corroborates the general division approach and the ascent model of love in Kant.

VI

Before moving to the main discussion, I would like to say a word or two about certain aspects of love to which I do not devote entire chapters but that also deserve mention. First, I approach the notion of love of beauty through the lens of sexual love (ch. 2.1). This is by no means the only strategy available, and love of beauty could also be considered for its own sake (even though there are only two direct passages on it in the *Critique of Judgment*). One could, for instance, begin one's discussion with the third *Critique*, establish that love of beauty is love of delight, and then try to establish links between these passages and Kant's discussions in the 'Doctrine of Virtue' and the Vigilantius notes on ethics with an eye to elaborating further on the general qualities of love of delight. But this kind of more experimental exegesis is beyond the scope of the present work. Love of beauty has been recently discussed by Anne Margaret Baxley (2005) and Gabriele Tomasi (2015), and with reference to their discussions I adopt a merely reactive attitude in ch. 2.1, pointing out that an exegetical problem concerning love in the *Critique of Judgment* is left untouched by these accounts. However, this is not the main point of the chapter, and in all honesty I do not provide a general account of love of beauty.

Second, I discuss *love of honour* under self-love. Love of honour is an ambiguous notion detached from the general division of love (in itself it is neither love of benevolence nor love of delight). Love of honour consistently marks a concern for respect (from others), but it comes in physical and moral variants, the physical variant belonging to the conceptual cluster of self-love and the moral variant being grounded in respect for the moral law. My discussion of love of honour is indebted to the careful accounts provided by Houston Smit and Mark Timmons (2015) and Lara Denis (2014), but I should still note that neither Smit and Timmons nor Denis attempt to connect love of honour to love's general concept. I consider the relationship between love of honour and love in general at the end of ch. 1.1. The moral ideal of *love for the law* is discussed in ch. 1.3 and especially in ch. 3.1. I consider *love of human beings* in conjunction with love of neighbour, especially in ch. 4.2.1.

Further, there are various 'aspects' of love that are mentioned by Kant only in passing, in singular isolated contexts or in adverbial constructions, but that are never elaborated on or systematically developed. Some of these might be more, some less important for someone interested in a general concept of love, but since they are not given substantial consideration by Kant in terms of love, I do not discuss them or incorporate them into my framework. Of such loves, the most prominent is undoubtedly parental love, yet even though the natural impulse toward the preservation of offspring belongs to 'animal mechanical self-love' in the *Religion* (R, 6:26.12–18), the only published reference to 'parental love' [*die Liebe der Eltern*] occurs in the *Prolegomena*, where Kant uses love of God and parental love as examples through which to explain, formally, the notion of an analogical relation as such (4:357fn.; cf. 28:1087–1088). Parents do have a duty to provide for their children, according to Kant, and children are said to have a duty of gratitude (which is a duty of love) towards their parents (MM, 6:280–281; cf. 9:482). When Kant discusses the difference between hatred and anger in the lectures on ethics, he mentions a parent's anger toward a child's bad behaviour as an example of anger that presupposes love (LE, 27:687.38–688.1). That parents love their children would seem to be implicit in Kant's writings, but he does not discuss the parent-child relation in connection with love to any great extent. Hence, I do not include parental love in my framework.

Love of truth is mentioned a couple of times in the lectures but never in the published works (see LE, 27:60–62; 27:448–449). In the first *Critique*, Kant writes that 'we shall always return to metaphysics as we would to a beloved woman with whom we have had a quarrel.' (C1, A850/B878)[5] Although this is an interesting metaphor, to my knowledge Kant never elaborates on it. Even more remote examples of 'briefly mentioned loves', which for the most part never appear in Kant's published works, include 'love of the fatherland', as contrasted with universal love of human beings (LE, 27:673; see my ch. 5.3), 'love of justice' (LE, 27:688–689), 'peace-loving' (C2, 5:61.10; see also LE, 27:687.2), and the carnivorous 'love of roast beef' (LA, 25:1361.8), none of which are developed further in terms of love. The existence of constructions like 'love of roast beef' merely shows that, in the most general terms, 'love' can be used to signify any kind of relatively intense liking or desire. From this *flexibility* of the concept of love it does not follow that the framework of love should be expanded *ad infinitum* to accommodate ever-new aspects or kinds of love. Rather, it shows the need to restrict the framework through careful, quasi-inductive evaluations, so that the concept of love can remain at the same time broad and informative.

---

5 'Man kann also sicher sein, [...] man werde jederzeit zu ihr wie zu einer mit uns entzweiten Geliebten zurückkehren'.

1 Self-Love

According to Kant, it is a basic fact of human nature that we all love ourselves. Human beings are imperfect rational creatures who want things to go well for themselves, and there is really no way around this fundamental trait of our species. We want to be happy. Indeed, Kant tends to describe self-love [*Selbstliebe, Eigenliebe*][1] as the basic principle of subjective happiness. Self-love is the natural motivational ground of action, to which the moral incentive (respect for the moral law) is opposed. Self-love is active within us, and it is only hindered by morality to the extent that it gives rise to contra-moral inclinations. There are duties in Kantian ethics, of course (e.g. the duties to perfect oneself and to promote the happiness of others), and in light of our duties we should keep self-love in check and diminish its influence. Self-love can often appear as selfishness, and as such it is prone to impede our striving for virtue. It may threaten the freedom and happiness of others.

But what does the above actually mean, and can something like this be said to be the whole picture of self-love in Kant? While the basics are relatively simple from the perspective of moral theory, self-love poses problems for Kant's ethics. It is a significant concept in his moral philosophy and has received attention from scholars. Treatments of self-love in the previous literature, however, can be quite varied. Some view self-love as 'an objective principle of practical reason' (Paton 1947, p. 91) or even as 'furthering morality' (Šimfa 2013, p. 107), whereas others hold that '*love* is not an attitude that clear-sighted and rational people could ever take toward themselves.' (Wood 1996, p. 144) Often, scholars touch upon self-love in discussing other issues, such as beneficence (Hill 1993), benevolence (Edwards 2000), or respect for the moral law (e.g. Reath 2006; Engstrom 2010)[2]. Yet none of the previous readings aim to provide a systematic, exegetical interpretation of the notion of self-love.

---

[1] I have been unable to detect a difference in meaning between the two German terms, even though it seems that Kant tends to use *Eigenliebe* when he is contrasting self-love with self-conceit [*Eigendünkel*] (see e.g. C2, 5:73.12–14).
[2] Thomas Hill's focus (1993, pp. 1–2) is generally on the possibility of altruism, and he draws from a loosely Kantian framework, stating explicitly that his aims are not exegetical. Jeffrey Edwards's reading focuses on the *Groundwork* and the second *Critique* and is in fact a defence of Hutcheson against the basic framework of Kant's mature moral philosophy. Andrews Reath and Stephen Engstrom analyse the moral incentive (or 'spring' [*Triebfeder*], as Engstrom puts it) and its relation to non-moral agency. In doing this, they also offer very helpful analyses of self-love, particularly in relation to self-conceit within the context of the second *Critique* (see Reath 2006, pp. 14–17, 23–25; Engstrom 2010, pp. 101ff.).

My fundamental goal is to understand the intricate structure of self-love and the role it plays in Kant's thought. What, for instance, does Kant mean when he says that self-love is a predisposition to the good (R, 6:26)? Or when he argues that it is the source of evil (R, 6:45)? What does he mean when he holds that all material practical principles fall under self-love (C2, 5:22)? What is the status of rational self-love (C2, 5:73; cf. R, 6:45–46fn.), and how does self-love relate to the general division of love into love of benevolence and love of delight? Finally, what is the place of self-love in the infinite progress towards moral perfection – will it continue to exist or not?

In what follows, I shall present what I call a 'three-level' interpretation of Kantian self-love, according to which the concept of self-love is divisible into ascending levels of rationality. I begin by discussing self-love at a rudimentary, non-rational level of the cognitive structure of the human being, where it figures as the strongest impulses of human nature. These fundamental animal impulses include self-preservation (love of life), preservation of the species (sexuality and parenting), and sociality. Together, they may be identified as 'animal mechanical self-love', and according to Kant they constitute *a predisposition to the good*. The main point of the first section is to lay the ground for the three-level interpretation of self-love (and for the ascent model of love in Kant more generally) by showing that Kant discusses the strongest impulses of human nature in terms of love. I will strive to understand why Kant calls these non-rational animal impulses 'love' in the first place, and why he thinks that they constitute a predisposition to the good. To this end, I will also problematise the relationship between animal self-love and the 'self-love of humanity' (the latter of which implies what I call the 'middle level' of self-love) by looking at notions of sociality and *love of honour* in this context.

Second, I analyse the middle level of self-love in more detail, from the perspective of Kant's moral philosophy. I argue that this level of self-love is best approached by acknowledging the operation of the general division of love as love of benevolence and love of delight. This level implies the actuality of reason, and here self-love can be considered to inform all non-moral ends the agent may have and the instrumental reasoning related to them. The middle level brings with it the notion of *self-conceit*, which Kant incorporates into the framework of self-love through very complicated discussions. Love of benevolence for oneself is willing one's own happiness (or love from others), and this is a permanent and acceptable part of humanity; self-conceit, by contrast, is a morally reprehensible, delusional delight [*Wohlgefallen*] taken in a sense of special self-worth in comparison with others. Self-conceit arises when one makes the self-love of benevolence an unconditional law. *Rational self-love*, on the other hand, refers to the middle level of self-love under moral conditions: it is prudence limited by morality (love of benevolence) or moral self-contentment (love of delight).

Third, I consider what would happen to self-love in the ideally rational state of moral existence, where the highest good as moral happiness is realised as closely as possible. Here, I argue that because the end of morality will necessarily involve happiness, it follows that self-benevolence and moral self-contentment will be present in the infinite approximation towards the highest good. I don't see a way to conceive of morally deserved happiness without including some kind of self-benevolence or moral self-contentment, both of which can arguably be cashed out in terms of self-love. Hence, the three levels of self-love in my interpretation consist of: 1) animal mechanical self-love; 2) the middle level or general division of self-love; and 3) self-love and the highest good.

I thus argue that while there is an important sense in which self-love is in tension with morality and constitutes an obstacle to moral progress, it is an irreplaceable component of human existence. In Kant's moral thought, there is no prescription (or even possibility) of a type of agency that is completely stripped of self-love (even though unselfish acts may very well be commanded). Self-love cuts through the ascending levels of the cognitive structure of the moral agent and can also be used to illuminate the notion of moral progress from a broader species perspective. Although the third and highest level of self-love is of course idealised, it functions in my argument to illustrate the *persistence* of self-love in the infinite approximation to the highest good. No matter how closely the moral happiness of all rational creatures is realised, the Kantian agent will still retain some minimum of an attitude of love towards herself.

Overall, then, the three-level interpretation of self-love has two exegetical functions: 1) it outlines the first relatively comprehensive analysis of the conceptual structure of self-love in Kant, and 2) it serves as a preliminary for the ascent view of Kant's conception of love as a whole.

1.1 Animal Mechanical Self-Love

We cry for food and flee from fire. We crave sex, even without seeing or thinking of anyone in particular to have sex with. We will do almost anything to keep our children alive. We are drawn to others of our kind for warmth, shelter, and acceptance. These notions clearly express fundamental human desires – desires that members of our species tend to share. But are these desires expressions of love? And if so, how?

Kant does think that crude self-preservation, sexuality and care for offspring, and our instinctive attraction to other human beings can be discussed in terms of love. But these loves, at their natural core, are not Kant's usual concern when he talks about love. They are not his concern when he writes in the *Religion:* 'Like *love* in general, *self-love* too can be divided into love of *benevolence* and love of *delight* (BENEVOLENTIAE ET COMPLACENTIAE), and both (as is self-evident) must be rational.' (R, 6:45.22–25)[3] As such, the crude natural loves, as fundamental impulses of desire, operate completely irrespective of reason. They are non-rational, and they are neither benevolence nor delight. Given that the first major claim of my book is that the general division of love into love of benevolence and love of delight is a key to understanding love in Kant, it may seem peculiar that I begin the overall argument by pointing to a love (or a set of loves) that is *not* grasped by the general division of love. I seem to begin with a counter-example to what I wish to argue for. But while the general division of love is indeed a key to understanding love in Kant, it does not follow that the concept of love in Kant is completely reducible to the general division. This leaves us with the problem of how to understand those loves that Kant discusses as love but that do not fall into the general division of love. It is this task that I will now undertake with respect to the 'lowest' possible level of human existence.

The main point of the first section is to show that *Kant thinks of the strongest impulses of human nature in terms of love.* Together, these non-rational drives may be identified as animal mechanical self-love. But to say *just that* is not very conducive to understanding Kant's view. While the main point is necessary for the argument of this chapter (and for the ascent model of love in Kant as a whole), it is equally important to ask what Kant *means* when he speaks of love as he does. In particular, there are two questions I find pressing in the context of animal mechanical self-love. Why does Kant call these non-rational drives 'love' in the first place? And what does he mean when he says that animal mechanical self-love is a 'predisposition to the good'? In this section I provide some answers to these questions.

In the first part of *Religion within the Bounds of mere Reason,* Kant asserts that there is an 'original predisposition to good in human nature' (R, 6:26.2–3[4]; see also 6:43.18–21). The original predisposition to the good consists of three aspects of the human being (or the whole species)[5] in an ascending order: 1) animality (life); 2) humanity (rational life); and 3) personality (rational responsible life). The third predisposition is about morality, which is not my con-

---

3 'Wie *Liebe* überhaupt, so kann auch *Selbstliebe* in die des *Wohlwollens* und des *Wohlgefallens* (BENEVOLENTIAE ET COMPLACENTIAE) eingetheilt werden, und beide müssen (wie sich von selbst versteht) vernünftig sein.'
4 'ursprünglichen Anlage zum Guten in der menschlichen Natur.'
5 See R, 6:25.17–20.

cern at this particular point, but the first two are explicitly articulated in terms of self-love. The first is about non-rational animal self-love, and the second is about a self-love for which reason is required. Because the latter is relevant to understanding the former, I will return to it later on in the section. With regard to the first predisposition, Kant writes:

> 1. The predisposition to ANIMALITY in the human being may be brought under the general title of physical and merely *mechanical* self-love, i.e. a love for which reason is not required. It is three-fold: *first*, for self-preservation; *second*, for the propagation of the species, through the sexual drive, and for the preservation of the offspring thereby begotten through breeding; *third*, for community with other human beings, i.e. the social drive. (R, 6:26.12–18)[6]

As this passage clearly shows, Kant thinks that certain non-rational animal drives – self-preservation, sexuality and parenting, and sociality – are species of 'self-love'. But why does Kant use the word 'love' at all in this context?[7] He speaks elsewhere of 'love of life' [*Liebe zum Leben*] and 'sexual love' [*Liebe zum Geschlecht*] in the context of depicting 'the strongest impulses of nature' [*die stärksten Antriebe der Natur*], linking love of life to self-preservation and sexual love to the preservation of the species (AP, 7:276.28–33). In one sense it is obvious why Kant might use the word 'love' in the context of sexuality: there has been a close association between love and sexuality ever since the ancients, as *Eros*, which is traditionally used to depict sexual desire, is precisely an elementary notion of love. Another well-documented point in the literature concerning the original predisposition in the *Religion* is the observation that Kant owes much of his discussion to Rousseau (e.g. DiCenso 2012, p. 48; Pasternack 2014, p. 94; see also Wood 2009, pp. 127–128)[8]. In the *Discourse on the Arts and Sciences*, for example, Rousseau famously holds that the human being is natu-

---

[6] '1. Die Anlage für die THIERHEIT im Menschen kann man unter den allgemeinen Titel der physischen und bloß *mechanischen* Selbstliebe, d.i. einer solchen bringen, wozu nicht Vernunft erfordert wird. Sie ist dreifach: *erstlich* zur Erhaltung seiner selbst; *zweitens* zur Fortpflanzung seiner Art durch den Trieb zum Geschlecht und zur Erhaltung dessen, was durch Vermischung mit demselben erzeugt wird; *drittens* zur Gemeinschaft mit andern Menschen, d.i. der Trieb zur Gesellschaft.'

[7] Even though the predispositions to the good have received attention in the literature (e.g. Wood 1999, pp. 118–120, see also pp. 210–212; Palmquist 2009, pp. xxiv–xxv; DiCenso 2012, pp. 46–50; Pasternack 2014, pp. 93–96), to my knowledge, their status *as love* has not been examined previously. The new *Kant-Lexikon* (Willachek et al. (Eds.), 2015) omits the predispositions (R, 6:26) altogether from the article on *Selbstliebe*.

[8] Interestingly, J.B. Schneewind views animal mechanical self-love as reminiscent of 'the Stoic view of our initial tendency toward self-preservation.' (Schneewind 2009, p. 107)

rally good, and that developments in the arts and sciences cause moral degeneration (Rousseau 1997 [1750], pp. 4–28). In the *Discourse on the Origin and Foundations of Inequality Among Men* he states: 'Man's first sentiment was that of his existence, his first care that for his preservation.' (Rousseau 1997 [1755], p. 161) Rousseau distinguishes between two types of self-love: *amour propre* and *amour de soi-même*. Amour de soi-même is 'a natural sentiment which inclines every animal to attend to its self-preservation, and which, guided in man by reason and modified by pity, produces humanity and virtue.' (Rousseau 1997, p. 218) *Amour propre*, on the other hand, originates in society, makes people prefer themselves to others, inspires evil, and is also 'the genuine source of honour' (Rousseau 1997, p. 218). So there is a relatively easy answer to the question: 'Why does Kant call these drives (self-)love, if he does not think of them in terms of his general division of love?' The easy answer is that sexuality has been called love ever since the dawn of our culture, and the rest he just picks up from Rousseau.

But there is a more interesting answer, I think, which does not avoid making reference to the ancients but is not similarly reliant on Rousseau's influence. The fact that Kant calls the animal impulses love may also be explained in terms of another, more general paradigm of love that has been with us at least since Plato. This paradigm of love can be called *love as desire*, and its origins trace back to Socrates' speech in the *Symposium*, where the love object is by definition something that the lover desires (and, according to Socrates, lacks) (see Plato 2006, 200a–201a). For Kant, the drives of animal mechanical self-love are directly connected to what he calls the faculty of desire [*Begehrungsvermögen*]. It is through the notion of desire and its connection to the classical paradigm of love *as* desire that we can shed light on the status of these impulses *as* love.

Further down in the *Religion*, Kant explains that 'there is no question here of other predispositions except those that relate immediately to the faculty of desire' (R, 6:28.22–23)[9]. By 'the faculty of desire', Kant is referring to 'a being's *faculty to be by means of its representations the cause of the reality of the objects of these representations*.' (C2, 5:9fn.[10]; see also MM, 6:211; 20:206) Kant divides desire into lower and higher faculties; where the lower faculty is sensuous, the higher faculty is associated with pure practical reason (C2, 5:24–25). All living beings act in accordance with the laws of the faculty of desire (C2, 5:9fn.), and as such, animal desire is necessitated by mechanisms of nature in contrast

---

9 'hier von keinen andern Anlagen die Rede ist, als denen, die sich unmittelbar auf das Begehrungsvermögen [...] beziehen.'
10 'das Vermögen desselben [eines Wesens], durch seine Vorstellungen Ursache von der Wirklichkeit der Gegenstände dieser Vorstellungen zu sein.'

with the moral laws of freedom (see LE, 27:344; C2, 5:95–97). Moreover, the faculty of desire is connected to pleasure and displeasure (see LE, 27:344; C2, 5:95–97; MM, 6:211–213; cf. Frierson 2014, p. 99).[11] In a typical case of a 'lower' desire, for example a desire for chocolate (or for eating chocolate), we represent (eating) chocolate as something pleasurable, and the faculty of desire motivates us to the action of eating chocolate, or in other words, it motivates us to be the cause of the reality of the pleasure of eating chocolate. But the animal impulses go cognitively even lower than that. In *Anthropology from a Pragmatic Point of View*, Kant speaks of the relationship between animality and the objects of desire in terms of *instincts*: 'the inner *necessitation* of the faculty of desire to take possession of this object before one even knows it, is *instinct* (like the sexual instinct, or the parental instinct of the animal to protect its young, and so forth).' (AP, 7:265.23–26)[12] It therefore seems that the primitive nature of desire in animal mechanical self-love can be understood such that acquaintance with an object is not even required for the impulse to be operative, and even when one encounters an actual object (say food or a sexually attractive other), the satisfaction of the animal impulse does not require that one be able to form a concept of the object.

In the early 'Observations on the Feeling of the Beautiful and Sublime',[13] Kant speaks of a man who loves women only as 'things that are to be enjoyed' [*genießbare Sachen*] (2:208.3–5) and who is capable of enjoying gratification

---

11 For Kant's general threefold classification of the faculties of the human mind into cognition, the feeling of pleasure, and desire, see (C3, 5:178; 20:206). Basically, through cognition we encounter objects in the first place, through desire we actualise certain objects, and through pleasure we have feelings for the objects (cf. Frierson 2014, p. 99). Frierson notes: 'Human action is caused by desire, which is caused by pleasure, which is caused by cognition.' (Frierson 2014, p. 99) This may be the case with the lower faculty of desire, but in the case of the higher faculty of desire pleasure cannot precede but can only follow the determination of the faculty of desire (MM, 6:212.27–213.2; see also 5:24.32–40). Frierson's focus is on empirical psychology, which may explain why he relates the higher faculty of desire not to pure practical reason (C2, 5:24.35–36) or pure rational principles (MM, 6:212.31) but more loosely to 'character' and 'maxims'. According to Frierson, the higher faculty of desire can have empirical determining grounds, as in the case of a 'person who smokes [cigarettes] from principle' (Frierson 2014, pp. 99–100). This reading contradicts Kant's account of the higher faculty of desire as laid out in his moral philosophy (cf. MM, 6:426.20–26).
12 'die innere *Nöthigung* des Begehrungsvermögens zur Besitznehmung dieses Gegenstandes, ehe man ihn noch kennt, der *Instinct* (wie der Begattungstrieb, oder der Älterntrieb des Thiers seine Junge zu schützen u. d. g.).' Note that here, the 'object' seems to refer to another living creature as such rather than the pleasure taken in interacting with it. This is an ambiguity that Kant does not clarify in his discussions of desire.
13 'Beobachtungen über das Gefühl des Schönen und Erhabenen'.

'without ever having to envy others or even being able to form any concept of others' (2:208.6–9)[14]. The feeling this man enjoys 'can occur in complete thoughtlessness' (2:208.14–15)[15]. Despite the slight difference in terminology, the example seems to match what Kant says about instincts in the *Anthropology* quite closely. As non-rational and instinctive, animal mechanical self-love (as in the case of the sexual impulse) operates thoughtlessly, without acknowledging the personhood of others, indeed even without a concept of others. In terms borrowed from Rae Langton, animal mechanical self-love can give rise to *solipsism* (Langton 2009, p. 316, see also pp. 325 ff.)[16], where the agent lets the rudimentary desires intrinsic to animal life override reason and understanding and ends up taking no account of the ends or the personhood of others, or her own personhood. This is how various vices can become grafted onto animal mechanical self-love.[17]

The animal within us is consumed by desire. It is drawn to others, but it does not understand that others exist as separate from itself, and it knows nothing of the moral vocation of the organism of which it is a constitutive part. The animal within us does not understand that others set ends autonomously and that they have a capacity to be happy. This helps to explain what puts the *love* in animal

---

14 'ohne daß sie andere beneiden dürfen oder auch von andern sich einen Begriff machen können'.
15 'bei völliger Gedankenlosigkeit statt finden können.'
16 Langton uses the term mainly in the context of sexuality and attaches it specifically to some of Kant's discussions of sexual desire or sexual love (see LE, 27:384 ff.; Langton 2009, p. 316). I discuss the issue of sexuality further in ch. 2.
17 These are vices of crudeness [*Rohigkeit*], such as gluttony [*Völlerei*], lust [*Wollust*], and wild lawlessness [*wilde Gesetzlosigkeit*] (see R, 6:26.18–27.3; cf. MM, 6:424–427). Because I have chosen to outline the general conceptual structure of self-love, and because my main focus is understanding the broadest conceptual divisions of love related to it, it is not possible for me to analyse specific vices (or the duties to which they are opposed) in detail. Since 'self-love' is the general term in Kant's moral philosophy to which the moral incentive and the overall framework of duties is contrasted, the points of contact between self-love and duties would be overabundant considering my aims. There are specific negative duties against suicide, unnatural sex, gluttony, and the misuse of substances, which are connected to the animal nature of the human being (MM, 6:421–427). Kant insists that these duties are grounded in the categorical imperative (not animal nature) (see MM, 6:422.31–423.6; 6:425.23–26; 6:427.5–19; GW, 4:429.15–25; 4:425.12–27; 4:421.24–423.14). The success of his various arguments has been widely debated in the literature (for suicide, see e.g. Paton 1947, pp. 150–154; Korsgaard 1996, pp. 87–92; Wood 1999, pp. 84–86; Allison 2011, pp. 183–184; cf. Timmermann 2007, p. 81; for unnatural sex, see Denis 1999 and Soble 2003). Here, I cannot add anything new to these debates, and a proper attempt to do so would throw me off course with respect to my chosen focus on seeking out and clarifying the most general divisions of (self-)love in Kant.

mechanical self-love: animal mechanical self-love is a form of self-centred or species-centred *desire* that does not take others into account. It is a kind of love but not a case of 'true love' [*wahre Liebe*] (see 8:337.33–34), which would require reason and respect.

We know that Kant grounded the moral good in pure practical reason and viewed rationality as that which distinguishes humanity from animality. How, then, is animal mechanical self-love a *predisposition to the good*? Scholarly discussion on this topic would appear to be scarce. In particular, previous commentators do not problematise the notion of a predisposition to the good in relation to animal mechanical self-love; they simply tend to assume that animal mechanical self-love is good without explaining how this could be so.[18] Before moving on to analyse the middle level of self-love in more detail, let us pause to consider this question.

'Predisposition' [*Anlage*] is originally a term from biology (see Shell 2015, p. 96). For Kant, a predisposition is a natural feature, property, or capacity of an organism (or species) that accounts for its developing in a certain way (see Allison 2009, p. 26fn.; cf. Wood 1999, p. 211; 2009, p. 113; see also 2:434–435; cf. MM, 6:399.11). In the *Religion*, Kant writes: 'By the predispositions of a being we understand the constituent parts required for it as well as the forms of their combination that make for such a being.' (R, 6:28.17–19)[19] If the being is not even possible without a given predisposition, then the predisposition is *original*, and if this is not the case then the predisposition is *contingent* (ibid., 6:28.19–21). As original predispositions, animal self-love, the self-love of humanity, and personality are all fundamental to the human species. As already noted, even though the predispositions are regularities, they are not static. They are not ready-made, rigid 'building blocks' of organisms but instead involve developmental processes. According to Kant, it is a general feature of nature (including human history) that '[a]ll natural predispositions of a creature are determined

---

[18] For instance, Gordon Michalson claims that: 'All three predispositions […] are good in themselves' and that they 'effectively constitute the hand we are initially dealt, while […] how we play it depends upon the way we ourselves introduce the wild card of freedom.' (Michalson 1990, pp. 39–40) Stephen Palmquist writes: 'Animal self-love predisposes living beings to do good by causing them to preserve themselves, propagate the species, and form social groups for mutual protection.' (Palmquist 2009, p. xxiv) In the same vein as Michalson, James DiCenso holds that Kant's 'discussion [of the predispositions] starts from an assumption of the goodness of our nature as such' (DiCenso 2012, p. 47), whereas Lawrence Pasternack notes merely that 'the Predisposition to Animality has a kind of innocence' (Pasternack 2014, p. 94).

[19] 'Unter Anlagen eines Wesens verstehen wir sowohl die Bestandstücke, die dazu erforderlich sind, als auch die Formen ihrer Verbindung, um ein solches Wesen zu sein.'

sometime to develop themselves completely and purposively.' (8:18.19–20)[20] In the human species, the unfolding of our higher, rational predispositions can only take place through a gradual, intergenerational, and indefinitely long cultural process (8:18–19). As Allen Wood and Paul Guyer remind us, Kant conceives of the natural predispositions of the human species teleologically (see Wood 1999, pp. 209–211; Guyer 2009, p. 145). The mature Kant views nature as if it were a system of ends or purposes, where the natural predispositions of the human being are ultimately referred to our moral vocation, which is connected to the ideal of the complete highest good (the morally deserved happiness of rational creatures) as the final purpose of the world (see e.g. C3, 5:429.29–32; 5:434–435; 5:451). Naturally, the highest good of the human species cannot be reached in a single lifetime or by an individual organism. At best, the species can gradually approximate the highest good.

But even if we reflect on animal mechanical self-love from the perspective of our moral vocation, its goodness, or the goodness to which it is predisposed, may still appear problematic. What exactly is the function of this self-love with respect to the good? In the second *Critique*, Kant distinguishes between two notions of the 'good' in the German language, using '*das Wohl*' for physical well-being or pleasure and '*das Gute*' for the moral good (C2, 5:59–60; see also 5:62–63).[21] In the *Religion* (written after the second *Critique*), it is '*das Gute*' that appears in the heading of Kant's discussion of the original predisposition. But as animal mechanical self-love is physical and not moral, in the light of the second *Critique* it should be impossible for animal mechanical self-love to be good [*gut*] 'in itself' or 'as such', against the claims of some commentators (see Michalson 1990, p. 39; DiCenso 2012, p. 47). Indeed, Kant is not making the unqualified claim that animal mechanical self-love is good [*gut*] as such. Here is Kant's own clarification: 'All these predispositions in the human being are not only negatively *good* (they do not conflict with the moral law) but they are also predispositions *to the good* (they further compliance with that law).' (R, 6:28.12–14)[22] 'The good' of which Kant speaks here is clearly the moral good, but it is not the case that animal mechanical self-love is (morally) good in itself. Kant does not elab-

---

20 'Alle Naturanlagen eines Geschöpfes sind bestimmt, sich einmal vollständig und zweckmäßig auszuwickeln.'
21 Note, however, that even here, where he explicitly defines the concept of the good [*das Gute*] in terms of morality, he allows the use of 'good' [*gut*] as an adjective in the context of instrumentally rational action from empirical determining grounds (C2, 5:62.30–31).
22 'Alle diese Anlagen im Menschen sind nicht allein (negativ) gut (sie widerstreiten nicht dem moralischen Gesetze), sondern sind auch Anlagen zum Guten (sie befördern die Befolgung desselben).' Translation modified following Pluhar.

orate on what he means by 'furthering' [*befördern*] the moral good in terms of animality, but the idea must be that animal mechanical self-love somehow helps, promotes, or facilitates moral progress or the formation of our moral character on the species level. But how?

Naturally, animal mechanical self-love is a necessary condition for any kind of progress on the part of the human species – it concerns the very possibility of our species as such. If the animal within us didn't struggle for its own preservation, if it were repulsed by all representations of sex, if it couldn't care less about its offspring (if any even appeared), and if it were prone to isolate itself completely from others of its kind, there would be no future for the human being. In this fundamental and necessary sense, animal mechanical self-love enables moral progress.

Admittedly, if the published *Anthropology* is included as evidence, Kant's use of the notion of the good in conjunction with animal mechanical self-love is more ambiguous than might be implied by the *Religion*. In contrast to the second *Critique*'s distinction between the physical '*das Wohl*' and the moral '*das Gute*' (C2, 5:59–60), the published *Anthropology* divides '*das Gute*' into physical and moral goodness (AP, 7:277.6–7)[23]. There, in a section titled 'On the Highest Physical Good' [*von dem höchsten physischen Gut*], the animal mechanical impulses of love of life (self-preservation) and sexual love (species preservation) are connected with what is *physically* best for the world [*das physiche Weltbeste*] (AP, 7:276.28–277.3):

> The strongest impulses of nature are *love of life* and *sexual love*, which represent the invisible reason (of the ruler of the world) that provides generally for the highest physical good of the human race by means of a power higher than human reason, without human reason having to work toward it. Love of life is to maintain the individual; sexual love, the species. (AP, 7:276.28–33)[24]

---

[23] Since the *Anthropology* contains material from several decades of Kant's thinking, one could conjecture that this distinction is a remnant of an earlier period of Kant's thought. Yet the sections that contain this use of '*das Gute*' in the published works are not to be found in Kant's earlier lectures on anthropology. This suggests that the material was added, or at least architectonically reorganised, well after the publication of the second *Critique*.

[24] 'Die stärksten Antriebe der Natur, welche die Stelle der unsichtbar das menschliche Geschlecht durch eine höhere, das physische Weltbeste allgemein besorgende Vernunft (des Weltregierers) vertreten, ohne daß menschliche Vernunft dazu hinwirken darf, sind *Liebe zum Leben* und *Liebe zum Geschlecht*; die erstere um das Individuum, die zweite um die Species zu erhalten'. Note that it is somewhat unclear whether *unsichtbar* refers to the invisibility of the reason or to the invisibility of the process the reason generates.

This does not have to be viewed as conflicting with the account in the *Religion*, but it adds another dimension to how animal impulses are predisposed to the good. The physically good must be understood in conjunction with pleasure. In the light of this evidence there is also a sense in which the strongest impulses of human nature (love of life and sexual love) are good because they give us pleasure, apparently via good meals (see AP, 7:278.10–12) and sexual intercourse.[25]

As already mentioned, no progress whatsoever is possible on the species level without animal mechanical self-love. This is the bare minimum that Kant must have in mind with respect to the relationship between animal mechanical self-love and the moral good.[26] There may, however, be stronger connections. I discuss the issue of sexual love further in ch. 2, but there is another link that can shed light on animal self-love as predisposed to the good. This link is the animal impulse of sociality [*Gemeinschaft; Gesellschaft*] (R, 6:26.17–18)[27]. The so-

---

25 This passage may also raise questions about the role of God's reason in this context. As we are here dealing with a *physical* good (pleasure) that human reason does not have to work for (AP, 7:276.30–31), it seems that Kant's reference to God's reason shouldn't (at least on the face of it) be primarily understood from the perspective of the moral postulate of God. Rather, the reference seems to point toward the notion of *providence* [*Vorsehung*], which Kant makes use of in the philosophy of history (see e.g. 8:30.19; 8:121.3; 8:123.23). Interpreted from this perspective, animal mechanical self-love yields physical pleasure according to a 'hidden plan of nature' [*der verborgene Plan der Natur*] (see 8:272–273), the final purpose of which is the complete development of all our predispositions (see 8:18.19–20). Relatedly, in *The Metaphysics of Morals*, love of life (self-preservation) and sexual love (species-preservation) are connected with 'an intelligent cause' [*der Ursache [...] Verstand*] in terms of the critical teleology (see 6:424.12–18). In the critical teleological framework articulated in the third *Critique*, all natural purposes must be thought of *as if* they were intelligently caused (even though we cannot know this theoretically) if they are to be systematically connected to the ideal or the final purpose of the highest good (the morally deserved happiness of rational creatures). The reason for this is that Kant thinks that the highest good is possible only if God is postulated (see ch. 3).
26 In Kant's *Lectures on Pedagogy*, the first principle of education is to discipline the wildness of animality, and hence the education related to animality is *negative:* 'To discipline means to seek to prevent animality from doing damage to humanity, both in the individual and in society. Discipline is therefore merely the taming of savagery.' (9:449.28–30; see also 9:441.18; 9:465.30) / 'Discipliniren heißt suchen zu verhüten, daß die Thierheit nicht der Menschheit in dem einzelnen sowohl als gesellschaftlichen Menschen zum Schaden gereiche. Disciplin ist also blos Bezähmung der Wildheit.' This supports the view that animality on its own does not play a positive role in moral progress.
27 In English, this animal impulse might also be termed 'sociability', since 'sociality' and 'sociability' are nearly indistinguishable. According to the Merriam-Webster dictionary, for instance, 'sociality' is 'sociability', but 'sociality' involves in particular 'the tendency to associate

cial impulse connects animal self-love with the self-love of humanity, and looking more closely at this connection might help to explain how animal mechanical self-love is predisposed to the good. Let us therefore turn to the predisposition of humanity:

> 2. The predispositions to HUMANITY can be brought under the general title of a self-love which is physical and yet *involves comparison* (for which reason is required); that is, only in comparison with others does one judge oneself happy or unhappy. Out of this self-love originates the inclination *to gain worth in the opinion of others*, originally of course, merely *equal* worth: not allowing anyone superiority over oneself, bound up with the constant anxiety that others might be striving for ascendancy; but from this arises gradually an unjust desire to acquire superiority for oneself over others. (R, 6:27.4–12)[28]

Kant's discussion implies what I call the actually rational 'middle level' of self-love, which I discuss from a moral theoretical perspective in the second section. Here, the passage in question connects particularly well with Kant's philosophy of history, where he uses these kinds of terms to discuss the development of human societies. Animal self-love makes us approach other animals of our kind for sex and nurturing and to live in their company, but our rational predisposition brings with it a comparative and competitive drive. As rational creatures who live in societies, we observe others and compare ourselves with them. We constantly evaluate their well-being, their various skills, their wealth, power, how good they are morally, and so on. We do not want to be worse than others, and we are afraid that they will strive to be superior to us. We also want them to think well of us. This rational but non-moral predisposition of self-love motivates us to emulate and compete. It gives rise to social antagonism, which Kant famously calls 'unsociable sociability' [*die ungesellige Geselligkeit*] (8:20.30)[29]. In

---

in or form social groups'. Since this belongs to the animal level, I use 'sociality' for the animal impulse and (unsocial) 'sociability' for the social self-love for which reason is required.

28 '2. Die Anlagen für die MENSCHHEIT können auf den allgemeinen Titel der zwar physischen, aber doch *vergleichenden* Selbstliebe (wozu Vernunft erfordert wird) gebracht werden: sich nämlich nur in Vergleichung mit andern als glücklich oder unglücklich zu beurtheilen. Von ihr rührt die Neigung her, *sich in der Meinung Anderer einen Werth zu verschaffen*; und zwar ursprünglich bloß den der *Gleichheit:* keinem über sich Überlegenheit zu verstatten, mit einer beständigen Besorgniß verbunden, daß andere darnach streben möchten; woraus nachgerade eine ungerechte Begierde entspringt, sie sich über Andere zu erwerben.'

29 The key text here is 'Idea for a Universal History with a Cosmopolitan Aim'. Kant's basic idea of unsocial sociability is not his own invention, and similar notions had been previously expressed by various authors. As noted above, Rousseau called the self-love related to social antagonism *amour propre* (see Rousseau 1997 [1755], p. 218; see also 1974 [1762], pp. 173–5 (begin-

unsociable sociability, self-love draws us together to form communities, and the same self-love also threatens to destroy them (see 8:20.30–33). Self-love can be a great source of evil, a source of arrogant self-conceit, greed, dominance, tyranny, and war, but competitive antagonism also drives culture forward and propels the development of natural human predispositions. The self-love of humanity makes us advance our various talents, taste, and the argumentative skills we need in our quest for knowledge (see Cohen 2014, p. 81). It motivates us to emulate the morality of others, and it is generally a source of our inclination for honour (see Denis 2014, p. 200). As Kant explains in 'Idea for a Universal History with a Cosmopolitan Aim'[30], this cultural process grounds a frame of mind 'which can with time transform the rude natural predisposition to make moral distinctions into determinate practical principles and hence transform a *pathologically* compelled agreement to form a society finally into a *moral* whole.' (8:21.14–17)[31]

This is at base how the self-love of humanity is predisposed to the good. What is particularly interesting from the perspective of animal mechanical self-love, and self-love and love more generally, is that the higher (though still physical and not moral) self-love is rooted in animal sociality. As Wood (2009, p. 115) notes, unsociable sociability is a 'modification' of the social animal predisposition. Being instinctively drawn to others grounds rational comparison with others, and the development of comparative self-love from this basis can somehow be morally transformative at the level of society.

Before concluding this section, let us turn to whether this idea can be made sense of by looking at the connection between animal sociality and what Kant calls *love of honour* [*Ehrliebe*]. According to Kant, the inclination to be equal to others gives rise to emulation, which we ought to cultivate and which 'serves merely to educate our animal nature and make it adequate to humanity, or the intellectual being within us, and to its laws.' (LE, 27:695.17–20)[32] This emulative tendency gives rise to love of honour (LE, 27:695.25–30; see Denis 2014, p. 200). Drawing from previous discussions on this topic (Smit & Timmons 2015; Denis 2014), I would suggest that there are two basic kinds of love of hon-

---

ning of Book IV)). For more detailed accounts of the historical influences behind Kant's idea of unsociable sociability, see Schneewind (2009) and Wood (2009, esp. pp. 114–117).
30 'Idee zu einer allgemeinen Geschichte in weltbürgerlicher Absicht'.
31 'welche die grobe Naturanlage zur sittlichen Unterscheidung mit der Zeit in bestimmte praktische Principien und so eine *pathologisch*-abgedrungene Zusammenstimmung zu einer Gesellschaft endlich in ein *moralisches* Ganze verwandeln kann.'
32 'sie dient nur zur Ausbildung unserer thierischen Natur, und um sie mit der Menschheit oder dem intellectuellen Wesen in uns und dessen Gesetzen angemessen zu machen.' Translation modified.

our in Kant: one *physical*, the other *moral*.³³ The first kind is emphasised in Kant's earlier lectures on ethics³⁴, while the latter plays a greater role in his mature moral philosophy. Physical love of honour is a natural impulse [*Trieb*] or inclination to secure respect and a 'favourable judgment' [*ein günstiges Urtheil*] from others (LE, 27:408.4–5; 27:408.29). Like the other drives connected to self-love and unsociable sociability, love of honour has an ambiguous nature. When we take the judgments of others into account in assessing our own actions, we indirectly pave the way for morality. This love of honour is a natural and in itself unselfish (see LE, 27:410.30–31) inclination merely not to be an object of contempt (LE, 27:408.35–37). As such, it is not directed to one's own advantage (27:408.5–7), but it can easily turn into an ambitious craving for honour, or arrogant self-conceit, such that we come to view others as inferior and think of ourselves as being entitled to their highest respect. In Kant's mature moral philosophy, on the other hand, it is respect for the moral law that grounds love of honour. In *The Metaphysics of Morals*, love of honour is a virtue based on the self-assessment of our dignity in comparison with the moral law (MM, 6:420.13–30; see LE, 27:609.5–610.9; 27:695–696; 27:667.12–21). Love of honour is also a basic claim to be respected by others because of one's fundamental standing (and equality with others) as a moral being (MM, 6:464.5–11; see Denis 2014, pp. 206–207). The moral love of honour is not based on external concern for the opinions of others: 'A lover of honour finds in himself no need to be known [for his merits]' (LE, 27:665.6–7)³⁵. Hence the two basic kinds of love of honour differ from each other with respect to their ground. Even though the physical love of honour can be unselfish, it must be classified under self-love in the broadest sense because it is based on inclination (and con-

---

33 The analyses of this topic offered by Smit and Timmons (2015) and Denis (2014) are extremely helpful. However, neither Smit and Timmons nor Denis make an attempt to connect love of honour with love's general framework – i.e. they do not problematise the status of love of honour *as love*. As with the animal impulses of self-love, Kant never discusses love of honour in terms of the general division of love. Given my previous analysis of love and desire, we can see why Kant might call the physical love of honour 'love': as an inclination, it is connected with the (lower) faculty of desire. There is also a long-running linguistic convention involved here: even Aristotle referred to desire for honour as 'love of honour' (1984; Nicomachean Ethics, Book IV, 1125b1–25; see Denis 2014, p. 203). On the other hand, as I will show below, moral love of honour comes close to respect.
34 In particular, I'm speaking about the Collins notes on ethics.
35 'Ein Ehrliebender findet in sich kein Bedürfnis, bekannt zu sein'.

nected with emulation).³⁶ Moral love of honour, or 'true love of honour' [*wahre Ehrliebe*] (see LE, 27:695.26) would seem to be a kind of self-respect.

For the mature Kant, of course, animality cannot serve as the basis of morality, which must be grounded in pure practical reason. In the Vigilantius notes on ethics, however, true love of honour can come about when animal nature is educated by cultivating the natural, inborn tendency to emulation, such that one learns gradually to test one's worth not against others but against the moral law (LE, 27:695.20–26). Kant does not elaborate on how one learns this, but it would probably be through moral education (see 9:446–449). My conceptual point is that by looking at love of honour, it is possible to detect a predisposition to the good in the animal self-love of sociality. Through the unsociably sociable self-love of humanity, animal sociality connects to love of honour and may thus be a contributing factor in the acknowledgment of the fundamental equality of all human beings as moral beings. But as Denis (2014, p. 205) warns us, maybe the continuity in Kant's accounts of love of honour shouldn't be exaggerated, and my basic claim in this section does not hinge on this tentative suggestion concerning the role of love of honour in mediating animality and morality.

The bulk of my discussion in this section has been motivated by a desire to understand. I have merely argued that Kant views the strongest impulses of human nature in terms of love, and that these impulses can be classified under animal mechanical self-love. Moreover, I am confident that animal mechanical self-love is *somehow* a predisposition to the good. The social impulse of animal self-love grounds the unsociably sociable self-love of humanity, which belongs to the history and teleology of moral progress. Love of honour is an interesting notion along this trajectory. At the very least, animal mechanical self-love is, for Kant, a necessary condition of the continued survival of our species.

1.2 The Middle Level of Self-Love

I shall now move on to what I call the broad middle level of self-love. The first section already identified this level from the perspective of the philosophy of history. Here, my focus will be moral philosophy. The moral perspective marks the self-love normally referred to in discussions of self-love in Kant, and it is clearly

---

36 The next section will show, with reference to the second *Critique*, that all inclination-based maxims fall under self-love, even if they are not 'selfish' in the sense of seeking one's own advantage.

this kind of self-love that Kant had the most to say about. In order to make sense of this notion, I will consider the operation of self-love in the mature period, focusing on the *Groundwork*, the second *Critique*, and the *Religion*, while also taking into account the Vigilantius lectures on ethics and *The Metaphysics of Morals*.

I will approach this level of self-love with an interpretative key provided in the *Religion*, according to which love in general, and self-love in particular, is divided into two distinct forms or types of love, namely love of benevolence and love of delight. For this reason, I will begin by grounding my interpretation in the *Religion* and then work my way back chronologically through the *Groundwork* and the second *Critique*. We might call this the general division approach to the middle level of self-love.

Considering the overall aims of the present chapter and this study as a whole, there are three main claims that I shall argue for in this section: 1) Kant's moral philosophy contains a notion of self-love that requires reason (and that is hence distinct from and cognitively 'higher' than animal mechanical self-love); 2) this self-love may be plausibly interpreted in terms of the general division of love, such that self-love is mainly benevolence toward oneself but also delight in oneself; and 3) while the latter especially brings with it the danger of self-conceit [*Eigendünkel*], which is evil, both forms of love are acceptable under moral conditions.

I take it that none of these claims are trivial, and they may be even more prone to objections than my assertions in the previous section. It would be possible to argue on the basis of certain passages in the *Groundwork* that animal mechanical self-love and 'higher' self-love are in fact not distinguishable from each other, and that the general division of love is simply a peculiarity of the *Religion*, and not supported by Kant's other major works. However, I hope to show that these lines of argumentation will not work. The textual evidence suggests that Kant developed his account of self-love substantially after the *Groundwork*, and since the later works are fairly consistent in outline among themselves, their picture of self-love is preferable. This is not to say that Kant essentially changed his mind on self-love after 1785 or that the period following the *Groundwork* was marked by complete uniformity. I wish only to suggest that certain distinctions that we find in later works were not yet clearly in place in 1785. A further possible objection against my claims is that, even if it were granted that part of self-love involves reason and that the general division of love has something to do with it, this self-love still contains elements, or some meaning, that cannot be grasped in terms of the general division. At face value, this objection seems to me to be the most promising, and its success hinges on whether or not the general division is robust enough to capture Kant's most all-encompassing formulations of self-love, where self-love informs all instrumentally rational non-moral activity. I believe the general division is indeed robust at the middle level and that the general division of love, together with the multilevel account of self-love, makes it possible to harmonise the self-love discussed in the *Groundwork* with the later works while continuing to appreciate their apparent differences.

As mentioned above, in the fourth section of the first part of the *Religion* ('Concerning the Origin of Evil in Human Nature')[37], Kant introduces the idea of a general division of love, which is applicable to self-love in particular: 'Like love in general, *self-love* too can be divided into love of benevolence and love of delight (BENEVOLENTIAE ET COMPLACENTIAE), and both (as is self-evident) must be rational.' (R, 6:45.22–25)[38] The first amounts to wanting [*wollen*] things to go well [*wohl*] for oneself, and it is rational insofar as the instrumental reasoning related to the pursuit of happiness [*Glückseligkeit*] or well-being [*Wohlergehen*] is apt. The rational maxims of love of benevolence for oneself are non-moral; they subordinate reason to natural inclination. (R, 6:45.25–32) Rational love of delight, on the other hand, has two senses, the first of which coincides with love of benevolence: 'we take delight in those maxims, already mentioned, which have for the end the satisfaction of natural inclination [...] and then it is one and the same with love of benevolence toward oneself' (R, 6:45.35–38)[39]. The second sense of love of delight for oneself is distinctive and seems to imply morality: 'Only the maxim of self-love, of *unconditional delight* in oneself (independent of gain or loss resulting from action), is however the inner principle of contentment only possible for us on condition that our maxims are subordinated to the moral law.' (R, 6:45.40–46.18)[40]

This passage supports point 1) above: there is *some sort of* rational self-love in Kant that is distinct from the way animal mechanical self-love is described (this point is corroborated by the existence of the 'self-love of humanity' discussed in the latter half of the previous section; see R, 6:27.4–12). Hence, it may be proposed that there are at least two 'levels' of self-love in Kant: a non-

---

[37] 'Vom Ursprunge des Bösen in der menschlichen Natur.'
[38] 'Wie *Liebe* überhaupt, so kann auch *Selbstliebe* in die des *Wohlwollens* und des *Wohlgefallens* (BENEVOLENTIAE ET COMPLACENTIAE) eingetheilt werden, und beide müssen (wie sich von selbst versteht) vernünftig sein.'
[39] 'wir uns in jenen schon genannten auf Befriedigung der Naturneigung abzweckenden Maximen [...] wohlgefallen; und da ist sie mit der Liebe des Wohlwollens gegen sich selbst einerlei'. Translation modified.
[40] 'Allein die Maxime der Selbstliebe des *unbedingten* (nicht von Gewinn oder Verlust als den Folgen der Handlung abhängenden) *Wohlgefallens* an sich selbst würde das innere Princip einer allein unter der Bedingung der Unterordnung unserer Maximen unter das moralische Gesetz uns möglichen Zufriedenheit sein.'

rational level and a rational level. What I wish to focus on next is claim 2), which concerns the viability of the general division of love in this context. By showing that the general division of love is indeed viable, I hope to provide the necessary conceptual tools for establishing and clarifying the meaning of 3) – the claim that self-love is acceptable under moral conditions while self-conceit is evil.

In the *Groundwork*, self-love is explicitly contrasted with respect for the moral law. The latter represents a worth that 'infringes' [*Abbruch thut*] on self-love (GW, 4:401.28–29fn.) in the sense that we are subject to the moral law 'without consulting self-love' (GW, 4:401.33fn.)[41]. When explaining the proper motivational ground of moral action, Kant uses *Selbstliebe* as a general term to capture those motivational grounds that are distinct from morally adequate motivation. Pure morality abstracts from the presentation of ends, and by implication self-love can be seen to refer generally to cases where an expected 'effect' [*Wirkung*] of conduct is made the motivational ground of action. It seems to be self-love that informs all our fears and inclinations. (GW, 4:401) In this sense, in the *Groundwork* picture, self-love simply denotes all of our non-moral interests (see also GW, 4:406) – a picture that is consistent with the second *Critique*. Throughout his writings, Kant assumes that what human beings (as imperfect rational creatures) naturally desire is happiness, and hence self-love may be identified as the principle of subjective non-moral happiness. In fact, it is the name given to the subjective interest in happiness.

But the *Groundwork* does not clearly distinguish between rational and non-rational aspects of self-love. In Section I, 'preservation' [*Erhaltung*] and 'prosperity' [*Wohlergehen*] are identified as the constituents of happiness, which according to Kant is better pursued with instinct rather than reason. Here, self-preservation (which Kant later calls 'love of life') is not distinguished from prosperity in terms of reason, as is the case in the *Religion* (GW, 4:395.4–12; R, 6:26.12–18; cf. 6:45fn.). However, happiness as the satisfaction of the sum of all one's inclinations (GW, 4:394.17–18; see Timmermann 2007, p. 20) in the *Groundwork* is a purpose that is assumed to be naturally necessary in all imperfect rational creatures (GW, 4:415.28–33). In other words, even though the distinction between animal mechanical self-love and rationally comparative self-love is not clear in the *Groundwork*, Kant says neither that self-love is non-rational or irrational nor that it is impermissible as such. We must interpret his idea such that, in the light of his basic division between nature and freedom/morality, self-love concerns our natural inclinations (it flows from the side of nature, as it were) but is entangled in our rational capacities.

---

[41] 'ohne die Selbstliebe zu befragen'.

In the *Groundwork*, the pursuit of happiness comes in the guise of 'hypothetical assertoric imperatives'[42], which means that the pursuit involves principles or quasi-commands (see GW, 4:414–415; cf. 4:418.28–32) stemming from means-end reasoning concerning the purpose of 'one's own greatest well-being' (GW, 4:416.2)[43]. In this limited and qualified sense, Herbert Paton (1947, p. 91) is correct: self-love in the *Groundwork* is 'an objective principle of practical reason', for it is assumed as actual in all finite rational beings. But the 'objective' here should not be confused with 'objectively necessary' in the moral sense. Self-love is not a duty, and as such it is not in the service of morality. Indeed, what is at issue in Kant's examples of the specific duties not to commit suicide and not to make false promises is 'the principle of self-love' [*Princip der Selbstliebe*] (GW, 4:422.7; 4:422.24), but the key point is that the self-love in question may not be universalised (see Timmermann 2007, p. 81). In Kant's examples of how the principle of self-love functions in moral life, what we encounter are immoral instances of self-love. Suppose, for instance, that I borrow money and falsely promise to repay it. This may well promote my 'own benefit' [*eigenen Zuträglichkeit*] and 'future well-being' [*künftigen Wohlbefinden*], but if universalised the promise would contradict itself, for then no one would believe others' promises (GW, 4:422.15–36).[44] Self-love may be objectively actual (its principle is active in all humans), but it is by no means objectively good (good 'as such' or 'in itself').

Can the natural but rational and principled self-love of the *Groundwork* be interpreted in terms of the general division of love found in the *Religion*? Instances of self-love in the *Groundwork* seem to refer to one's own happiness or well-being, and in this sense self-love in the *Groundwork* may well be viewed along the lines of love of benevolence in the *Religion*. In short, it consists in wishing or willing that things will go well for oneself. There is no talk in the *Groundwork*

---

[42] According to Kant, a rational being is endowed with a will – that is, the capacity of acting from principles, which are representations of laws. Objective principles are rational commands, the formulae of which are imperatives. Imperatives are further divided into hypothetical and categorical; hypothetical imperatives concern means-end reasoning, whereas only categorical imperatives are moral and do not refer to other ends. Hypothetical imperatives are further divided into problematic and assertoric practical principles, where the former concern possible purposes and the latter actual purposes. Moral imperatives are apodictically practical principles. (GW, 4:412–415) However, hypothetical imperatives are not commands strictly speaking but rather 'counsels' [*Anrathungen*] (GW, 4:418.31). In the second *Critique*, the hypothetical imperatives of self-love are, properly speaking, theoretical; they merely point out empirical causal connections and do not necessitate universally in determining the will. (C2, 5:25–26)
[43] 'seinem eigenen größten Wohlseyn'.
[44] I do not aim here to determine whether this argument is ultimately successful.

of any specific pleasure or delight taken in the maxims of self-love, which would seem to exclude the possibility of interpreting the self-love of the *Groundwork* directly in terms of love of delight. In the *Groundwork*, Kant writes that 'skill in the choice of the means to one's own greatest well-being can be called *prudence*' (GW, 4:416.1–3)[45], even though the subjective concept of happiness cannot be determined with complete certainty (GW, 4:418). In the *Religion*, love of benevolence is rational if it is 'consistent with' [*zusammen bestehen*] and 'apt' [*tauglich*] with regards to happiness at the level of one's choices (R, 6:45.27–30). These rationality criteria seem to match the *Groundwork* definition of prudence quite closely. This supports the idea that while the non-rationality/rationality divide in the *Groundwork* is occasionally fuzzy when it comes to self-love, the principle of self-love discussed in the *Groundwork* is indeed love of benevolence. Hence, while the general division of self-love is not explicitly operative in the *Groundwork*, the principle of self-love may be plausibly interpreted in terms of it, which lends support to claim 2) above.[46]

I now move on to the second *Critique*. For explanatory purposes, we can roughly divide Kant's treatment of self-love in this work into two 'phases' according to the *function* of self-love in the discussion. It seems to me that the function of self-love in the first chapter of the 'Analytic' is more or less equivalent to how self-love operates in the *Groundwork*: according to Kant's dualistic conception of possible determining grounds of the will, self-love functions as a general term for the determining ground of a will not determined by the moral law (see fig. 1). In the third chapter, on the other hand, Kant discusses how the moral law ought to influence the will *as regards self-love* and the moral danger that ensues if this

---

[45] 'kann man die Geschicklichkeit in der Wahl der Mittel zu seinem eigenen größten Wohlsein Klugheit [...] nennen.' Note that in this passage Kant speaks of prudence 'in the narrowest sense' [*im engsten Verstande*]. It is unclear what the broader sense would be, but Kant explains in a footnote that prudence divides into 'worldly prudence' [*Weltklugheit*] and 'private prudence' [*Privatklugheit*]. The former is the skill of using others for one's purposes; the latter, the unification of one's purposes to one's 'enduring advantage' [*daurenden Vortheil*] (GW, 4:416.30–33). I take it that private prudence is the broader of the two, but this is in tension with the equally plausible notion that skill or insight [*Einsicht*] to unite one's purposes belongs to skill in choosing the means to one's 'own greatest well-being' (which is prudence in the narrowest sense). (Cf. Kain 2003, pp. 247, 263fn.60)

[46] Note that even if my interpretation of self-love in the *Groundwork* is rejected, we might still need to accept the general division interpretation of the middle level of self-love on the basis of the relative harmony between the second *Critique* and the *Religion*. In this case, we would need a weighty argument as to why the doctrine of self-love in the *Groundwork* overrides the combination of the second *Critique* and the *Religion*. However, it is difficult for me to see how this could be charitable, and I don't have such an argument in sight.

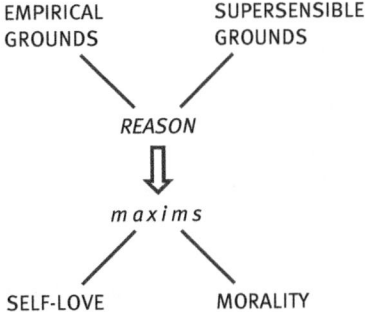

Figure 1. Determining Grounds of the Will

does not take place properly (the problem of self-conceit). I will now consider both of these 'phases' in the light of the general division.

The lion's share of the first chapter of the second *Critique* is dedicated to establishing that the practical principles of self-love (which Kant calls 'material') are not the principles generated by the moral law (which is 'formal').[47] The basic idea is summarised in Kant's famous statement: 'All material practical principles as such are, without exception, of one and the same kind and come under the general principle of self-love or one's own happiness.' (C2, 5:22.6–8)[48] Equally telling is the following: 'The direct opposite of the principle of morality is the principle of *one's own* happiness made the determining ground of the will' (C2, 5:35.7–8)[49]. We learn that in the case of self-love, the determining ground of the will always rests on expectations of pleasure or displeasure, 'agreeableness' [*Annehmlichkeit*] or 'disagreeableness' [*Unannehmlichkeit*]. The fact that pleasure is involved makes it plausible to suppose that the self-love at issue might be love of delight. This conjecture is supported by the fact that

---

47 As Jens Timmermann has pointed out to me, the discussion is also directed against rival ethical schools, most notably the hedonism of Epicurus (see C2, 5:24.15–20).
48 'Alle materiale praktische Principien sind, als solche, insgesammt von einer und derselben Art und gehören unter das allgemeine Princip der Selbstliebe oder eigenen Glückseligkeit.' It is important to note that the broad formulation of self-love implies that even beneficent love of neighbour, if based on inclination, is technically subsumed under self-love. However, this does not mean that loving one's neighbour out of inclination is selfish; it merely means that in the choice of the objects of beneficent love from inclination we are prone to a 'second order self-partiality' (see Wood 1999, p. 271). Note also that Kant occasionally distinguishes between sympathy [*Sympathie*] and self-love [*Philautie*] (C2, 5:85.12).
49 'Das gerade Widerspiel des Princips der Sittlichkeit ist: wenn das der *eigenen* Glückseligkeit zum Bestimmungsgrunde des Willens gemacht wird'.

there are no instances of 'benevolence' [*Wohlwollen*] in the first chapter of the 'Analytic'. With this said, is 'delight' [*Wohlgefallen*] mentioned in this context?

As Gregor notes, 'Kant [...] uses a variety of words for "pleasure"' (C2, p. 157fn.a), and words such as *Lust, Vergnügen, Zufriedenheit* and *Wohlgefallen* are all quite close to each other. As determining grounds of the will, they belong to the 'lower faculty of desire' [*unteres Begehrungsvermögen*], as opposed to the 'higher faculty' [*oberes Begehrungsvermögen*], which alone is moral and furnished by pure practical reason irrespective of sensibility. And indeed, under Remark I of the basic theorem of self-love (Theorem II), we find a chain of signifiers that goes from 'satisfaction' [*Vergnügen*], 'joys' [*Freuden*], 'amusements' [*Ergötzungen*][50], and 'enjoyment' [*Genuß*] back to 'satisfaction' [*Vergnügen*], and finally the word *Wohlgefallen* appears (C2, 5:24.11–12). The point is that even though the pleasures we take in 'overcoming obstacles opposed to our plans' (C2, 5:24.4–5)[51] are 'more refined because they are more in our control than others' (C2, 5:24.6–7)[52], the determining ground of this delight is nevertheless our own happiness, or the lower faculty of desire – i.e. self-love.[53] (C2, 5:24)

It thus seems plausible to identify the self-love at issue in Chapter I of the 'Analytic' as love of delight. But does this create an inconsistency with the *Groundwork*, where I identified self-love as love of benevolence? In both cases, the basic point is clearly that self-love and the moral law constitute two opposing grounds of action or determination of the will. How is this apparent similarity regarding the function of self-love to be explained if we are dealing with two different dimensions of the general division of love? Quite easily, I think, if we recall that Kant explains in the *Religion* that the first sense of love of delight is in fact identical to love of benevolence (R, 6:45fn., see above). In this case, love of delight simply denotes taking pleasure in the inclination-based maxims of love of benevolence (insofar as these maxims yield successful results) 'like a mer-

---

50 I here follow Timmermann's suggestion (private discussion) when it comes to translating *Ergötzungen*. Gregor uses 'delights', but this would be confusing as I render *Wohlgefallen* 'delight'. In this context, Gregor has *Wohlgefallen* as 'pleasure'.
51 'Überwindung der Hindernisse, die sich unserem Vorsatze entgegensetzen'.
52 'feinere [...], weil sie mehr wie andere in unserer Gewalt sind.'
53 Cf. Christine Korsgaard (1997, p. 220), who argues, in a supposedly Kantian fashion, that the instrumental reason related to pursuing our aims shares 'a common normative source' with moral reason in the autonomy of the agent. Even though specifically moral aims also often require auxiliary instrumental reasoning, I think that Korsgaard's account, at least from an exegetical perspective, does not sufficiently appreciate Kant's basic distinction between self-love and the moral law as two opposing sources of motivation for action, which he so vehemently holds in both the *Groundwork* and the second *Critique*. Korsgaard's views have been forcefully criticised by Camilla Kong (2012).

chant whose business speculations turn out well and who, because of the maxims he adopted therein, rejoices in his good insight' (R, 6:45fn.)⁵⁴. The fact that Kant identifies this taking of pleasure with 'wanting things to go well for oneself' implies that the notion of pleasure is implicitly included in the love of self-benevolence as such. The general division therefore helps to make clear that, at a general level, the self-love of the first chapter of the second *Critique* is not only consistent with the self-love of the *Groundwork* but can also be viewed as an elaboration of it.⁵⁵

However, in the 'second phase' of Kant's discussion of self-love in the second *Critique*, things become exegetically more complicated. In Chapter III, 'On the Incentives of Pure Practical Reason' (C2, 5:72.27)⁵⁶, Kant discusses the effects of the moral law on the mind as an incentive or 'spring' [*Triebfeder*] (see Engstrom 2010, pp. 91–93). Because Kant's basic system of the mental structure of the agent relies on the dualism of the moral law and sensibility, the effects of the moral law must be felt as effects on sensibility. We know that allowing the sensuous side of our nature to determine the will is equated with self-love in a broad sense, and thus the effects of the moral law are necessarily effects on self-love (inclinations, feeling). A will determined by the moral law must reject all such self-love that is opposed to the law. In this context, Kant refines the conceptual framework of self-love, introducing new systematic distinctions:

> All the inclinations together (which can be brought into a tolerable system and the satisfaction of which is then called one's own happiness) constitute *regard for oneself* (SOLIPSISMUS). This is either the self-regard of *love for oneself*, a predominant *benevolence* toward oneself (PHILAUTIA), or that of *delight* in oneself (ARROGANTIA). The former is called, in particular, *self-love*, the latter, *self-conceit*. Pure practical reason merely *infringes* upon self-love, inasmuch as it only restricts it, as natural and active in us even prior to the moral law, to the condition of agreement with this law, and then it is called *rational self-love*. But it *strikes down* self-conceit altogether […]. (ibid., 5:73.9–18)⁵⁷

---

54 'wie ein Kaufmann, dem seine Handlungsspeculationen gut einschlagen, und der sich wegen der dabei genommenen Maximen seiner guten Einsicht erfreut.' Pluhar's translation.
55 I am not claiming that the two accounts are technically identical. For instance, there are differences in the way Kant construes his treatment of hypothetical imperatives, but I cannot discuss these differences in detail here.
56 'Von den Triebfedern der reinen praktischen Vernunft'.
57 'Alle Neigungen zusammen (die auch wohl in ein erträgliches System gebracht werden können, und deren Befriedigung alsdann eigene Glückseligkeit heißt) machen die *Selbstsucht* (SOLIPSISMUS) aus. Diese ist entweder die der *Selbstliebe*, eines über alles gehenden *Wohlwollens* gegen sich selbst (PHILAUTIA), oder die des *Wohlgefallens* an sich selbst (ARROGANTIA). Jene heißt besonders *Eigenliebe*, diese *Eigendünkel*. Die reine praktische Vernunft thut der Eigenliebe blos *Abbruch*, indem sie solche, als natürlich und noch vor dem moralischen Gesetze in uns

Is the general division of love into love of benevolence and love of delight operative in this passage? Yes and no. What Kant generally calls self-love in other parts of the *Groundwork* and the second *Critique* is now called self-regard [*Selbstsucht*]. Here, Kant seems to use the term 'self-love' [*Selbstliebe, Eigenliebe*] in a more restrictive sense: self-love 'in particular' [*besonders*] is benevolence towards oneself, and it is distinguished from delight in oneself, which is 'self-conceit' [*Eigendünkel*][58]. The basic notions of the general division of love, benevolence and delight, are explicitly operative, but 'self-love' is here connected only to benevolence. This suggests that love of benevolence is a more paradigmatic form of self-love. But what should we make of the fact that delight is discussed here not in terms of love but in terms of self-conceit, which, as implied by the context, is obviously reprehensible? Does this cast doubt on the 'acceptability-thesis' of claim 3) above, according to which both benevolence for oneself and delight in oneself are somehow acceptable? Or does it mean that the delight in oneself that is under discussion here is not part of self-love? And if delight as self-conceit does not belong to self-love, what are the implications for the success of the general division approach in the particular context of self-love?

I will address from three different directions the problem of how self-love, delight in oneself, and self-conceit interrelate, which will clarify the status of the general division of love in this context and bring to a close my discussion of the middle level of self-love. These three directions are 1) the generality of self-love, 2) the problem of rationality in self-love, and 3) the Vigilantius notes.

1) Firstly, there is a sense internal to the second *Critique* in which both benevolence and delight in Chapter III can be, or even must be, interpreted as belonging to self-love in the broadest middle-level sense. Kant's description of self-regard as the sum of inclinations (as a tolerable system) necessarily falls under the basic description of self-love in 'Theorem II', where self-love includes 'all material practical principles' (C2, 5:22.6)[59]. We can understand the relation between self-regard and self-love (in the broad sense of the second *Critique*) either such that they are equivalent, insofar as the system of self-love is 'tolerable' [*erträglich*], or such that self-regard is a name used for self-love when everything that

---

rege, nur auf die Bedingung der Einstimmung mit diesem Gesetze einschränkt; da sie alsdann *vernünftige Selbstliebe* genannt wird. Aber den Eigendünkel *schlägt* sie gar nieder'.

58 For an earlier, pre-autonomy treatment of self-love and self-conceit, see the Collins notes on ethics, where self-love or *philautia* is described as love of delight and contrasted with self-conceit (LE, 27:357).

59 'Alle materiale praktische Principien'.

falls under self-love is *taken together* (see above, 5:73.8–19). In both cases, any instance of benevolence for oneself or delight in oneself is subsumed under self-love (irrespective of whether the system is 'tolerable'). Further along in Chapter III Kant explains that self-love is the propensity to turn 'subjective determining grounds of choice into the objective determining ground of the will in general', whereas 'if self-love makes itself lawgiving, it can be called *self-conceit.*' (C2, 5:74.15–19)[60] The latter passage confirms that self-conceit belongs to self-love: it is self-love that arrogantly takes the place of the moral law.[61] Thus the fact that Kant distinguishes between self-love and self-conceit cannot as such be taken to warrant the interpretation that the latter does not belong to the former. The viability of the general division approach is not threatened on the mere basis of the existence of such a division.

2) In the light of the second *Critique* and the *Religion*, we now have at least three different senses of 'rational self-love', which may or may not turn out to be equivalent. In the *Religion*, love of benevolence as willing one's own happiness is 'rational to the extent that with respect to the end only what is consistent with the greatest and most abiding well-being is chosen, and that also the most apt means for each of these components of happiness are chosen.' (R, 6:45.27–30)[62] In the second *Critique*, love of benevolence is rational when it is 'infringed' by the moral law 'to the condition of agreement with this law' (C2, 5:73.15–17)[63]. If we interpret consistency 'with the greatest and most abiding well-being' as implying that one does not act immorally, then the two senses of rational love of benevolence in the *Religion* and the second *Critique* can indeed be viewed as equivalent. This would imply that they cohere with the prudence discussed in the *Groundwork* and that Kantian prudence as such implies

---

60 'den subjectiven Bestimmungsgründen seiner Willkür zum objectiven Bestimmungsgrunde des Willens überhaupt' / 'welche [*die Selbstliebe*], wenn sie sich gesetzgebend und zum unbedingten praktischen Princip macht, *Eigendünkel* heißen kann.'
61 The self-love that serves as the ground of self-conceit can now be viewed as either love of benevolence toward oneself (wanting things to go well for oneself) or love of delight as taking pleasure in the maxims of the former (which would amount to the same thing as the former on the basis of the *Religion*). For detailed discussions of self-conceit, see Reath (2006, pp. 14–17, 23–25), Engstrom (2010), and Moran (2014).
62 'vernünftig, als theils in Ansehung des Zwecks nur dasjenige, was mit dem größten und dauerhaftesten Wohlergehen zusammen bestehen kann, theils zu jedem dieser Bestandstücke der Glückseligkeit die tauglichsten Mittel gewählt werden.'
63 '*Abbruch* thut' / 'auf die Bedingung der Einstimmung mit diesem Gesetze'.

a moral side constraint: the prudent agent does not act immorally.[64] This interpretation is charitable, for it renders the mature period consistent in this respect. But the interpretation is not necessary, and the text remains ambiguous. It is equally possible that there are two different rationality criteria for love of benevolence, such that rationality implies mere instrumentality irrespective of morality in the case of the *Religion* (and, supposedly, the *Groundwork*) and the 'stronger', morally constrained instrumental rationality appears only in the second *Critique*. Fortunately, my argument does not hinge on this point. The third type of rational self-love concerns love of delight (as distinct from love of benevolence). In the *Religion*, the condition of rationality for this self-love is quite simply morality in the sense in which morality was first opposed to self-love in the *Groundwork* and the second *Critique*. For this reason, Kant has doubts about the appropriateness of the term 'rational self-love' in this case:

> We could call this love a *rational love* of oneself that prevents any adulteration of the incentives of the power of choice by other causes of contentment consequent upon one's actions (under the name of happiness to be procured through them). But, since this denotes unconditional respect for the law, why needlessly render more difficult the clear understanding of the principle with the expression *rational self-love*, when this self-love is however *moral* only under the latter condition, and we thus go around in a circle (for we can love ourselves morally only to the extent that we are conscious of our maxim to make respect for the law the highest incentive of our power of choice)? (R, 6:46.21–30)[65]

Is this the same sense in which rational love of benevolence is described as 'rational' in the second *Critique*? Clearly not, since the rationality criterion for rational love of benevolence in the second *Critique* is morality merely in the negative sense: reason may still be used in the service of inclination, and it suffices that the prudential maxim is not contra-moral. Yet the rational moral love of delight in the *Religion* implies a contentment [*Zufriedenheit*] that is only possible through 'unconditional respect for the law'. It is also worth noting that in the second *Critique* passage quoted above (C2, 5:73.9–18), 'self-love' is not mentioned in

---

64 Note, however, that even in this case there is nothing moral about the self-love as such. It is just negatively constrained by morality.
65 'Man könnte diese die *Vernunftliebe* seiner selbst nennen, welche alle Vermischung anderer Ursachen der Zufriedenheit aus den Folgen seiner Handlungen (unter dem Namen einer dadurch sich zu verschaffenden Glückseligkeit) mit den Triebfedern der Willkür verhindert. Da nun das letztere die unbedingte Achtung fürs Gesetz bezeichnet, warum will man durch den Ausdruck einer *vernünftigen*, aber nur unter der letzteren Bedingung *moralischen Selbstliebe* sich das deutliche Verstehen des Princips unnöthigerweise erschweren, indem man sich im Zirkel herumdreht (denn man kann sich nur auf moralische Art selbst lieben, sofern man sich seiner Maxime bewußt ist, die Achtung fürs Gesetz zur höchsten Triebfeder seiner Willkür zu machen)?'

the context of delight in oneself, which is defined as self-conceit. Does this mean that the doctrines of self-love in the second *Critique* and the *Religion* are incompatible, or at least that they cannot be plausibly harmonised in terms of the general division of love? No, for in the second *Critique* we do find a notion of acceptable delight in oneself that is not self-conceit and that appears to coincide with the description of moral rational love of delight in the *Religion*. In the section on the 'Critical Resolution of the Antinomy of Practical Reason' (C2, 5:114)[66], Kant introduces the notion of a satisfaction or delight [*Wohlgefallen*] in oneself that is not based on material determining grounds and instead rests solely on the direct determination of the will by the moral law. (C2, 5:116.25 – 33) This is 'contentment with oneself' [*Selbstzufriedenheit*], which is 'a negative delight in one's existence, in which one is conscious of needing nothing.' (C2, 5:117.28 – 31)[67] It denotes 'mastery over one's inclinations' [*der Obermacht über seine Neigungen*] rather than 'complete independence' [*gänzliche Unabhängigkeit*] from them. (C2, 5:118.26 – 33) I interpret its negativity to mean that it is a delight that is not based on the positive satisfaction of any inclination (unlike the first sense of love of delight in the *Religion*) and merely follows from consciousness of being able to 'negate' inclinations through respect for the moral law. There are therefore two kinds of delight in oneself in the second *Critique*: self-conceit [*Eigendünkel*] and contentment with oneself [*Selbstzufriedenheit*]. The former (self-love as the unconditional practical principle in C2, 5:74.17 – 19) is practically identical with the *Religion*'s idea of self-love as the spring of evil: 'self-love [...], when adopted as the principle of all our maxims, is precisely the source of all evil.' (R, 6:45.14 – 15)[68] Self-contentment in the second *Critique* comes close to the second sense of love of delight in the *Religion*, which is also contentment [*Zufriedenheit*] with oneself through respect for the moral law. Hence, while the conceptual systems of self-love in the second *Critique* and the *Religion* seem different, these differences can be considered superficial. The respective notions of self-love can be harmonised, which provides support for claims 2) and 3) above concerning the

---

66 'Kritische Aufhebung der Antinomie der praktischen Vernunft'.
67 'ein negatives Wohlgefallen an seiner Existenz andeutet, in welchem man nichts zu bedürfen sich bewußt ist.'
68 'Selbstliebe [...], als Princip aller unserer Maximen angenommen, gerade die Quelle alles Bösen ist.' It now seems to me that the reason self-conceit is not discussed in terms of rational self-love either in the second *Critique* or in the *Religion* is that while the notion of self-conceit implies the existence of the rational capacity (its possibility belongs to the predisposition to humanity), it involves a morally improper use of reason, and in this sense it is *irrational*. Recall that the ground of evil cannot be located in a natural impulse and that its rational origin remains inscrutable (R, 6:32 – 43).

middle level of self-love: the general division of love is in operation, and both love of benevolence for oneself and love of delight in oneself are acceptable under moral conditions.[69]

3) The Vigilantius notes on ethics from 1793–94 corroborate the picture of the middle level of self-love I have drawn thus far. They explicitly confirm that Kant's use of the general division is not simply an anomaly found only in the *Religion* but is rather foundational to how Kant viewed self-love in the mature period. They also explain the relation between the conceptual systems of the second *Critique* and the *Religion*. In the Vigilantius notes, self-love is discussed as *philautia*. *Philautia* is divided into love of benevolence and love of delight. It is implied that love of benevolence means the inclination or the will to promote one's own ends, and there is no reason to view the account as differing significantly from Kant's previous discussions.[70] Love of benevolence is assumed to be active in all human beings, and it is acceptable. If the duty of love towards others[71] is excluded from consideration, love of benevolence is 'solipsism' [*Solipsismus*][72] or 'egoism' [*Eigennutz*], in which case it becomes a moral flaw. (LE, 27:620) Love of delight, on the other hand, is more complex, and as we would assume on the basis of the combination of the second *Critique* and the *Religion*,

---

[69] In general, the *Religion* asserts that both love of benevolence and love of delight 'must be rational'. This should now be understood in both a descriptive and a normative sense: these forms of self-love are rational on their own as a matter of definitional necessity (they imply the level of reason), and they appear under a normative requirement to be harnessed by reason or *made rational*. Even if love of benevolence is construed as being completely non-moral, the demand of aptness in instrumental reasoning imposes quasi-normative constraints on the operation of self-love. Love of delight may be moral as a consequence of the operation of pure practical reason (see also Section III of my Introduction).

[70] In comparison with the second *Critique* and the *Religion*, the main shift of emphasis in Kant's discussion of self-love in the Vigilantius notes (and *The Metaphysics of Morals*) is that whereas self-love (as love of benevolence) was previously mainly about the maxims of actions and wanting things to go well for oneself, in the latter two sources *philautia* is mainly about regarding oneself as worthy of being loved by others [*Liebenswürdig*]. Arrogance, on the other hand, is an unwarranted claim to respect, and I believe at least part of the explanation for this shift of emphasis has to do with the fact that the distinction between love and respect has such a prominent place in the 'Doctrine of Virtue'. Since self-love (as willing that things go well for me or that others love me) brings about self-conceit if made an unconditional law, it seems that somehow the will to be happy and loved by others brings about unjustified claims to respect from others if universalised absolutely (see LE, 27:621).

[71] See ch. 4.2.2.

[72] Note that the notion of *Solipsismus* seems more restrictive and negative in tone here than in the second *Critique* (see C2, 5:73).

three meanings of love of delight can be detected in Kant's treatment. Even though love of delight forms the other half of the division of *philautia* in these notes, it seems that Kant reserves the paradigmatic meaning of *philautia* for love of benevolence.[73] The first meaning, in which love of delight may be considered equivalent to love of benevolence, is skimmed over in passing in the very first sentence, the latter part of which already implies the danger of irrational self-conceitedness: 1) 'This, too, is *philautia*, if it is exclusively entertained towards oneself, but also becomes unreasonable' (LE, 27:621.18–19)[74]. We then learn that in comparison with others, love of delight becomes 'self-estimation of oneself' [*Selbstschätzung seiner selbst*], which has two possible outcomes: 2) 'arrogance' [*Arroganz*] and 3) 'true self-esteem' [*wahre Selbstschätzung*]. (LE, 27:621.26–622.5) The first is a faulty, unjustified claim to respect from others, and given that in the second *Critique* Kant defined self-conceited delight precisely as arrogance, we may take it that this is the same delight that was at issue in Kant's previous discussion of self-conceit. This arrogant delight is now discussed explicitly in terms of love of delight. True self-esteem, on the other hand, is based on 'a close examination of oneself' (LE, 27:621.29)[75] and is only warranted on the condition of performing imperfect meritorious duties. As a morally conditioned and permissible delight in oneself, this corresponds roughly to the moral love of delight in the *Religion* (which implies unconditional respect for the moral law) and the negative moral delight of the second *Critique* (which implies moral freedom or mastery over inclinations). In Vigilantius, however, the emphasis shifts from negative to positive: 'we thereby add a supplement to morality' and 'can thus acquire merit in relation to others' (LE, 27:622.17–20)[76]. There is a positive moral delight in oneself in Vigilantius, which seems very close to the concept of 'ethical reward' in the actual *Metaphysics of Morals*, a reward which is similarly occasioned by the performance of wide duties and is 'a moral pleasure that goes beyond mere contentment with oneself (which can

---

[73] This was the case in the second *Critique*, where *philautia* was love of benevolence and distinct from self-conceited delight (C2, 5:73). This is also the case in *The Metaphysics of Morals*, where *philautia* is contrasted with self-conceit (MM, 6:462.5–10). The Vigilantius notes, however, allow for the construal of false claims of moral merit in *Wohlgefällige Selbstliebe* as *philautia* (LE, 27:624–625). The context would seem to imply that this love of delight for oneself is in fact the self-conceit of the published works, but my argument does not hinge on this, and I do not wish to force the interpretation.
[74] 'Auch diese ist Philautie, wenn sie ausschließend gegen sich selbst ausgeübt wird, wird aber auch vernunftwidrig.'
[75] 'vorgängiger genauer Prüfung seiner selbst'.
[76] 'wir geben dadurch der Moralität einen Zusatz' / 'Verdienste können wir indeß nur dadurch gegen andere enlangen'.

be merely negative)' (MM, 6:391.12–13)[77]. Based on the combination of these passages, the interpretation must be that there are actually two possible forms of morally acceptable love of delight in oneself: negative self-contentment and positive moral pleasure from merit[78] (both of which, however, involve the danger of self-conceit).

Let us take stock of what we've learned about the middle level of self-love thus far. I hope to have shown: 1) that there is a self-love that involves reason (one that is 'higher' than mere animal nature); 2) that even though the conceptual system of this level of self-love varies throughout the mature period, these variations can be made sense of by using the general division of love in a way that renders the outlines and main tenets of Kant's discussion (relatively) consistent; and 3) that self-love is, paradigmatically, an acceptable love of benevolence for oneself common to all human beings, but it is also love of delight for oneself. I have also shown that love of delight may be 1) simply equivalent to love of benevolence, or 2) an acceptable moral self-contentment (negative) or self-esteem in a feeling of merit (positive), but it may also be 3) self-love turned into morally reprehensible self-conceit or arrogance. On this basis, the structural outline of the middle level of self-love may be presented in the form of a diagram (see fig. 2).

1.3 Self-Love and the Highest Good

We saw above that the only kind of self-love that Kant explicitly rejects is self-conceit or arrogance. Self-love that is made an unconditional law is 'the source of all evil', and the moral law 'strikes down' such self-conceit. But we have also seen that self-love is scarcely reducible to self-conceit, and that there are various

---

[77] 'einer moralischen Lust, die über die bloße Zufriedenheit mit sich selbst (die blos negativ sein kann) hinaus geht'.
[78] In relation to others, the positive pleasure might actually be derived from a sympathetic reaction to the recipient of the moral action whose happiness is promoted by the virtuous act (see 6:391.16–21). I thank Jens Timmermann for making me aware of this (in private discussion). However, Timmermann's line nevertheless leads to the question of why, then, Kant uses the term *'moral* pleasure' [*moralische Lust*], if this pleasure is based on sensuous sympathy. One clue is that Kant is speaking of moral pleasure here in terms of 'receptivity' [*Empfänglichkeit*] (MM, 6:391.11). Moral pleasure might therefore be connected to Kant's discussion of 'moral feeling' [*das moralische Gefühl*] in Section XII of the Introduction to the 'Doctrine of Virtue', where the natural predisposition of moral feeling is described as *Empfänglichkeit* to moral pleasure and displeasure (MM, 6:399.19; 6:400.18). Perhaps the moral pleasure here is not a sympathetic reaction but a positive dimension of 'moral feeling'.

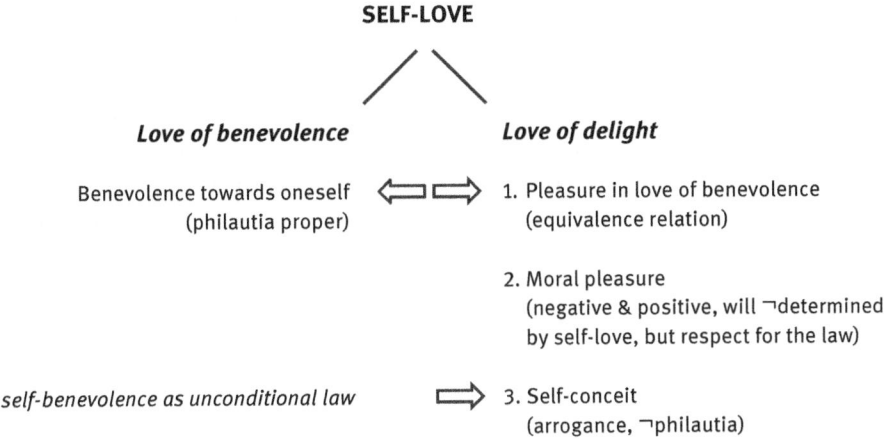

Figure 2. The General Division of Self-Love

kinds of self-love that Kant views as necessary elements of our animal nature (animal mechanical self-love) and our humanity (love of benevolence). Arguably, there are also forms of self-love that Kant accepts on the basis that they are produced by morality (negative and positive moral love of delight). It must therefore be said that any strong interpretative claim made in direct opposition to self-love, such as Wood's assertion that '*love* is not an attitude that clear-sighted and rational people could ever take toward themselves' (Wood 1996, p. 157), is very difficult to sustain.[79] It is only applicable to self-conceit, and then the picture of 'an attitude of *love*' becomes implausibly narrow.

But isn't there a demand in Kant to the effect that we should aim to mitigate or diminish our self-love? As a determining ground of the will, self-love is clearly opposed to the moral law, and it is equally obvious that we should aim to further and strengthen the position of the moral law as an incentive to our actions. When speaking of 'love for the law'[80] in the second *Critique*, Kant proposes that we ought to strive for a moral disposition such that we have no inclinations that are in tension with what morality commands. This would be a state of subjective moral perfection, where one's attitude towards the moral law would be

---

[79] Towards the end of his article, Wood also suggests that 'Kant holds that people of virtuous disposition will limit their claims on happiness to those of reasonable self-love.' (Wood 1996, p. 157) However, Wood does not explain why reasonable self-love should not be considered an attitude of love towards oneself, and for this reason I admit to finding the main claim of his argument ambiguous.

[80] I discuss love for the law in detail in ch. 3.1.

not respect but actually love or liking [*Zuneigung*]. (C2, 5:83–84) Insofar as self-love is a general name for inclinations and is opposed to the moral law as a determining ground of the will, with love for the law self-love in this sense would cease to exist, and love for the law seems to be something that is called for. Similarly, the *Religion* asserts that what is required of us is a dispositional 'revolution' [*Revolution*] or a 'change of heart' [*Änderung des Herzens*], which consists in adopting the moral law as our supreme maxim and a gradual and laborious reworking of our conduct on this basis (R, 6:47–48).

But does this mean that we ought to get rid of self-love? Or in other words, is there or ought there to be an endpoint of human moral progress in which self-love is no longer a part of the constitution of our cognitive framework? I don't think so. The second *Critique* discussion of love for the law makes very clear that because we are imperfect creatures, love for the law can never actually be achieved. We 'can never be altogether free from desires and inclinations', and love for the law remains a 'constant though unattainable goal of [...] striving' (C2, 5:84.4–15)[81]. It is of course the case that from a decidedly moral perspective Kant expresses a strong dislike of inclinations. In the *Groundwork*, inclinations 'are so far from having an absolute worth [...] that to be entirely free from them must rather be the universal wish of every rational being' (GW, 4:428.16–17)[82]. In the second *Critique*, inclinations 'are always burdensome to a rational being' who wishes 'to be rid of them' (C2, 5:118.7–9)[83]. These statements are not surprising, since the basic business of pure practical reason is to disregard inclinations altogether when determining the will (see e.g. C2, 5:118.16–18). As already mentioned, however, even though inclinations can be disregarded in moral decision-making, Kant holds that ridding ourselves of inclinations entirely is not possible. When he considers the human being more broadly – as both a moral-rational and a natural-physical creature – his tone with regard to inclinations is different. In the *Religion*, he holds not only that we cannot rid ourselves of inclinations but also that we *should not*: '*Considered in themselves* natural inclinations are *good*, i.e. not reprehensible, and to want to extirpate them would not only be futile but harmful and blameworthy as well; we must rather only curb them' (R, 6:58.1–4)[84]. He clearly does not reject inclina-

---

[81] 'niemals von Begierden und Neigungen ganz frei sein' / 'beständigen, obgleich unerreichbaren Ziele [...] Bestrebung'.
[82] 'haben so wenig einen absoluten Werth [...] daß vielmehr, gänzlich davon frey zu seyn, der allgemeine Wunsch eines jeden vernünftigen Wesens seyn muß.'
[83] 'sind sie einem vernünftigen Wesen jederzeit lästig' / 'ihrer entledigt zu sein'.
[84] 'Natürliche Neigungen sind, *an sich selbst betrachtet, gut*, d.i. unverwerflich, und es ist nicht allein vergeblich, sondern es wäre auch schädlich und tadelhaft, sie ausrotten zu wollen; man

tions or self-love as such. Kant understands full well that although we have a moral vocation, we are also natural creatures. Even though all inclinations lack moral worth and any inclination can be contra-moral at the token level[85], some inclinations, such as sexual inclination, can be viewed as predisposed to the good at least in the sense of being necessary for the continued survival of the species. Some inclinations can even be beautiful results of moral action (such as the benevolent inclination of love towards others that arises from being beneficent to others from duty) (C2, 5:82.18–20; MM, 6:402; see ch. 4 below). I therefore think that aiming for 'love for the law' does not constitute a demand not to have inclinations at all; rather, it involves strengthening the moral incentive within us so that inclinations have less power over us. This moral striving also involves the cultivation of at least some inclinations (such as the inclination of benevolence for others), to the end that our emotional dispositions harmonise with moral demands (see ch. 4.2.2.A). Striving for a morally better character therefore means making the moral law the supreme incentive in the sense that it is *capable* of overriding self-love.[86]

There is thus no real demand in Kant's moral philosophy to eradicate self-love from our lives. The most precise formulations of the thought that self-love should be *limited* or *conditioned* can be found in the second *Critique* and *The Metaphysics of Morals*. The way in which it is permissible to make self-love or love of benevolence lawlike for ourselves is by limiting the maxim of our own happiness with the happiness of others. We can call this the *universalisability condition of the maxim of one's own happiness*. My own happiness 'can become an *objective* practical law only if I include in it the happiness of others.' (C2, 5:34.31–32)[87] In this case, as we learn from the second *Critique*, self-love may acquire 'objective validity' [objective Gültigkeit], as the determining ground of the will is not self-love but the lawful form, through which self-love is limited and the notion of happiness is applied to all finite beings. In *The Metaphysics of Morals*, we find a mirror image of the same idea, now concerning 'practical love', or the grounding of the duty of active rational benevolence toward others [*Liebe des*

---

muß sie vielmehr nur bezähmen'. 'Curbing' or taming [*bezähmen*] our inclinations successfully is once again called 'prudence' [*Klugheit*] (R, 6:58.7). Note also that the 'goodness' of inclinations is not unqualified but merely negative: they are not 'reprehensible'.

85 I thank Jens Timmermann for reminding me of this. Consider, for example, a father who (out of inclination-based benevolent love) rushes to buy a birthday present for his child and on his way to the toy store neglects to help someone who is drowning in a nearby pond.

86 This general view is inspired by Baron (1995).

87 'kann nur alsdann ein *objectives* praktisches Gesetz werden, wenn ich anderer ihre in dieselbe mit einschließe.'

Wohlwollens]. Assuming that self-love is a universal aspect of humanity, it is now the case that in order for there to be a duty to love others practically, one must include oneself in the universalised maxim of love as an *object of love*:

> I want everyone else to be benevolent toward me (BENEVOLENTIA); hence I ought also to be benevolent toward everyone else. But since all *others* with the exception of myself would not be *all*, so that the maxim would not have within it the universality of a law, which is still necessary for imposing obligation, the law making benevolence a duty will include myself, as an object of benevolence, in the command of practical reason. (MM, 6:451.4–10)[88]

Kant explains that the above does not make self-love a duty but merely 'permits' [*erlaubt*] self-love [*Liebe des Wohlwollens*] on the condition of one's 'being benevolent to every other as well' (MM, 6:451.16–17)[89]. Thus the moral permissibility of self-love as love of benevolence depends on adopting the maxim of practical love of benevolence towards others (I discuss practical love in more detail in ch. 4.2.2).[90]

But still, the more virtuous we become, the less we will entertain self-regarding inclinations, and the more we will be dedicated to pursuing our imperfect duties of love towards others. Is there some sort of limiting value in our striving to approximate the highest good as our own moral perfection[91] – a limiting value where the maxim of practical love towards others has taken over and the maxim of self-love has been reduced to some absolute minimum, such that it only continues to exist as a part of the formal condition of our duty to love others?

In the second *Critique*, the highest good is defined from the perspective of the agent. It contains the moral law as its determining ground or supreme condition (C2, 5:109) and consists of two elements: virtue (morality) and happiness. Virtue and happiness have to be combined in the concept of the highest good, but as they rely on basically opposing principles (those of morality and self-

---

88 'Ich will jedes Anderen Wohlwollen (BENEVOLENTIA) gegen mich; ich soll also auch gegen jeden Anderen wohlwollend sein. Da aber alle *Andere* außer mir nicht *Alle* sein, mithin die Maxime nicht die Allgemeinheit eines Gesetzes an sich haben würde, welche doch zur Verpflichtung nothwendig ist: so wird das Pflichtgesetz des Wohlwollens mich als Object desselben im Gebot der praktischen Vernunft mit begreifen'.
89 'unter der Bedingung, daß du auch jedem Anderen wohl willst'.
90 For further discussion of the problem of self-benevolence in this context, see Schönecker (2013, pp. 334–339).
91 There are several aspects of the highest good, which I will discuss in more detail in chs. 3 and 5.

love, respectively), their combination is very difficult to conceive.⁹² Kant thinks that if a concept includes two determinations that are necessarily combined in the concept (as must be the case with the concept of the highest good), the determinations must be thought of in terms of 'ground and consequent' [*Grund und Folge*]. According to Kant, this kind of connection is either a logical (analytic) or a causal (synthetic) connection. (C2, 5:111.6–10) Because the two principles in question are heterogeneous, Kant holds that their combination cannot be thought of analytically (in terms of identity) but must be a synthetic relation of cause and effect. This implies that the purely intellectual moral law must be conceived as a cause of sensible happiness. For this to be possible, it must be assumed that one's moral disposition belongs both to the 'noumenal' realm and to the empirical realm of appearances, for happiness as a sensible effect requires that its cause be empirical. (C2, 5:111–115) The type of satisfaction, or the 'analogue of happiness' [*Analogon der Glückseligkeit*] (C2, 5:117.27), that may come about this way is precisely the delight that I previously identified (drawing on the *Religion*) as *negative moral* love of delight in oneself. It is the morally acceptable self-contentment felt upon being 'free from inclinations' in the sense of being able to override them morally. This type of self-love would therefore be a part of a world in which the highest good, as the subjective combination of virtue and happiness, has been realised. It seems possible, however, that a being that no longer had any inclinations that ran contrary to the moral law would lose its ability to feel satisfaction in being able to override them (but Kant does not address this issue). Recall, moreover, that the evidence I provided for the interpretation that the negative delight of the second *Critique* is in fact self-love is indirect⁹³. In the *Religion*, Kant both *defines* moral delight in oneself as self-love and *expresses doubts* about calling it self-love.

The above considerations to the side, insofar as the highest good involves one's own happiness and the happiness of others (which it must), it necessarily involves self-love. If we conceive of a world (or better, an infinite approximation towards a world) where our selfish inclinations have been reduced to an absolute minimum, there must still be something that makes us happy. Where can this happiness come from? Since happiness according to Kant's paradigmatic definition is the sum total of satisfied inclinations, it seems to me that the first main

---

92 Kant calls this the antinomy of practical reason. For a pessimistic view of his discussion, see Beck (1960, pp. 245–247). Here, my intention is not to work with the details of the antinomy as such but only to further articulate the role and structure of self-love in relation to it.

93 The basis of the identification was that the second sense of love of delight in the *Religion* was *Zufriedenheit* in oneself based on respect for the moral law, and the second *Critique* spoke of a *Wohlgefallen* that was also *Zufriedenheit* in oneself and also based on respect for the law.

candidate for a possible source of happiness is animal mechanical self-love (enjoyment of nutrition and sexuality, the preservation of offspring, and natural sociality). The second option is that, since humans in such a world would be largely unselfish, a source of happiness might be the benevolent practical love [*Liebe des Wohlwollens*] that we would shower on and receive in abundance from others around us. It seems possible that there is something intrinsic to loving others as well as ourselves that makes us happy.[94] In Kant's philosophy, we are *receptive* to benevolent love because we *wish to be happy* or *wish to be loved*, which is precisely love of benevolence for ourselves. The third option is the moral delight discussed in the above paragraph, which, despite the doubts I have expressed, may plausibly be interpreted in terms of love of delight.

Admittedly, Kant is ambiguous about the nature of the happiness involved in the highest good. Because approximation to the subjective highest good is infinite, it must involve the practical postulate of immortality. This is the only way to conceive of the infinite ascent towards perfect happiness proportionate to perfect virtue in terms of a single agent. But if immortality or the practically postulated afterlife is an immaterial state of being (as we have good reason to assume), and if we know that the ground of inclination is material, then how can the afterlife contain satisfied inclinations? Kant does not seem to consider this problem, especially given the many passages in which there is no implication that the virtuous life is devoid of inclinations.[95] Our approximation to the highest good may eventually become completely devoid of all inclination-based happiness, but this is unclear; it depends on our interpretation of the postulate of immortality and involves bracketing actual intergenerational moral progress on the species level, where inclinations will clearly continue to exist. Even if we decide to bracket the species level and conceive of approximation toward the highest good as involving the abolition of inclinations, what is left is negative moral delight in oneself, which may arguably be called love of delight for oneself.

---

[94] In ch. 4 we will learn that Kant holds that loving others from the incentive of the moral law (with practical love of benevolence) will cause us to love them from inclination too. There is a pleasure connected with beneficent love (LE, 27:419.4–7; cf. MM, 6:402.19–21), and in the highest good as an ultimate end 'human beings seek something that they can *love*' (R, 6:7.27–28) / 'sucht der Mensch etwas, was er *lieben* kann'. Neighbourly love from inclination must be subsumed under the basic theorem of self-love (C2, 5:22.6–8).

[95] However, Kant does problematise his conception in terms of the *end of all time*. Since the final end of all things is a non-temporal, unchanging state, its possible qualities are beyond our comprehension. In 'The End of All Things' [*Das Ende aller Dinge*], Kant, somewhat jokingly in my opinion, envisions this kind of bliss as the universal congregation's eternal repetition of the same song ('Alleluia!' or monotonous wailing), which indicates a complete absence of change (8:334.36–335.3).

Perhaps the real source of morally deserved happiness lies in all three elements (animal desire, loving others and the need to be loved benevolently, and one's own virtue). All in all, I find it highly difficult to conceive of the possibility of happiness in the infinite approximation towards the comprehensive highest good without reference to self-love. I call this general finding *the persistence of self-love*.

1.4 Self-Love Persists on Three Levels

In the first chapter, I argued for a 'three-level interpretation' of self-love, according to which self-love can be plausibly divided into three 'levels' utilising a vertical metaphor to describe ascending levels of rationality.

I held firstly that there is a low, arational 'ground level' of self-love, which I identified as 'animal mechanical self-love'. Animal mechanical self-love includes the strongest impulses of human nature and divides into love of life (self-preservation), sexual love and parenting (preservation of the species), and sociality. The existence of these terms shows that Kant discusses the strongest impulses of human nature in terms of love. I pointed out how animal mechanical self-love can be understood as desire and how it is generally a predisposition to the good, at least in the sense that it is a necessary condition of species-level moral progress. Further, I showed how the social impulse can be seen as the ground of the unsociably sociable self-love of humanity, which belongs to the history and teleology of moral progress. I also discussed the role of love of honour in this context.

Second, I argued that there is a higher level of self-love that implies reason and which I called the 'the broad middle level of self-love'. I showed how this level can be analysed in terms of the general division of love into love of benevolence and love of delight. Self-love is fundamentally the principle of one's own happiness: it is love of benevolence towards oneself, which consists in wanting things to go well for oneself and being loved by others. This love of benevolence is morally permissible on the condition that one includes the happiness of others in one's maxim. I identified three separate notions of love of delight in oneself: 1) pleasure in love of benevolence towards oneself (in which case love of benevolence and love of delight are equivalent); 2) a feeling of self-contentment (as 'negative' freedom over inclinations) or a feeling of positive moral merit due to the performance of imperfect duties; and 3) morally reprehensible arrogance or self-conceit, which is an unjustified claim to respect from others that arises from making the maxim of love of benevolence towards oneself an unconditional practical law.

Third, I argued for the *persistence of self-love* by analysing the place of self-love in what I call the third or highest level of self-love. Unlike the two lower levels of self-love, which are actual, the third level is an idealised notion that includes close proximity to the moral-physical highest good (the virtue and happiness of all rational creatures). Since happiness involves self-love by definition – and since even negative moral self-contentment can plausibly be interpreted as love of delight – I concluded that self-love is an irreducible aspect of even the highest stages of moral happiness. This conclusion is in line with Kant's view that there is no reason to rid ourselves of inclinations as such. Further, benevolence towards others [*Liebe des Wohlwollens*], which figures as a path towards universal moral happiness, can only be viewed as conducive to happiness under the supposition that human beings want things to go well for themselves or want to be loved by others. In Kant, then, love can make us happy only if an element of self-love persists.

2 Sexual Love

While Kant's views on sex differences and sexual morality have been under discussion for several decades, it seems that, somewhat surprisingly, there are no previous exegetical analyses of sexuality in Kant specifically from the perspective of *love*. As we saw in Chapter 1, sexuality as a natural impulse of procreation belongs at bottom to 'animal mechanical self-love'. Hence, the sexual impulse is basically a component of the broad conceptual cluster of self-love. We also learned that, as a vehicle of (human) species-level sustenance, sexual love is a 'predisposition [*Anlage*] to the good'. Yet even a brief glance at Kant's discussions of love in the context of sexuality reveals that several questions were left unanswered in the first chapter: 1) Are the sexual impulse and sexual love one and the same – or what is their relationship? 2) Just how is sexual love predisposed to the good – or how are teleology and morality related to sexual love? 3) What is the relationship between sexual love and love of beauty? 4) Is the general division of love operative in sexual love – and if so, what is its role? 5) How does the notion of love illuminate the status of sex and gender differences in Kant as regards the equality of human beings?

These issues form the underlying framework for the discussion of this chapter. Two main exegetical claims emerge from my reading: 1) In Kant's earlier works, there is a strong connection between sexuality and love of beauty, but this link wanes towards the 1790s. Beauty can be seen to mediate between sexuality and morality in terms of love, but the extent to which Kant holds on to this picture during the mature period is unclear. 2) In general, sexual love may be divided into *narrow* and *broad* sexual love, such that narrow sexual love is simply the natural impulse of procreation, whereas broad sexual love combines sexual inclination with moral love in the context of heterosexual marriage. My interpretative distinction between narrow and broad sexual love will also clarify the status of the general division of love within this framework. Narrow sexual love remains basically outside the grasp of the general division, but broad sexual love proceeds from the narrow when the sexual impulse or sexual inclination unites with moral love of benevolence for another human being.[1]

---

1 Note that Kant uses at least the words 'impulse' [*der Antrieb*], 'inclination' [*die Neigung*], and 'instinct' [*der Instinkt*] to describe the nature of sexuality. A distinction can be found between inclination and instinct, so that inclination presupposes acquaintance with the object whereas instinct is blind (LE, 27:417.26–27; cf. LA, 25:1114.18–19; both cited in Tomasi 2015). Impulses seem to generally imply the species level, whereas inclinations sometimes presuppose a given agent. Often, however, Kant seems to use these terms interchangeably, and my argument does not hinge on these distinctions. Therefore, I will not analyse them in further detail (see

In accordance with the two main claims, the chapter is divided into two parts. In the first part, I analyse the relationship between sexuality and love of beauty. I begin by discussing love in the precritical 'Observations on the Feeling of the Beautiful and Sublime' and then track the link between the notions of sexual love and the beautiful through the contexts of Kant's philosophy of history (in the 'Conjectural Beginnings of Human History'[2]) and the third *Critique*. This discussion will also serve as a preliminary for the interpretative distinction between narrow and broad variants of sexual love. In the second part of the chapter, I establish the division between narrow and broad sexual love in greater detail by analysing how the word 'love' operates in an array of passages on sexuality in various works by Kant. When showing the existence of broad sexual love, I focus especially on the perspectives of morality in marriage right on the one hand and teleology on the other.

Unlike the other chapters, this one also contains an evaluative element. This is because most of the previous research on sexuality in Kant is specifically feminist in orientation. The existence of these secondary discussions is reflected in the way I treat this particular topic. Many scholars hold that Kant's views on women are deplorable (see e.g. Schott 1997, esp. Schröder 1997; see also Wood 1999; Marwah 2013; cf. Herman 1993), and his insights were criticised even by his contemporaries.[3] Recent feminist debate on this issue mainly concerns the question of just *how* deplorable Kant's views are. From this perspective, Kant is by no means a forerunner of feminism, and the more charitable interpretations tend to assert that his opinions are not '*quite* so deplorable as critics make them out to be' (Baron 1997, p. 166; see Mikkola 2011, p. 92). The scholars who take the more charitable route sometimes also hold that if we bracket Kant's substantial discussions on sexual difference as such, we may still use the universalistic, supposedly gender-neutral groundings of Kant's mature moral theory as emancipative conceptual tools for approaching contemporary problems of equality (gender issues among others) – and in this 'formal' sense, Kant's moral philosophy can be beneficial to feminism (e.g. Nagl-Docekal 1997; Baron 1997; cf. Mikkola 2011, p. 105). On the other hand, some draw on the connections between sexual love (or marriage) and friendship in Kant in approaching questions of solipsism and objectification (Langton 2009, pp. 318–327, 362–365), reciproci-

---

ch. 1.1). As regards sexual love, the main concern for me is the distinction between nature (instinct, impulse, inclination) and morality, and how this distinction is mediated.
2 'Muthmaßlicher Anfang der Menschengeschichte'.
3 For instance, Goethe saw a remark of Kant's as being befitting of 'an old bachelor' [*Hagestolz*] (Goethe 1970 [1798], p. 518), and Schleiermacher accused Kant of treating the female sex 'completely as a means' [*durchaus als Mittels*] (Schleiermacher 1799, p. 306) (see Hull 1996, p. 313).

ty and responsibility (Korsgaard 1996, pp. 194–196), or with the specific intent of revising Kant's original positions (Denis 2001b). With all these discussions in mind, I wish to show that while an interpretative endeavour such as mine cannot bracket Kant's sexual teleology and/or his anthropological opinions on sexual difference, the notion of broad sexual love developed below nevertheless supports the idea that Kant was *less misogynistic* than is often assumed.

All in all, my analysis of sexual love in Kant shows that despite his seemingly negative remarks on sexuality and his apparent conservatism in sexual philosophy, there is no need to reject the basic idea that for Kant, (narrow) sexual love is a strong and necessary natural impulse of procreation and a predisposition to the good. Moral restrictions only allow the impulse to operate within heterosexual marriage, where the rights of the sexes are *nominally* equal but the husband is *de facto* the leader. In Kant's early work, the union of the sexual impulse and moral love in the husband may be viewed through the notion of love of beauty. Promoting their wives' happiness through the moral practical love of benevolence remains the most important duty that husbands have towards their spouses, whereas wives are described as being generally more prone to love from inclination. Women serve an auxiliary purpose in the moral progress of human kind, and while they ultimately (or at least arguably) share the same rational capacities as men, they are domestic creatures in Kant's sexual teleology. The status of women as legal and moral persons is ambivalent and limited, and in this sense there is an inconsistency or an *insoluble tension* between Kant's formal moral egalitarianism and his philosophy of sex. In comparison with some of the contemporary statements in the feminist debate around Kant, I hope my argument will also point toward a more balanced interpretation of the status of sex difference in his philosophy.[4]

---

[4] By focusing on sexual love in heterosexual relationships, I do not wish to suggest that homosexuality is irrelevant or devoid of love. My chosen focus follows from my Kant immanent exegetical method: Kant's narrow basic notion of sexual love is the natural impulse of procreation, and he does not discuss homosexuality in terms of love. As one who was not particularly progressive in this respect, still less a sexual libertine, Kant viewed homosexuality as a horrendous moral flaw. I will also have to omit a detailed discussion of Kant's condemnation of masturbation, even though masturbation, too, relates to the sexual impulse, and hence to sexual love in the narrow sense. For criticisms of Kant's notorious views on these topics, see Denis (1999) and Soble (2003). Here, I limit my treatment to the kind of sexuality that Kant explicitly discusses in terms of love: sexuality between men and women.

2.1 Sexual Love and Love of Beauty

'Observations on the Feeling of the Beautiful and Sublime' (1764) begins with a distinction between two different kinds of pleasurable feelings an agent may have. The first kind represents the simple satisfaction of inclinations. This kind of pleasure is mere 'gratification' [*Vergnügen*] and may occur without any special talents on the part of the agent, without a morally virtuous disposition, and apparently even without the use of rational capacities: it 'can occur in complete thoughtlessness' (2:208.14–15)[5], 'without their having to envy others or even being able to form any concept of others' (2:208.7–9)[6]. As examples of this type of pleasure Kant mentions things like food and drink, hunting, business profits, and a kind of sexual pleasure. The sexual feeling is defined in terms of love. It is the feeling of a man 'who loves the opposite sex only insofar as he counts it among the things that are to be enjoyed' (2:208.3–5)[7]. If we compare this kind of sexual love with what is said about 'animal mechanical self-love' in the *Religion*, we see that the terms attributed to sexuality in both cases seem equivalent. The animal mechanical impulse of sexuality in the *Religion* is arational and does not involve comparison – or, more precisely, does not involve an evaluation of the happiness of others in comparison with one's own happiness. Similarly, the sexual love mentioned in the beginning of the 'Observations' need not involve thought, envy, or even the formation of a concept of another human being.[8] The similarity of these descriptions of sexuality in the

---

5 'bei völliger Gedankenlosigkeit statt finden können.'
6 'ohne daß sie andere beneiden dürfen oder auch von andern sich einen Begriff machen können'.
7 'derjenige, der das andre Geschlecht nur in so fern liebt, als er es zu den genießbaren Sachen zählt'.
8 Considering that the sexual impulse may hinder the use of one's rational capacities, one might like to think of the impulse in terms of 'passion' [*Leidenschaft*], for the hindering of reason is constitutive of what a passion is for Kant. However, in the *Anthropology* Kant explains that 'one cannot list any physical love as passion, because it does not contain a *constant* principle with respect to its object.' (AP, 7:266.12–13) / 'keine physische Liebe als Leidenschaft aufführen kann: weil sie in Ansehung des Objects nicht ein beharrliches Princip enthält.' According to Kant, sexual desire disappears (at least temporarily) once it is satisfied, and passions are more like long-term obsessions. In the *Anthropology*, however, Kant also lists sexual inclination (alongside the inclination to freedom) as a 'passion of natural inclination' (AP, 7:267.35–268.1; see also MM, 6:426.26). As a natural passion, sexual inclination relates to *affects*, which are rash, sudden, overwhelming feelings (see AP, 7:252). In the discussion that follows, though, he again distinguishes between sexual inclination (of mere animals) and passion (AP, 7:269.13–14) and does not say anything about it in terms of passion (or affect) (cf. LA, 25:1361). Perhaps he means that obsessive (or simply long-term) sexual love for a person can

general framework of the concept of love serves as preliminary evidence that there might be such a thing as *narrow sexual love* in Kant, which consists merely of the animal impulse to sex and the pleasurable satisfaction of this impulse. Since this kind of sexual love seems to involve viewing the other as a 'thing' [*eine Sache*], it also suggests that there is a kind of *solipsism* related to sexuality (see Langton 2009, 325–327) – that is, the objectification or depersonalisation of the other human being in the context of the animal impulse.

What interests me most in the first section of this chapter is the relationship between the sexual impulse and the notion of the beautiful. The question is: how does love of beauty proceed from crude or narrowly construed sexuality? Kant's essay quickly moves on to distinguish the abovementioned 'lower' feelings from feelings of a 'finer' [*feinere*] sort. The finer feelings are feelings for the beautiful and the sublime.[9] In general, Kant analyses the finer feelings by attributing them to various topics, such as landscapes, morality, national characteristics, and sexual difference. In the sphere of sexuality, Kant's basic idea is that women are marked out by the notion of the beautiful, men by the sublime. This basic distinction corresponds to a distinction Kant makes concerning morality: 'Subduing one's passions by means of principles is *sublime*', and 'true virtue alone is sublime' (2:215.5–24)[10], whereas 'tenderheartedness that is easily led into a warm feeling of sympathy is beautiful and loveworthy' (2:215.33–35)[11]. This latter, feminine virtue is, however, 'weak and always blind.' (2:215.37–216.1)[12] As some commentators (like Patrick Frierson (2011)) have noted, Kant's idea is not that women are *not at all* sublime and men *not at all* beautiful. It is rather that individuals of both sexes express these qualities in varying degrees, such that *in comparison with men* women are for the most part more beautiful and less sublime, and vice versa (Kant does not discuss whether the qualities might be reversed within a particular individual, or whether a given woman might be

---

be a 'passion' (see MM, 6:426.20–26). The distinctions around §82 and §83 of the *Anthropology* appear particularly unclear (AP, 7:267–270).
9 These concepts are seminal to the domain of aesthetics, and their history runs through Edmund Burke's *A Philosophical Enquiry into the Origin of Our Ideas of the Sublime and Beautiful* (1757) down to Longinus' treatise *On the Sublime* (around 100 AD). Both texts were widely read and very influential in Kant's time, even though they are not mentioned by Kant in the 'Observations' (for Kant's later discussions of Burke, see C3, 5:277; 20:238).
10 'Bezwingung seiner Leidenschaften durch Grundsätze ist *erhaben*.' / 'ist wahre Tugend allein erhaben.'
11 'Weichmüthigkeit, die leichtlich in ein warmes Gefühl des *Mitleidens* gesetzt wird, ist schön und liebenswürdig'.
12 'schwach und jederzeit blind.' On the whole, the passage anticipates Kant's mature discussion of sympathetic participation, or *Teilnehmung*, in (MM, 6:456–457).

more sublime than a given man, or a man more beautiful than a woman). Kant asserts further that general education and societal relations pertaining to sexual difference should be organised so that the defining characteristics of both sexes are emphasised. As Frierson points out, Kant's distinction between the beautiful and the sublime as regards sex is *both descriptive and normative*. (Frierson 2011, pp. xxix–xxx)[13]

Kant emphasises that the beauty of women, regarding both their looks and their demeanour in a broader sense, is based on the sexual drive, which is dependent on the aims or purposes of nature: 'no matter how far one might try to go around this secret, the sexual inclination is still in the end the ground of all other charms' (2:234.21–23)[14]. Further down he writes:

> This whole enchantment is at bottom spread over the sexual drive. Nature pursues its great aim, and all refinements that are associated with it, however remote from it they seem to be, are only veils, and in the end derive their charm from the very same source. (2:235.19–22)[15]

In the 'Observations', the great end of the beautiful and the sublime as regards the character of the sexes is marital happiness. This is the proper object of refined sexual love, and it is in this context that the broader notion of love of beauty develops out of the crude and arational, narrowly conceived sexual impulse. What is of importance here is that beauty occasions love, and sublimity esteem. Hence, in the 'Observations' Kant holds that love in the broader sense does not operate symmetrically between the sexes. The experience of sexual beauty is aroused by nature's procreative aim through the male sexual impulse.[16] Even

---

[13] Kant's notorious comments on women's education, which was a hotly debated public issue during his time, derive from his normative insistence on the supposedly natural characteristics of the sexes (see Petschauer 1986). As Baron points out (1997, p. 167), Kant does not imply that women are not capable of higher learning; he apparently opposes their education on the basis that it would compromise their beauty. And as Peter Petschauer (1986, p. 285) correctly argues, Kant's views on women's education 'remain static' between the 'Observations' and the published *Anthropology*. In terms of Kant's near contemporaries, gender-equal education was advocated by the mayor of Königsberg, Theodor von Hippel (see Schröder 1997).
[14] 'man mag nun um das Geheimniß so weit herumgehen, als man immer will, die Geschlechterneigung doch allen den übrigen Reizen endlich zum Grunde liegt'.
[15] 'Diese ganze Bezauberung ist im Grunde über den Geschlechtertrieb verbreitet. Die Natur verfolgt ihre große Absicht, und alle Feinigkeiten, die sich hinzugesellen, sie mögen nun so weit davon abzustehen scheinen, wie sie wollen, sind nur Verbrämungen und entlehnen ihren Reiz doch am Ende aus eben derselben Quelle.'
[16] It is, however, implicitly clear throughout Kant's writings that the sexual impulse is active in both sexes, and I know of no scholars who deny this.

though it seems that women might perhaps be generally more prone than men to experience a (non-sexual, neighbourly) feeling of love[17], it is men who love women rather than the other way around. The man appreciates the noble [*das Edle*] in himself and the beautiful in the woman, whereas the woman's feeling is for the beautiful in herself and for the noble in the man (2:240.26–32). Transported into the sphere of love, this idea means that 'the man [...] can say: *Even if you do not love me I will force you to esteem me*, and the woman, [...]: *Even if you do not inwardly esteem us, we will still force you to love us.*' (2:242.5–9)[18] However, this should not be understood in terms of squabbling or a crude struggle for power. The marital couple is 'a single moral person, which is animated and ruled by the understanding of the man and the taste of the wife.' (2:242.14–16)[19] The end is *mutual* happiness, and it is moral love and beautiful obligingness that yield the proper flavour of marital life: 'the more sublime a cast of mind is, the more inclined it also is to place the greatest goal of its efforts in the satisfaction of a beloved object, and on the other side the more beautiful it is, the more does it seek to respond to this effort with complaisance.' (2.242.18–22)[20] In fact, Kant seems to propose that the man should ultimately come to love his wife not because she is beautiful but because she is his wife. (2.220.30–221.7)

The love (of beauty) at issue in marriage in the 'Observations' is thus not merely the crude sexual impulse, or the mere desire to derive pleasure from the use of another person as a sexual object; at least from the man's perspective, it is a combination of sexual desire and what Kant later comes to call love of be-

---

17 Kant states that women 'do something only because they love to, and the art lies in making sure that they love only what is good.' (2:232.1–2) / 'thun etwas nur darum, weil es ihnen so beliebt, und die Kunst besteht darin zu machen, daß ihnen nur dasjenige beliebe, was gut ist.' And later on: 'the feeling of love of which she is capable and which she inspires in others is fickle but beautiful' (2:236.29–30) / 'das Gefühl der Liebe, dessen sie fähig ist und welche sie anderen einflößt, ist flatterhaft, aber schön'. The association of women with inclination and beauty seems to parallel the ideas put forth later in the *Groundwork*, and especially in the second *Critique*, according to which beneficence from inclination or love lacks proper moral worth but is nevertheless *beautiful* (C2, 5:82.18–20). Note, however, that the verb used in the first 'Observations' passage above is not *lieben* but *belieben*, which according to the Grimm and Adelung dictionaries can be close to love but can also imply liking in a much more general sense.
18 'der Mann [...] sagen können: *Wenn ihr mich gleich nicht liebt, so will ich euch zwingen mich hochzuachten*, und das Frauenzimmer [...]: *Wenn ihr uns gleich nicht innerlich hochschätzet, so zwingen wir euch doch uns zu lieben.*'
19 'eine einzige moralische Person [...], welche durch den Verstand des Mannes und den Geschmack der Frauen belebt und regiert wird.'
20 'so ist eine Gemüthsart, je erhabener sie ist, auch um desto geneigter die größte Absicht der Bemühungen in der Zufriedenheit eines geliebten Gegenstandes zu setzen, und andererseits je schöner sie ist, desto mehr sucht sie durch Gefälligkeit diese Bemühung zu erwiedern.'

nevolence for another human being – that is, practical love or active rational benevolence. In this context, love of beauty denotes a man's sexual love for a woman *in the broad sense*, and hence the 'Observations' supports the basic claims of the chapter. There is a close connection between sexuality and beauty in terms of love: the beauty of women is grounded in the sexual impulse, and the love this beauty occasions is not merely animal mechanical self-love but a broader kind of sexual love of beauty.

In 'Conjectural Beginning of Human History' of 1786, we find an even stronger statement concerning the relationship between sexuality, love, and beauty. In a rather playful manner, Kant here imagines a possible developmental history for the human species, the beginning of which he models on the biblical account of Genesis – starting with the first human couple (8:110.11). In this early state of human existence, the impulses of animal mechanical self-love are in operation: 'After the instinct of nourishment, by means of which nature preserves each individual, the *instinct of sex* is most prominent, by means of which nature preserves each species.' (8:112.27–29)[21] Kant's story then begins to unfold as an account of the effect of reason on the foundational natural impulses or instincts. His description of the effect of reason on sexuality is particularly interesting. Reason marks a separation between the human stimulus to sex and the mostly periodic impulse found in animals. By means of reason and imagination, the human being can uphold sexual desire, which is something animals are unable to do. Kant appeals to the example of the use of fig leaves to cover genitalia to illustrate this point. When the sexual object is concealed (that is, when the genitals are covered with a fig leaf), imagination strengthens and prolongs sexual desire (8:112.31–113.3).[22] Through concealing the sensory object and postponing immediate desire satisfaction, imagination and reason lead sexuality from mere animal mechanical sensibility to a level of rational ideality. Most importantly, and more specifically, they inform the transition from animal sexuality to love, and finally to the notion of beauty (even as detached from human objects):

> *Refusal* was the first artifice for leading from the merely sensed stimulus over to ideal ones, from merely animal desire gradually over to love, and with the latter from the feeling of the

---

[21] 'Nächst dem Instinct zur Nahrung, durch welchen die Natur jedes Individuum erhält, ist der *Instinct zum Geschlecht*, wodurch sie für die Erhaltung jeder Art sorgt, der vorzüglichste.'

[22] As Wood correctly notes, Kant's slightly satirical position seems to imply 'that Adam and Eve first put on figleaves not out of shame but to excite one another's sexual desires' (Wood 2007, p. 161).

merely agreeable over to the taste for beauty, in the beginning only in human beings but then, however, also in nature. (8:113.7–11)[23]

In the 'Conjectural Beginning', the sexual impulse is clearly distinguished from love. What is implied is that when reason and imagination operate on the sexual impulse, the resulting love must be differentiated from animal mechanical self-love. The 'Conjectural Beginning' does not make clear what this higher love is like, but we know it is occasioned by the working of reason on sexuality, and the overall context of the essay suggests that it is moral and, as related to sexuality, predisposed toward general species-level progress, 'gradually from the worse toward the better' (8:123.25)[24]. The 'Conjectural Beginning' also supports the idea that love of beauty is occasioned by sexual love. The trajectory above is from an animal impulse to love and from love to a taste for beauty, which in turn starts with human beauty but may then be somehow generalised to the rest of nature.[25] The claim is obviously stronger than that made in the 'Observations', where sexuality is presented merely as the ground of female beauty; here, it is presented as the ground of the taste for both human beauty and non-human natural beauty. Based on the combination of the 'Observations' and the 'Conjectural Beginning', the naturalistic ground of beauty (that is, beauty in a quite general sense) is animal sexuality, and the transition between the two is mediated by reason and love. But there is an obstacle to this interpretation.

Kant's most extensive discussion of beauty is located in the third *Critique*, where it forms nearly half of the entire work. At first glance, there seems to be a striking discontinuity between Kant's discussion of beauty here and his earlier works. Even though 1) the division between the beautiful and the sublime is still in operation, 2) the 'Analytic of the Beautiful' [*Analytik des Schönen*] in the third *Critique* relates the beautiful to aesthetic pleasure [*Wohlgefallen*][26], and 3) Kant's general idea is to show how the notion of the beautiful mediates between nature and morality, there is *hardly any link between sexuality and beauty* in the mature

---

23 '*Weigerung* war das Kunststück, um von bloß empfundenen zu idealischen Reizen, von der bloß thierischen Begierde allmählig zur Liebe und mit dieser vom Gefühl des bloß Angenehmen zum Geschmack für Schönheit anfänglich nur an Menschen, dann aber auch an der Natur überzuführen.'
24 'vom Schlechtern zum Besseren allmählig'.
25 We hear echoes of Diotima's speech in Plato's *Symposium*.
26 Pluhar rightly warns that in the third *Critique*, *Wohlgefallen* simply means liking, and we should not attach special meaning to the word as such and should instead attend to the context (C3, 49fn.14). In particular, we should not assume that *Wohlgefallen* automatically denotes love of delight. Insofar as there are links between love and *Wohlgefallen* in the third *Critique*, these must be established via context-specific argument.

work. The paradigmatic case of the beautiful is aesthetic reflection of beautiful natural forms, and the notion of the beautiful is then secondarily applied to artistic works. We do find two statements that link aesthetic judgment concerning the beautiful to love, but they do not seem to provide the necessary connection with sexuality that we would expect, based on the earlier works.[27] How can we reconcile this lack of sexual love of beauty in the third *Critique* with Kant's pre-critical position and the position he continued to hold in philosophy of history, according to which beauty is based on sexual impulse?

There is one passage in the third *Critique* that concerns human feminine beauty. When discussing the beauty related to fine art, Kant notes as an aside that judgments of beauty regarding certain animate objects of nature take their objective purposiveness into account. In such cases, the aesthetic judgment is grounded in a teleological one, as with women's beauty: 'Thus if we say, e. g., That is a beautiful woman, we do in fact think nothing other than that nature offers us in the woman's figure a beautiful presentation of the purposes [inher-

---

[27] First: 'The beautiful prepares us for loving something, even nature, without interest' (C3, 5:267.35–36) / 'Das Schöne bereitet uns vor, etwas, selbst die Natur ohne Interesse zu lieben'. This is neither about sexual love (since sexual love has an interest) nor, perhaps, even about loving the beautiful, and the love hinted at (but in no way elaborated) in this remark is probably some kind of love of delight toward other beings that neither reduces to self-interest nor takes an interest in the other's well-being, but that acquires some sort of reflective quasi-moral status in disinterested pleasure. It may be possible to interpret the notion of being 'without interest' in terms of not involving *an intention to use the love object* (see MM, 6:443.2–9). Second, love of natural beauty may denote a direct, non-selfish interest in the existence of the objects in question, yet without assigning a purpose or an end to them. Someone 'who contemplates the beautiful shape of a wild flower, a bird, an insect, etc., out of admiration and love for them, and would not want nature to be entirely without them [...] is taking a direct interest in the beauty of nature' (C3, 5:299.8–14) / 'welcher [...] die schöne Gestalt einer wilden Blume, eines Vogels, eines Insects u. s. w. betrachtet, um sie zu bewundern, zu lieben und sie nicht gerne in der Natur überhaupt vermissen zu wollen, [...] nimmt ein unmittelbares und zwar intellectuelles Interesse an der Schönheit der Natur.' According to Kant, this kind of directly interested love requires that one have a prior interest in the moral good, or at least a predisposition to it (C3, 5:300.35–36). Thus, in the third *Critique*, the experience of beauty in general does not necessarily imply love but may serve as preparation for a quasi-moral love (which does not hinge on sexuality). Moreover, the love of beauty directly addressed in this work rests on explicitly moral presuppositions about the agent. In her discussion of love of natural beauty in Kant, Baxley argues that natural beauty may be valued 'both for its own sake [...] as well as for the sake of [...] the moral message we take from it' (Baxley 2005, p. 42). I think this is correct, but Baxley does not problematise the status of the two seemingly different types of love at play: love without interest and directly interested love. This distinction is also not noted by Tomasi (2015). Unfortunately, I cannot provide a highly detailed investigation of this issue here since my chosen perspective focuses on the particular relationship between sexual love and love of beauty.

ent] in the female build.' (C3, 5:312.1–4)[28] The purpose Kant has in mind here is undoubtedly the preservation of the species through procreation. Hence, in the case of women, their beauty remains grounded in the teleology of sexual desire, and we can at least say that there isn't an absolute discontinuity between the earlier works and the third *Critique*. Unlike the 'Conjectural Beginning', however, this passage cannot be taken to suggest that sexuality is the foundation from which aesthetic judgments in general are ultimately derived. Furthermore, in a comment on the moral proof of God's existence in the 'Critique of Teleological Judgment'[29], Kant implies that historically, judging the beauty (of nature) was grounded on the existence of morally practical reason: 'Indeed, it was in all probability through this moral interest that people first became attentive to the beauty and the purposes of nature.' (C3, 5:459.1–3)[30] There is no hint of beauty's being generally grounded in sexuality in the third *Critique*. Did Kant change his mind on the issue in the late 1780s?

This is possible, and quite clearly the link between sexual love and love of beauty wanes towards the 1790s, as does the association between women and the beautiful. *Anthropology from a Pragmatic Point of View*, published in 1797, does not discuss women in terms of beauty.[31] Does this mean that Kant did not think that beauty was grounded on sexuality in the end? It seems to me that when Kant began his search for a priori foundations for judgments of beauty, he was forced to shift the focus of beauty away from women, who remained paradigmatically closer to empirical inclinations in comparison with men (even though arguably equipped with rational capacities). On the other hand, the critical distinction between the aesthetic and the teleological forced Kant to ground judgments of beauty on something other than the objective purposiveness of nature. Objective purposiveness (as in the sexual impulse) was now a matter of teleological judgment, not a matter of aesthetics. As noted above, in the third *Critique* the beauty of women is construed as an isolated special case of beauty that

---

28 'In einem solchen Falle denkt man auch, wenn z. B. gesagt wird: das ist ein schönes Weib, in der That nichts anders als: die Natur stellt in ihrer Gestalt die Zwecke im weiblichen Baue schön vor'.
29 'Kritik der teleologischen Urtheilskraft'.
30 'Auch wurde aller Wahrscheinlichkeit nach durch dieses moralische Interesse allererst die Aufmerksamkeit auf die Schönheit und Zwecke der Natur rege gemacht'. Note that the German is slightly ambivalent regarding whether *die Schönheit* refers to the beauty of nature or to beauty in general. Pluhar opts for the first alternative, which does seem more likely.
31 The anthropology lectures confirm this shift: the Friedländer notes from 1775–1776 treat beauty equally as a property of men and women (LA, 25:665), and in the Mrongovius notes from 1784–1785 we even find a startling Platonic claim, according to which beauty is essentially masculine (LA, 25:1330.20–21).

is grounded in teleology. Importantly, however, the third *Critique* simply does not make specific conjectures about the possible arational foundation of beauty – a topic which was dealt with in the 'Conjectural Beginning'. All in all, I don't think it's sufficiently clear whether Kant meant to renounce what he had previously said about the connection between the sexual impulse and love of beauty. I am forced to take the position that in the precritical phase and in the philosophy of history, Kant views love of beauty as grounded in the sexual impulse, but this picture is indeed blurred by the third *Critique* and the development of the anthropology. All we can say is that men's moral sexual love of beautiful women (which I will call broad sexual love) is grounded in the objectively purposive sexual impulse (which I will term narrow sexual love). This finding on sexual love of beauty nevertheless supports the basic claims of the chapter: 1) Kant's earlier works show a strong connection between sexuality and beauty in terms of love, and 2) sexual love can be plausibly said to divide into narrow and broad variants.

2.2 Narrow and Broad Sexual Love

In this section, I hope to illustrate in further detail how Kant's notion of sexual love indeed divides into *narrow and broad sexual love*. As we've seen, the basic idea behind this interpretative distinction is that narrow sexual love consists merely in the animal impulse of procreation, whereas broad sexual love combines sexual inclination with moral love in the context of heterosexual marriage. I will establish this claim by analysing how the word 'love' operates in Kant's discussions of sexuality, first from the perspective of nature, then from the perspective of morality and marriage right, and finally from the perspective of teleology. If we look at the various passages in which Kant addresses this topic, we see that the relationship between the two variants of sexual love is both additive or accumulative and transformative. In other words, it seems to me that when animal sexuality unites with morality in marriage, the rudimentary form of sexual love both remains in place and is transformed into something more tender and compassionate. When the operation of pure practical reason imposes restrictions on animal desire and other kinds of demands on how the agent acts within the interpersonal relationship originally founded on the natural impulse, the resultant love is reminiscent of both the original sexual instinct and the kind of practical love of neighbour that one may also express towards strangers. But the loves are different: broad sexual love is milder than sheer lust or animal craving for sex and more intimate, more caring, than beneficence simply from rational benevolence.

2.2.1 Narrow Sexual Love

Is there really such a thing as narrow sexual love in Kant? The literature in this area is scarce. Of the few who have touched on the topic, Langton most clearly perceives that Kant does use 'sexual love' for 'sexual desire' (Langton 2009, p. 325)[32], but on the other hand Wood holds that for 'Kant, sexual desire is not a form of love, because love seeks the good of its object whereas sexual desire does not.' (Wood 2008, p. 225) A position like Wood's is certainly not an absurd position to maintain, and we should carefully put together a more comprehensive picture of the evidence before deciding on the matter. In the Collins notes on ethics, which Wood cites, Kant does state the following: 'But if he loves them merely from sexual inclination, it cannot be love; it is appetite.' (LE, 27:384.22–23)[33] Indeed there is further evidence for his position in the Mrongovius notes on anthropology, in the 'Conjectural Beginning', and in *The Metaphysics of Morals*. In the Mrongovius notes, sexual inclination is distinguished from 'genuine love' [*eigentliche Liebe*] (LA, 25:1361.6–7), and as we saw in the previous section, the 'Conjectural Beginning' contrasts 'animal desire' with love (8:113.7–11). Finally, from *The Metaphysics of Morals* we learn that sexual inclination does not belong to love's general division into love of benevolence and love of delight: 'it cannot be classed with either the love that is delight or the love of benevolence' (MM, 6:426.26–28)[34].

But even though this may seem like a lot, it is hardly the complete picture of the evidence, and if we investigate further we find that there is more to be said for the view that does include sexual inclination or the natural sexual impulse in the general concept of love. Let me rehearse the evidence for the existence of narrow sexual love discussed thus far, connect it with further evidence, and then try to provide a balanced summary of the overall situation.

Recall the passage on animal mechanical self-love in the *Religion*:

---

[32] Interestingly, Langton speaks of an 'optimistic' and a 'pessimistic' Kant in the context of sexual love (Langton 2009, pp. 320–321, cf. 325–326). It seems to me that Kant's 'pessimistic' remarks on sexual love relate to moral problems in the context of what I would call 'narrow sexual love', whereas the 'optimism' that Langton also sees in Kant is close to my 'broad sexual love' (the difference is that Langton emphasises the similarity between sexual love and friendship in describing Kant's 'optimism' (Langton 2009, pp. 320–321, 327, 363), whereas I emphasise love of benevolence in my description of 'broad sexual love').

[33] 'Allein wenn er sie bloß aus Geschlechts-Neygung liebt, so kann dies keine Liebe seyn, sondern Appetit.'

[34] 'Sie kann [...] weder zur Liebe des Wohlgefallens, noch der des Wohlwollens gezählt werden' (cf. LE, 27:417.27–28).

1. The predisposition to ANIMALITY in the human being may be brought under the general title of physical and merely *mechanical* self-love, i.e. a love for which reason is not required. It is three-fold: *first*, for self-preservation; *second*, for the propagation of the species, through the sexual drive, and for the preservation of the offspring thereby begotten through breeding; *third*, for community with other human beings, i.e. the social drive. (R, 6:26.12–18)[35]

In the *Religion* the sexual drive is clearly a form of love. It belongs to 'animal mechanical self-love' and is therefore part of love's overall concept. Remember also that in the 'Observations', Kant used the word 'love' to describe something felt by a man who only wants to use women for his own pleasure (2:208.3–5). In *The Metaphysics of Morals*, we encounter the claim: 'Sexual inclination is also called *love* (in the narrowest sense of the word)' (MM, 6:426.20–21)[36]. Against this, one could argue that Kant's use of the passive voice means that what he is addressing is not in fact his own view but a view generally held by other people. Yet the fact that he concedes that what is at issue is the 'narrowest meaning of the word' seems to imply that it is a use that he accepts – for why else would he use the word 'narrowest' [*engsten*]? Further evidence for narrow sexual love can be found in *Anthropology from a Pragmatic Point of View*: 'The strongest impulses of nature are *love of life* and *sexual love*, […] Love of life is to maintain the individual; sexual love, the species.' (AP, 7:276.28–33)[37] And finally, once more from *The Metaphysics of Morals*: 'Just as love of life is destined by nature to preserve the *person*, so sexual love is destined by it to preserve the *species*; in other words, each of these is a *natural end*' (MM, 6:424.12–14)[38].

If we now weigh the evidence, we see one published and two unpublished instances that detach sexual inclination or animal desire from love or 'genuine love', one published instance that detaches sexual inclination from love's general division, and five published instances that explicitly connect the sexual drive, sexual inclination, or the sexual impulse to love's overall framework. It seems to me that a balanced interpretation has no option but to hold that there is such a

---

[35] '1. Die Anlage für die THIERHEIT im Menschen kann man unter den allgemeinen Titel der physischen und bloß *mechanischen* Selbstliebe, d.i. einer solchen bringen, wozu nicht Vernunft erfordert wird. Sie ist dreifach: *erstlich* zur Erhaltung seiner selbst; *zweitens* zur Fortpflanzung seiner Art durch den Trieb zum Geschlecht und zur Erhaltung dessen, was durch Vermischung mit demselben erzeugt wird; *drittens* zur Gemeinschaft mit andern Menschen, d.i. der Trieb zur Gesellschaft.'
[36] 'Die Geschlechtsneigung wird auch *Liebe* (in der engsten Bedeutung des Wortes) genannt'.
[37] 'Die stärksten Antriebe der Natur […] sind *Liebe zum Leben* und *Liebe zum Geschlecht*; die erstere um das Individuum, die zweite um die Species zu erhalten'.
[38] 'So wie die Liebe zum Leben von der Natur zur Erhaltung der *Person*, so ist die Liebe zum Geschlecht von ihr zur Erhaltung der *Art* bestimmt; d.i. eine jede von beiden ist *Naturzweck*'.

thing as narrow sexual love. It is also very important to see that, more generally, the existence of narrow sexual love supports the view that even though the general division of love into love of benevolence and love of delight is a powerful key for understanding much of what Kant says about love, on the whole his conception of love is irreducible to the general division. The sexual impulse belongs to love but remains outside the grasp of the framework of love of benevolence and love of delight. But to account for the contrasting evidence presented above, it must be noted that narrow sexual love is love only in a highly restricted sense; it is non-rational and sometimes distinguished from love. It denotes merely 'the strongest possible sensible pleasure in an object.' (MM, 6:426.21–22)[39]

2.2.2 Broad Sexual Love

I will now move on to showing how the broader notion of sexual love accumulates on top of the narrow. As noted above, broad sexual love is essentially the non-rational sexual inclination united with moral love in the context of heterosexual marriage. In the recent literature, Kant's 'philosophy of marriage' has been strongly criticised. Scholars often speak of things like Kant's 'steely cynicism on the subject of marriage' (La Vopa 2005, p. 1), or argue that even at its best Kantian marriage is 'a system of mutual exploitation' (Wood 1999, p. 257), or that it marks 'the self-destruction of the categorical imperative' (Schröder 1997, p. 282). I think these kinds of views are unnecessarily one-sided and are largely due to lack of analysis of the concept of love within the context of marriage. For instance, the view that Kant conceived of marriage as merely mutual exploitation is, I think, a distorted position that results from placing improper weight on his discussion of marriage right (the tone and vocabulary of which is at least in part set by its necessarily legalistic context) and from neglecting his discussions of the duties of the spouses and how love operates in relation to those duties. I argue that if sexual love in marriage is analysed in terms of the broader notion of love I call 'broad sexual love', many pessimistic readings of Kantian marriage will thereby be mitigated.

Now it is true and generally well known that sexual desire or narrow sexual love is morally problematic for Kant. For instance, Kant compares the satisfaction of the sexual appetite to sucking the juice of a lemon and then throwing it away: 'As soon as the person is possessed, and the appetite sated, they are thrown away, as one throws away a lemon after sucking the juice from it.'

---

[39] 'die größte Sinnenlust, die an einem Gegenstande möglich ist'.

(LE, 27:384.31–33)⁴⁰ He speaks of sex as being like eating roast pork (LE, 27:386.35–36) or even like cannibalism (MM, 6:359.33–360.7). Since we know that the sexual impulse is, at bottom, a non-rational animal instinct, we may say that sexual desire on Kant's view, in its natural crudity, operates completely irrespective of the humanity and the personhood of the other agent. The desire may not even require the concept of another human being to yield enjoyment or fulfil its purpose (see R, 6:26; cf. 2:208.1–15). As such, the impulse does not take into account that the other human being to which it is directed has a capacity to set ends and make moral choices. However, as an inclination directed towards a particular human other, the sexual inclination has a profound connection to the person or the personhood of both parties. Kant emphasises that sexual desire itself is not directed to the humanity of the other; it is not a desire for a human '*qua* human' [*als Menschen*] (LE, 27:385.16) but rather a physical or animal desire for the other's sex [*Geschlecht*] (LE, 27:385.15–22; 27:386.36–37; 27:387.28–29; 27:637.37–638.2; 27:638.10–20; see also MM, 6:277–278).⁴¹ However, Kant thinks that it is precisely through this base mechanism that the *humanity* or the *person* of the other is possessed, enjoyed, or used as a thing (LE, 27:384.30–31; 27:385.23–35; 27:386.30–39; 27:387.25–29; MM, 6:426.1–15). For Kant, sexual desire is directed to a part of the human being, the use or enjoyment of which implies the use of the whole human being: 'a person is an absolute unity' (MM, 6:278.4–15)⁴², and 'if someone concedes a part of himself to the other, he concedes himself entirely' (LE, 27:387.29–31⁴³; see also MM, 6:278.32–279.12; Herman 1993, p. 55). In this way, desiring a part comes to mark the enjoyment of the whole. As Langton puts it, 'the extensional object of sexual desire is in fact a person [...] but the desire is for that person *qua body*' (Langton 2009, p. 368). Since

---

40 'So bald sie nun die Person haben, und ihren Appetit gestillet so werfen sie dieselbe weg, eben so, wie man eine Citrone wegwirft, wenn man den Saft aus ihr gezogen hat.'
41 Pace Korsgaard, who asserts that for Kant the object of sexual desire is a person *qua* person, even though she also sees Kant as 'sometimes changing his ground' (Korsgaard 1996, pp. 194, 214). In support of her claim, she quotes the Collins notes: 'They themselves, and not their work and services, are its [sexual desire's] Objects of enjoyment'. (LE, 27:384.3–5; cited in Korsgaard 1996, p. 194; see also Langton 2009, p. 367) However, the construction 'they themselves' is a peculiarity of the translation Korsgaard is using and is not at all contained in the original German. The German speaks of man's desire as immediately directed to 'other human beings as objects of his enjoyment'. This phrasing of course requires interpretation. 'Der Mensch hat eine Neigung die gerichtet ist auf andre Menschen, nicht, so ferne er die Arbeit und die Umstände anderer genießen kann, sondern unmittelbar auf andre Menschen als Objecte seines Genußes.' (LE, 27:384.3–5)
42 'Person [...] eine absolute Einheit ist'.
43 'wenn der Mensch einen Theil von sich dem andern überläßt, so überläßt er sich ganz.'

the person is used as an object of enjoyment, and since this does not involve consideration of the higher ends of humanity (since what is at issue is merely the satisfaction of an animal impulse), the person becomes a thing. Because 'each partner dishonors the humanity of the other' (LE, 27:385.31–32)[44], the same happens to both parties. In this way, sexual desire turns both the self and the other into mere objects or things from which sensual pleasure is derived. Kant therefore holds that sexuality is morally degrading. One both makes oneself an object and fails to treat the humanity of the other as an end in itself, rendering that other a mere means. However, it must still be emphasised that, contra certain interpreters, it does not follow that Kant thinks 'that by its very nature sexuality is bad' (Singer 2009, p. 377). For Kant, the sexual impulse remains predisposed to the good. In *The Metaphysics of Morals*, the proper natural end of the sexual impulse is even more crucial than self-preservation. It is 'an end even more important than that of love of life itself, since it aims at the preservation of the whole species and not only of the individual.' (MM, 6:425.3–5)[45]

From the perspective of love, however, what is most important in this context is that throughout his writings Kant holds that the sexual impulse can unite with neighbourly, other-regarding love: 'The sexual inclination can admittedly be combined with love of human beings, and then it also carries with it the aims of the latter' (LE, 27:384.34–36)[46]. Interpreted in the light of Kant's later discussions of love of human beings [*Menschenliebe*], the love in the above quotation from the Collins notes on ethics is most likely the rational love of benevolence as found in the general division of love and developed as practical love in the 'Doctrine of Virtue'. It is active rational benevolence by which one adopts the ends of another as one's own. The roots of this idea trace back to the precritical 'Observations', which I quoted at the beginning of this chapter: 'the more sublime a cast of mind is, the more inclined it also is to place the greatest goal of its efforts in the satisfaction of a beloved object, and on the other side the more beautiful it is, the more does it seek to respond to this effort with complaisance.' (2:242.18–22)[47] It is not the case that Kant held a cynical view concerning the possibility of moral sexuality. The sexual end of humanity is 'to preserve the spe-

---

44 'einer entehrt des andern seine Menschheit'.
45 'Zweck der Natur [...] noch wichtigern, als selbst der der Liebe zum Leben ist, weil dieser nur auf Erhaltung des Individuum, jener aber auf die der ganzen Species abzielt.'
46 'Die Geschlechts-Neigung kann zwar mit der Menschenliebe verbunden warden, und denn führt sie auch die Absichten der Menschenliebe mit sich'. Translation modified.
47 'so ist eine Gemüthsart, je erhabener sie ist, auch um desto geneigter die größte Absicht der Bemühungen in der Zufriedenheit eines geliebten Gegenstandes zu setzen, und andererseits je schöner sie ist, desto mehr sucht sie durch Gefälligkeit diese Bemühung zu erwiedern.'

cies without forfeiture of the person' (LE, 27:391.23–24)[48]. The aim of this resultant, broader notion of sexual love is thus not only procreation or sensible pleasure but also the happiness of the other human being. This point is confirmed in *The Metaphysics of Morals*, where sexual inclination is distinct from, but may unite with, moral love: 'this ardor has nothing in common with moral love properly speaking, though it can enter into close union with it under the limiting conditions of practical reason'. (MM, 6:426.29–32)[49] The properly moral love of *The Metaphysics of Morals* is at least the practical love of benevolence, but it might also refer to intellectual love of delight, the attributes of which I will elaborate on in the chapter on love of neighbour. For Kant, the way sexual inclination and moral love can be united is through marriage. In other words, marriage occasions the transition from narrow to broad sexual love.

It seems that the moral love Kant is speaking about is really a husband's love for his wife; Kant never explicitly considers wives as loving their husbands in the moral-practical sense of active rational benevolence. Furthermore, as feminist scholars like Hannelore Schröder (1997) have argued, there do seem to be restrictions to women's moral personhood that become apparent in the context of marriage. The most charitable recent interpretation of Kantian marriage in this regard, by Mari Mikkola, asserts that Kant's 'entire account of marriage is aimed at safeguarding women so that they are not reduced from persons to things.' (Mikkola 2011, p. 106) There is much to be said for Mikkola's view. As already noted, as such, human heterosexuality is directed only at the use of the sexual attributes or the sexual organs of the other human being, but since Kant views persons as essentially indivisible wholes, he thinks that the use of the sexual organs implies the use of the whole person (LE, 27:387–388). As constitutive, rudimentary parts of one's nature on the animal level, sexual organs are essential components of one's overall personhood. The justification of their use in marriage relies on the condition that both parties acquire the lifelong possession of (or right to use) the sexual attributes of the other. Because use of the sexual attributes implies use of the whole person, a default consequence of marriage is that all property rights that the spouses have prior to marriage become correspondingly mutual (even though the spouses may decide otherwise with a separate contract) (LE, 27:639–640). In line with the egalitarian foundations of his mature moral philosophy, Kant rejects polygamy, concubinage, and morganatic marriage on the grounds that these arrangements place women in an inferior po-

---

[48] 'die Erhaltung der Arten ohne Wegwerfung seiner Person'.
[49] 'das Brünstigsein hat mit der moralischen Liebe eigentlich nichts gemein, wiewohl sie mit der letzteren, wenn die praktische Vernunft mit ihren einschränkenden Bedingungen hinzu kommt, in enge Verbindung treten kann.'

sition: in polygamy, wives possess only a fraction of the husband; in concubinage, only the prostitute is possessed; and in morganatic marriage, property rights remain unfairly on one side (generally that of the man). (MM, 6:278–279) These moral and legal restrictions on the sexual contract clearly support Mikkola's view, or at least the view that Kant is not insensitive to the protection of the personhood of women and their rights (see also Korsgaard 1996, p. 195). It is the mutuality of possession in marriage that supposedly secures the personhood of the parties: 'while one person is acquired by the other *as if it were a thing*, the one who is acquired acquires the other in turn; for in this way each reclaims itself and restores its personality.' (MM, 6:278.10–13)[50] The basic set-up of marriage right thus clearly assumes the personhood of both sexes.

With this said, the status of women's personhood in Kantian marriage is more ambiguous than Mikkola's proposition implies. A closer look at Kant's doctrine supports a less charitable view. What we are dealing with is rather a *nominally equal* arrangement that constitutes what Jane Kneller aptly calls an 'illusion of equality' (Kneller 2006, p. 468). The relevant paragraphs in the 'Doctrine of Right' [*Rechtslehre*] suggest that even though possession is mutual and equal in marriage, it is really the men who possess the women. First of all, in the opening clause regarding this question, Kant unambiguously declares that 'a *man* acquires a *wife*' (MM, 6:277.3–4)[51]. The point about possession's being mutual appears only later, as if justifying the first clause. Further, in response to the immediate criticism launched against his views (see La Vopa 2005, pp. 8–9; Rauscher 2012, ch. 5), Kant objects that 'if I say "my wife", this signifies a special, namely a rightful, relation of the possessor to an object as a *thing* (even though the object is also a person).' (MM, 6:358.31–33)[52] The 'wife' is mentioned here just as an example, but it is telling that Kant does not think of constructing the relationship the other way around. Most importantly, Kant does seem to hold that in marriage, natural equality is not in conflict with the masterhood of the man:

> If the question is therefore posed, whether it is also in conflict with the equality of the partners for the law to say of the husband's relation to the wife, he is to be your master (he is

---

50 'indem die eine Person von der anderen *gleich als Sache* erworben wird, diese gegenseitig wiederum jene erwerbe; denn so gewinnt sie wiederum sich selbst und stellt ihre Persönlichkeit wieder her.' Barbara Herman's interpretation of this is eloquent: 'Perhaps it goes this way: I give myself (or rights over me) and you give yourself; but since you have me, in giving yourself to me you give me back to me.' (Herman 1993, p. 60)
51 'Der *Mann* erwirbt ein *Weib*'.
52 'Sage ich [...]: mein Weib, so bedeutet dieses ein besonderes, nämlich rechtliches, Verhältniß des Besitzers zu einem Gegenstande (wenn es auch eine Person wäre), als *Sache*.'

the party to direct, she to obey): this cannot be regarded as conflicting with the natural equality of a couple if this dominance is based only on the natural superiority of the husband to the wife in his capacity to promote the common interest of the household [...]. (MM, 6:279.16–25)[53]

In the *Anthropology*, as to who has supreme command in the household Kant writes: 'there certainly can be only one who coordinates all transactions in accordance with their ends.' (AP, 7:309.28–30)[54] Even though it seems possible that Kant leaves room for cases where the husband is not naturally superior in the sense required for legal dominance, Kant's naturalistic vocabulary appears to support the notion that he does not view the legally subordinate status of women as merely contingent. This is corroborated by the essay on 'Theory and Practice'[55] (1793), where the *natural* requirement for being a citizen (or eligible to vote) is not being a child or a woman (8:295.14–15). By implication, women are *naturally* not citizens (cf. Mikkola 2011, p. 101).[56] As Schröder puts it: 'Men are both the owners of women and yet their equal partners.' (Schröder 1997, p. 294) Kantian marriage is not just about safeguarding the personhood of women; it also affirms the dominance of men. It is precisely this that has led scholars to describe marriage as 'a stress point' (La Vopa 2005, p. 5) or as constituting a 'deep tension' (Kneller 2006, p. 469) in Kant's ethical system. I agree with the critical voices that despite the nominal equality of the marital relationship, there is an inconsistency or insoluble tension between the universalistic notion of personal autonomy and Kant's *de facto* doctrine of women. For Kant, women are *quasi-persons,* subordinate to their husbands, and the publish-

---

[53] 'Wenn daher die Frage ist: ob es auch der Gleichheit der Verehlichten als solcher widerstreite, wenn das Gesetz von dem Manne in Verhältniß auf das Weib sagt: er soll dein Herr (er der befehlende, sie der gehorchende Theil) sein, so kann dieses nicht als der natürlichen Gleichheit eines Menschenpaares widerstreitend angesehen werden, wenn dieser Herrschaft nur die natürliche Überlegenheit des Vermögens des Mannes über das weibliche in Bewirkung des gemeinschaftlichen Interesse des Hauswesens [...] zum Grunde liegt'.
[54] 'denn nur Einer kann es doch sein, der alle Geschäfte in einen mit dieses seinen Zwecken übereinstimmenden Zusammenhang bringt.' Translation modified. The Louden translation speaks of a single end, whereas the German is in the plural. The syntax implies that the ends might be 'his' [*Einer*], but it's also possible that the *seinen* refers back to the 'household' [*Haus*] mentioned in the previous sentence, and I've tried to preserve this ambiguity. It is unclear to me what the function of the *dieses* in the construction is.
[55] 'Über den Gemeinspruch: Das mag in der Theorie richtig sein, taugt aber nicht für die Praxis'.
[56] In the Vigilantius notes, however, the wife's belonging to the husband in servitude 'is due merely to her lesser ability to provide for herself' (LE 27:642.20–21) / 'so rührt dies blos von deren Schwäche, sich selbst zu erhalten, her'.

ed evidence would seem to suggest that he viewed this not as a contingent fact but as *natural*.

2.2.3 The Teleology of Sexual Love

To conclude the argument of this chapter, especially regarding the distinction between narrow and broad sexual love, I turn finally to the question of teleology. As I noted in the beginning, in the *Religion* Kant holds that the non-rational animal impulse of sex (narrow sexual love) is somehow predisposed to the good. But what does this mean? How is sexual love predisposed to the good, and what is the status of sex difference in this respect?

There are basically three ways to understand what Kant might mean by 'good' here. It might mean the moral good, it might mean the physical good as sensible happiness, or both. With all its dangers in terms of sensible happiness, sexuality can be viewed as being conducive to the physical good to the extent that it produces the strongest possible sensible pleasure in an object. The context in the *Religion*, however, suggests that Kant is talking about the moral good, or good in both senses (see ch. 1.1). But how can the crude physical impulse of sexuality be a predisposition [*Anlage*] to moral goodness? I think there are two possible answers to this question. First, we can take a weak notion of *Anlage* and hold that the impulse is predisposed to the moral good merely in the sense that it is a necessary condition of the continued existence of the species. The sexual impulse works to preserve the species, and in this sense it enables moral progress in the long term. On the other hand, we may take a stronger notion and suggest that there is something in the sexual impulse that, despite its non-moral character, is still somehow conducive to moral goodness, perhaps in the sense that it serves to occasion moral love between the sexes. In other words, narrow sexual love is predisposed to the good in the sense that we may judge that it leads to broad sexual love.

Most likely, all of the above is the case, even though Kant does not elaborate on the connection between sexuality and the good in much detail. In this respect, *Anthropology from a Pragmatic Point of View* (1798) is a key source.[57] In

---

[57] For scholars seeking a charitable interpretation of Kant's views on sexuality or sexual difference, one method is to reject or 'bracket' the anthropological remarks altogether, as they do seem to conflict with Kant's mature moral universalism. This is the strategy taken, for instance, by Mikkola (2011, p. 105). But most of what Kant says about sexual difference is actually contained in the anthropological discussions, and if this evidence is ruled out there is not much left to interpret. Kant did teach an anthropology course every winter for twenty years (so it is

the chapter 'On the Highest Physical Good' in the *Anthropology*, sexual love is associated with progress towards species-level happiness in the physical sense. There, love of life (self-preservation) and sexual love represent God's 'reason [...] that provides generally for the highest physical good' (AP, 7:279.29 – 30)[58], irrespective of human reason. I believe the passage is a remnant of an earlier period in Kant's philosophy, where he had not yet worked out the critical notion of teleological judgment. The statement regarding God's role seems too strong in the light of the third *Critique* (see C3, 5:447 ff.; see also my ch. 1.1), but the point must at least be that love of life and sexual love provide the species with sensuous happiness. In the same passage, however, Kant seems to go slightly further, connecting sexual love and cultural progress:

> For by means of the general mixing of the sexes, the life of our species endowed with reason is *progressively* maintained, despite the fact that this species intentionally works toward its own *destruction* (by war). Nevertheless, this does not prevent rational creatures, who grow constantly in culture even in the midst of war, from representing unequivocally the prospect of a state of happiness for the human race in future centuries, a state which will never again regress. (AP, 7:276.33 – 277.4)[59]

We know from Kant's philosophy of history that the kind of progress described above must involve a moral element and that, in fact, the proposition of cultural progress cannot even be understood as a merely descriptive prediction of how things will work out. 'The prospect of a state of happiness' is a regulative ideal, approximation to which requires moral striving on the part of human agents. Kant is not naïve about progress. It is of course possible to provide a

---

clearly a part of his thinking). He also authorised the publication of *Anthropology from a Pragmatic Point of View*, which was put together from his own notes and for which he also wrote a preface – even if his mental powers were already weakening at that time. Because of this, and because we can follow the development of Kant's anthropology through the lecture notes of the 1770s and 1780s, I take it that its published form is a real source and ought not to be bracketed off, at least when one's goals are exegetical. The *Anthropology* does of course contain a lot of material that we would call *precritical*, but then the proper approach is to read it cautiously, together with other sources, when seeking an overall interpretation of Kant's position on a given question.
58 'das physische Weltbeste allgemein besorgende Vernunft'.
59 'da dann durch Vermischung der Geschlechter im Ganzen das Leben unserer mit Vernunft begabten Gattung *fortschreitend* erhalten wird, unerachtet diese absichtlich an ihrer eigenen *Zerstörung* (durch Kriege) arbeitet; welche doch die immer an Cultur wachsenden vernünftigen Geschöpfe selbst mitten in Kriegen nicht hindert, dem Menschengeschlecht in kommenden Jahrhunderten einen Glückseligkeitszustand, der nicht mehr rückgängig sein wird, im Prospect unzweideutig vorzustellen.'

weak interpretation of the passage: sexual love is merely the necessary enabling condition for any kind of future for the human species. We may, however, be reminded of the passage in 'Conjectural Beginning' (8:113.7–11), where animal desire gives rise to a higher kind of love, which in turn brings about a general appreciation of beauty, which again (as we know from the third *Critique*), is closely linked to morality or even functions as a bridge between nature and the moral good. A thorough investigation of the *Anthropology* reveals that even though we do not find an explicit link between sexuality and beauty, there is indeed a kind of quasi-moral aspect involved in the way sexual teleology is discussed.

In the chapter on 'The Character of the Sexes' [*Der Charakter des Geschlechts*], Kant assigns a specific teleological role to women, and *only women*, in the moral progress of the species. Kant holds that if one wishes to characterise women or their role in species-level progress, one must rely on considerations of natural teleology rather than considerations of morality or virtue: 'One can only come to the characterization of this sex if one uses as one's principle not what we *make* our end, but what *nature's end* was in establishing womankind' (AP, 7:305.29–32)[60]. Nature's purpose or end [*Zweck*], which Kant also describes in terms of nature's *wisdom* [*Weisheit*] concerning womankind, is twofold: '(1) the preservation of the species, [and] (2) the cultivation of society and its refinement by womankind.' (AP, 7:305.35–306.2)[61] The first purpose is familiar from the context of narrow sexual love. Given this purpose, nature instils in women a fear that something will happen to the foetuses they carry in their wombs. Thus the first purpose makes women seek male protection out of fear of physical injury. The second purpose assigns women a place in the moral development of *men*. Kant thinks that the sexual union generally requires that each partner be in some way superior to the other – otherwise, the self-love of each would bring about mere 'squabbling' [*Zank*] (AP, 7:303.14–19).[62] While men are superior in physical strength and economic status, women rule men through controlling male desire by demands of 'gentle and courteous treatment' (AP, 7:306.14)[63].

---

60 'Man kann nur dadurch, daß man, nicht was wir uns zum Zweck *machen*, sondern was Zweck der Natur bei Einrichtung der Weiblichkeit war, als Princip braucht, zu der Charakteristik dieses Geschlechts gelangen'.
61 '1. die Erhaltung der Art, 2. die Cultur der Gesellschaft und Verfeinerung derselben durch die Weiblichkeit.'
62 What this boils down to is characterised by Kant in terms of a distinction between dominating [*herrschen*] and governing [*regieren*]. According to Kant, 'inclination dominates, and understanding governs' (AP, 7:309.32–33) / 'die Neigung herrscht, und der Verstand regiert.' The wife dominates the household, but only insofar as the governing husband approves.
63 'sanfte, höfliche Begegnung'.

Women therefore lead [*bringen*] men, 'if not to morality itself, to that which is its cloak, moral decency, which is the preparation for morality and its recommendation.' (AP, 7:306.16 – 18)⁶⁴ It is unclear what exactly this means, but the idea is probably that because women are equipped with 'finer feelings [...] of sociability and propriety' and tend to express 'modesty' and 'eloquence' in comparison with men (AP, 7:306.10 – 11)⁶⁵, men are more prone to adopt behavioural patterns appropriate to these kinds of 'feminine' traits when associating with women within various social contexts.

In his recent criticism of Kant's sexual teleology, Inder Marwah suggests that Kant's teleological view of sex difference 'requires women to adopt an explicitly non-moral character' and that women are therefore reduced 'to the status of means' in the moral development of humanity. (Marwah 2013, p. 559) The first question to ask is of course: if women are reduced to means for the moral development of the species, who or what is using them as means?⁶⁶ Possible answers to this question include men as individuals, men as a group of individuals, and nature itself. The context suggests that, since the natural purposes here are not about what 'we make our end', the 'agent' responsible for using women as means can only be 'nature'. Regardless of the stance one takes toward this question, I do think there is a sense in which Marwah is correct. First, the teleological role of women is primarily a supportive function: by protecting and nurturing children, women promote the physical existence of the species. Second, through the procreative sexual bond, women serve to make men more moral. It is telling, though, that the role seems to be only preparative: real morality is something men must accomplish for themselves. There is no clear prescription or teleological judgment in Kant to the effect that women should or will attain a proper moral status, even though Kant does not seem to suggest that they in principle lack the requisite rational structures.⁶⁷ In the teleology of sexual love, women's

---

64 'wenn gleich dadurch eben nicht zur Moralität selbst, doch zu dem, was ihr Kleid ist, dem gesitteten Anstande, der zu jener die Vorbereitung und Empfehlung ist'. The Mrongovius notes on anthropology make the same point more bluntly: 'The female sex is for the cultivation of the male sex' (LA, 25:1394.12 – 13) / 'Das weibliche Geschlecht ist zur Cultur des männlichen'.
65 'die feineren Empfindungen [...] der Geselligkeit und Wohlanständigkeit' / 'Sittsamkeit' / 'Beredtheit'. Note how the word *feinere* carries with it an allusion to the 'finer feelings' of beauty and sublimity in the early 'Observations'.
66 I thank Alix Cohen for posing this question to me.
67 Admittedly, the evidence in this area is ambiguous and inconclusive. Kant doubts women's capacity for principles (2:232.2 – 3; LA, 25:722.23 – 25) but also views them as being capable of morality (LA, 25:705.16 – 27) and recognising moral worth (C2, 5:153.19 – 23.). In the essay 'An Answer to the Question: What is Enlightenment' [*Beantwortung der Frage: Was ist Aufklärung*] (1784), we can plausibly read Kant as saying that 'the entire fair sex' [*das ganze schöne Ges-*

ends are subordinate to the moral progress of men. In this sense of sexual teleology, women are means.

But are women mere means? Did Kant view them as 'natural serfs or animals', as Schröder suggests (1997, p. 296)? Or did he see them as *belonging* to humanity's moral development 'in the worst sense of the word', as Marwah proposes (2013, p. 564)? In this chapter, I have argued that if the notion of sexual love is accounted for in the broad sense, the picture of Kantian sexual relations is much less grim than commonly thought. From the precritical 'Observations' up until the final published version of the *Anthropology*, Kant maintains that if there is to be marital love in the broadest, proper meaning, it is the happiness of the wife that the husband must make his principal aim. The earlier works make the same point by making use of the concept of the 'finer feeling' of love of beauty. From this perspective, to love the beautiful, be it in woman or non-human nature, is to experience non-instrumental delight [*Wohlgefallen*], which prepares one for virtue. The comprehensive notion of teleology, which includes the highest good as the moral happiness of rational creatures, must also include the happiness of both men and women. The highest good cannot involve the misery of either sex. In the Mrongovius notes on anthropology, for instance, we encounter the statement: 'Nature wanted the happiness of both sexes.' (LA, 25:1392.24)[68] And if women are to participate in happiness, they must also be capable of virtue[69] (but Kant never directly addresses this point). The *Anthropology* confirms that women's happiness is principally achieved via their husbands' making their happiness their primary aim: 'The husband's behavior must show that to him the welfare of his wife is closest to his heart.' (AP, 7:309.33–310.1)[70] This clearly includes the general principle of practical love [*Liebe des Wohlwollens*] on the part of the husband: the husband must adopt his wife's ends as his own. Therein lies the teleological function of *broad* sexual love: it aims at the happiness of women. Even though Kant does give women a subordinate role in his sexual teleology, the broader notion of love that Kant consistently insists on ensures that women are not mere means but also ends in themselves.

---

chlecht] is in a state of 'self-incurred minority' [*selbst verschuldete Unmündigkeit*], which implies that in principle they might in the future mature and come to use their own understanding without external direction (8:35). I thank Martin Sticker for convincing me of this last point over the course of several informal discussions.
68 'Die Natur hat die Gluckseeligkeit beydes Geschlechts gewollt.'
69 I thank Jens Timmermann for bringing this to my attention.
70 'Das Betragen des Ehemanns muß zeigen: daß ihm das Wohl seiner Frau vor allem anderen am Herzen liege.'

In this way, the transition from morally problematic narrow sexual love to broad sexual love, which acknowledges and promotes the happiness of women, can also be seen to provide what Langton calls 'an escape from solipsism' (Langton 2009, p. 321), even if, in this case, only from a male perspective. Perhaps broad sexual love could be generalised so that it involves a reciprocal and equal relationship of love and respect between the spouses (or lovers in general), and the relationship based on sexual love would then actually be a relationship of friendship. Ideas along these lines have been presented in the literature, and writers like Korsgaard and Langton have rightly pointed out the similarity between some of Kant's discussions of sexual love and friendship in the Collins notes, in terms of the reciprocity of 'self-surrender and retrieval' (Korsgaard 1996, p. 195; see Langton 2009, pp. 319, 363). In both marriage and friendship, one yields oneself to the other and gets oneself back through the other (LE, 27:388.23–37; cf. 27:423.37–424.6). As Langton shows (2009, p. 320), in his correspondence Kant speaks of both marital love and love in friendship as assuming 'the same mutual respect', writing that this virtuous love common to both 'wants to communicate itself completely' (11:331.31–332.2)[71].

On the other hand, Denis (2001b) has listed six ways in which marriage and friendship differ from each other in Kant: 1) the basis of marriage is more sensuous and less intellectual than that of (moral) friendship; 2) marriage requires a relation of dominance in which husbands are ultimately superior to their wives; 3) women are generally inferior to men; 4) because of this, reciprocity in mutual disclosure is less likely between husband and wife than between friends (and women can't really keep secrets)[72]; 5) the proper distance required for respect is unlikely in marriage; and 6) friendship is more loving than marriage. (Denis 2001b, pp. 13–16) Denis's aim is to revise Kantian marriage into a 'moral marriage' on the basis of a Kantian model of friendship, and for the most part her characterisation of Kantian marriage is accurate. Yet her sixth point, the point about love, paints a picture of Kantian marriage nearly exclusively in terms of *narrow* sexual love, and while she acknowledges that 'marriage promises partners some measure of practical love' (Denis 2001b, p. 16), she mostly neglects the passages on which my notion of *broad* sexual love is based. Friendship is indeed not the same as sexual love or marriage, and my aim here is not to venture beyond Kant but merely to do him justice. From this per-

---

[71] 'gleiche gegenseitige Achtung' / 'will sich gänzlich mittheilen.' For a dramatic story about the correspondence between Kant and Maria von Herbert, which also illuminates the relationship between various aspects of Kant's life and his philosophy, see Langton's 'Duty and Desolation' (in Langton 2009, pp. 197–222).
[72] See AP, 7:304.1–2.

spective, broad sexual love may provide us with further resources when it comes to seeing the 'optimistic' Kant described by Langton (Langton 2009, p. 321). This optimism is missing from Denis's characterisation of Kant's (non-revised) account of love in marriage. However, if we are to generalise the notion of broad sexual love such that it operates symmetrically between the sexes, the basic premise we would need to add to Kant's framework (in a much more powerful way than he does) is that women and men are equal. Only then would something like 'sexual friendship' be possible in Kantian terms. But this is beyond the scope of my present work.

It is true that Kant's views on women are generally not very enlightened, even by the standards of his day. It is particularly true that Kant was opposed to women's higher education, and that the role he saw for women was a domestic one. The problem was, and is, that he could not see that women's happiness might reside outside the domestic sphere, in the public – in practicing science or striving for moral self-perfection based on principles. The distinction I have drawn between narrow and broad sexual love reveals a Kant who is by no means a feminist but whose views on sexuality are not as cynical or negative as is often thought, and who clearly reserves a place for loving morality and loving affection within the sexual sphere. The ascent of sexual love can thus be said to mark a transition from narrow to broad sexual love, from the merely natural to the natural-moral. The Mrongovius lectures on anthropology summarise this idea:

> as long as it [sexual inclination] is brutal and aims merely at enjoyment, it is only animal instinct. – But as soon as it is connected to benevolence and aims at the happiness of the other, it becomes genuine love. It must not be like love of roast beef, which one devours. (LA, 25:1361.4 – 8)[73]

---

[73] 'sie ist nur thierischer Instinkt so lange sie brutal ist und bloß auf den Genuß geht – Sobald sie aber mit Wohlwollen verbunden ist und auf die Gluckseeligkeit des andern geht; so wird sie eigentliche Liebe. Sie muß nicht sein wie Liebe zum RinderBraten den man destruirt'.

3 Love of God

In this chapter, my task is to locate the term 'love' in the context of Kant's considerations of God [*Die Liebe Gottes, Gottesliebe*] and to analyse the precise functions that love is given within these contexts. Since Kant's 'rational religion' is based on a moral philosophical interpretation of Christian scripture, and since love of God is a foundational notion in Christianity, it is fair to assume as a working hypothesis that love of God is a significant concept in Kant's approach to religion, and hence in his overall project.

If one takes into account that Kant sometimes viewed religion as 'rooted in the love of God' (LE, 27:720.25–26)[1], was sympathetic to the Christian idea that God *is* love[2] (R, 6:145.21; LE, 27:721.2), and held in the concluding remark of his late moral philosophical work *The Metaphysics of Morals* that the intention of the world's author 'can have only love for its basis' (MM, 6:491.2–3)[3], it is almost surprising that very little has been written about this topic in the literature.

As was the case with self-love and sexual love, there seem to be no systematic exegetical interpretations of love of God available. There are, however, discussions of Kant's reading of Jesus' basic commandment to love God above all, and your neighbour as yourself[4]. Ina Goy, for instance, observes that for humans, the commandment to love God results in an 'unattainable ideal'[5] (Goy 2014, p. 19), whereas Moors claims that 'the love of God equals […] moral self-love' (Moors 2007, p. 256, see also 269). On the other hand, some interpreters seem to view God's love for human beings as equatable to the ideal of love for the moral law (Palmquist 2000, p. 261; Axinn 1994, p. 119; Reardon 1988, p. 143), while some posit generally that Kant's God is loving (Wood 1970, p. 248), and others that his God is not loving (Goy 2014, p. 23).

While I think that all the previous propositions in this area are interesting and merit discussion, if taken as accounts of love of God they are ultimately problematic. The problem is first of all methodological: the propositions are not intended as systematic discussions of the issue but are rather brief comments made in the midst of other interpretative concerns.[6] Second, I think a sim-

---

[1] 'in der Liebe Gottes beruhet.'
[2] As expressed in the Gospel of John in the New Testament of the Christian Bible: 'The one who does not love does not know God, because God is love.' (1. John 4:8)
[3] 'die nur Liebe zum Grunde haben kann.'
[4] Mark 12:28; similar in Matt. 22:34. See my ch. 4.1.
[5] 'ein […] unerreichbares Ideal.'
[6] The case is different in Moors's article, where he goes so far as to claim that he is formulating 'a general evaluation of Kant's philosophy of love' (Moors 2007, p. 266). But Moors's eclectic ap-

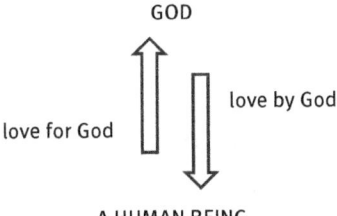

Figure 3. The Two-Directionality of Love of God

ple yet essential structural feature of love of God has not been fully acknowledged by the previous commentators: the fact that love of God works in two different directions. It can either mean the human being's love for God, or it can mean God's love for human beings, so that there is an 'upward' direction from human beings to God and a 'downward' direction from God to human beings (see fig. 3).[7]

This chapter aims to determine more precisely the relationship between these two directions and the extent to which they are distinguishable from each other. Drawing in part from previous research in this area, I shall build my discussion around the following questions: What is the relationship between love of God and love for the moral law? Does love for the law relate to love *for* God, to love *by* God, or to both – or do love of God and love for the law mean the same thing? What is the place of the general division of love (as love of benevolence and love of delight) in love of God – does the general division even play a

---

proach has other problems, as noted by Goy: He is insensitive to the dynamic temporal structure of the Kantian corpus and does not use source criticism when choosing the passages on which he bases his interpretations (see Goy 2014, p. 6). I discuss Moors's evaluation in my general introduction to this study. On the other hand, Dennis Vanden Auweele's (2014) 'For the Love of God: Kant on Grace' focuses solely on grace and does not provide an interpretation of how love functions in this context.

7 Goy (2014, p. 16) appears to recognise this structure but does not make interpretative use of it, whereas Moors fruitfully acknowledges that in the Vigilantius notes love for God is dependent on God's love. However, by claiming that the duty of love is there grounded on a 'theologico-metaphysical idea' of God's love (Moors 2007, p. 258), Moors downplays the point that for Kant, duties can only be grounded in pure practical reason. Moors is not entirely unaware of this moral grounding of duty, but his notion of a 'theologico-metaphysical basis' of duty and love (Moors 2007, p. 259) seems overly religious from a moral perspective. The overall context of Kant's writings on religion suggests that the idea of God's love is moral-rational (something that reason gives to itself) rather than 'theologico-metaphysical'. I hope to show this more clearly toward the end of the chapter.

role? Is love of God somehow reducible to rational or moral self-love? And finally, is Kant's God loving or not?

I will divide my treatment roughly into two exegetical parts. In the first, I will investigate human love for God; in the second, God's love for humans. The third section analyses the relationship between love of God and self-love and makes more general remarks concerning the place of God in Kant's philosophy. Within the two thematic sections, I will proceed chronologically with an eye to tracking the possible evolution of Kant's thought, focusing on the most relevant works from the mature period: the second *Critique*, the *Religion*, and *The Metaphysics of Morals* (as well as the Vigilantius notes on ethics). I will thus walk up the same path twice, but using a different perspective each time so as to gain an accurate overall picture.

I will show that love for the law is ideally related to love for God (rather than love by God) and that love for God can be meaningfully discussed in terms of a *scale structure*. I will also point out that the general division of love is operative in love of God and that by using the general division God's love can be divided into an *end account* and a *ground account*. Love of God will be seen as irreducible to rational or moral self-love. On the whole, and in its perfection, love of God is a necessary and sufficient condition for the complete highest good. Kant's God is ultimately a rational idea, or an ideal rational construction, and the evidence suggests that this God is a loving God, even though Kant remains puzzled about the relationship between God's love and God's justice. I will call the overall picture arrived at in this investigation *the ascent model of love of God*.

3.1 Love for God

For Kant, religion is very much about the cognition [*Erkenntnis*] of our duties as divine commands (C2, 5:129.18–19; R, 6:153.28–29; MM, 6:443.27–31). Morality is the proper stuff of religion, but it is morality viewed or cognised from a particular perspective, mainly that of Christianity. This perspective includes assumptions or beliefs that have a practical significance but that are absent from morality considered merely in itself. It appears that Kant, at least from the Herder lectures (1762–1764) onwards, never accepts that morality is grounded in religion and instead maintains that the concept of morality leads us to believe in God (see LE, 27:73–74; 27:306–308; C2, 5:129; see also Timmermann 2016a, p. 1). Morality is the necessary condition of religion – that is, religion in the proper, moral sense, and not as a mere cult (e.g. LE, 27:305; R, 6:51–52; see also 6:12–13). However, as Timmermann has shown, up until the 'Canon' [*Kanon*] of the *Critique of Pure Reason*, Kant thinks that belief in God is necessary if we are to have a sufficient motive to moral action. Even though the source of moral laws can be judged to lie in reason, an external lawgiver with threats and rewards is needed as an incentive for compliance with those laws. Without God, moral laws would be 'idle chimeras' [*leere Hirngespinste*] without reality (C1, A811/B839). This picture changes with the *Groundwork*, where moral motivation is connected with the new notions of autonomy and respect for the moral law. From that point on, belief in God is no longer necessary as a motive for moral action, but God and religion are still necessary conditions of our hoping for and aiming toward the highest good (as the morally deserved happiness of rational creatures). (Timmermann 2016a; see C3, 5:450–541; cf. MM, 6:443.35)

In the first section of this chapter, I investigate human love for God. As we would assume, Kant's treatments of this topic take place at the intersections of morality and religion. What remains constant in his discussions is the idea that human love for God is about viewing our duties as divine commands and about *striving to practice these duties gladly* [*gern*]. In Kant's mature period after the *Groundwork*, this striving is developed in terms of a regulative ideal that Kant calls 'love for the law', which is the unattainable goal of one's striving for gladness in fulfilling all of one's duties. The exegetical problems I wish to address in this section are as follows: What is the relationship between human love for God and love's general division? Is human love for God equatable with love for the law, or do they remain somehow discernible from each other? I will answer these questions toward the end of the section.

It seems that Kant does not write about love of God directly prior to the second *Critique*. To be sure, he recognises from the early 1760s onwards that there might be an obligation to love, but in its earliest formulations this obligation is not explicitly associated with God and is apparently discussed more as an interpersonal issue.[8] By contrast, it is equally the case that the earlier Kant recog-

---

8 See 'Attempt to Introduce the Concept of Negative Magnitudes into Philosophy' [*Versuch den Begriff der negativen Größen in die Weltweisheit einzuführen*] (1763) (2:183.35–36) and 'Inquiry Concerning the Distinctness of the Principles of Natural Theology and Morality' [*Untersuchung über die Deutlichkeit der Grunsätze der natürlichen Theologie und der Moral*] (1764) (2:300.2), as well as the Herder lectures on ethics (27:65–66). Goy (2014, pp. 15–16) speculates interestingly whether love of God might already be located in the aforementioned 'Inquiry', because the principle of mutual love is discussed in the same paragraph as the proposition to do 'what is in accordance with the will of God' / 'das, was dem Willen Gottes gemäß ist' (2:300.17). Goy is correct to note that the link between mutual love and love of God (and the commandment to love one's neighbour) is unclear, and I therefore think that she is stretching the rather vague evidence too far when she claims that in the 'Inquiry' love of God (and love of neighbour) are 'examples of the "many simple feelings of the good"' (Goy 2014, p. 16; see 2:299.33). It is not clear whether love of God is even meant to be at issue in the 'Inquiry', and it certainly isn't mentioned in that text.

nises that we have traditional obligations to God (e.g. 2:300.16–18), but these are not explicitly discussed in terms of love. It is also noteworthy that the later Kant of *The Metaphysics of Morals* specifically denies that there could be duties *to God* [*gegen Gott*]. The duties we may have *with regard to* [*in Ansehung*] a transcendent being (of which reason provides us an idea) are, properly speaking, duties to ourselves. (MM, 6:443.27–444.8)

The first time that love for God actually comes up in the Kantian corpus is in the Collins notes on ethics. Kant's mature theory of moral motivation is not yet in place, but his several remarks clearly anticipate the later works and indicate continuity in his treatment. In the Collins notes, Kant states, for instance, that 'the disposition to performance of duties is to be cultivated, and this is what the teacher of the gospels says: that we should do everything from the love for God. But to love God is to do His commands gladly.' (LE, 27:274.13–15[9]; similarly at 27:300.6–9; 27:335.35–37; see also 27:322.23–25) An important interpretative key is provided in the above passage: human love for God is closely connected with the notion of 'cultivating'[10] one's disposition to perform duties gladly. Later on in the lectures, in Kant's discussion of duties (and love) towards other people, we learn that to do something gladly is connected with doing it willingly, from one's 'own impulse' [*aus eignem Triebe*] or from 'inclination' [*aus Neygung*] (LE, 27:413.18–19).

In terms of Kant's mature moral philosophy from the *Groundwork* onwards, the idea of a commandment to do something out of inclination or inclination-based love may seem puzzling. In the foundational terminology of Kant's mature moral philosophy, duty and inclination are opposing terms: if an action is done from duty, it is not done from inclination, and conversely, if something is done from inclination, it is done from a sort of natural liking and therefore not from duty. But as we shall learn next, it is not the case that the commandment to love God in Kant's mature period prescribes practicing duties *from* inclination; instead, it prescribes practicing duties *with* a facilitating or corresponding inclination, and hence gladly. What will remain impossible for humans is the complete attainment of a love for the moral law (see ch. 1.3). We will always have inclinations that run contrary to what morality demands, which also means that we can never love God perfectly.

---

9 'ist die Gesinnung der Leistung der Pflichten zu cultiviren, und dieses ist das, was der Lehrer des Evangelii sagt, daß man alles aus Liebe zu Gott thun soll. Gott lieben ist aber seine Gebothe gerne thun.' Translation modified.
10 I discuss the notion of cultivation in ch. 4.2.2.A.

Kant's main discussion of love for God occurs in the second *Critique*. In the chapter 'On the Incentives of Pure Practical Reason'[11] Kant engages in philosophical interpretation of Jesus' basic commandment to love God above all and one's neighbour as oneself. I will read this passage by first pointing out the implied existence of the general division of love in this context, and then by looking at the way the adverb 'gladly' functions, in order to analyse how Kant understands the relationship between love for God and love for the law.

The starting point of Kant's enquiry is the idea that the twofold religious commandment is in agreement with the notion that while we are the lawgivers of morality, we are also its subjects: 'For, as a commandment it requires respect for a law that *commands love* and does not leave it to one's discretionary choice to make this one's principle. But love for God as inclination (pathological love) is impossible, for he is not an object of the senses.' (C2, 5:83.5–7)[12] Here, in the context of love for God, Kant seems to rely implicitly on the same division between inclination-based love and reason-based love that he uses extensively in the context of neighbourly love. In my chapter on love of neighbour, I will show how this distinction can be understood in terms of love's general division into love of delight and love of benevolence (both of which can be either intellectual/moral or pathological). Assuming these results, it seems that what is excluded in the passage quoted above is the possibility of loving God in the sense of inclination-based love of benevolence or pathological love of delight (or, even more obviously, the crude animal impulse of sex). We can hence plausibly say that love for God at least makes implicit reference to love's general division and can be analysed in conjunction with that division.

Kant goes on to conclude that since inclinations (and love in particular) cannot be directly commanded, the commandment to love can only concern practical love, i.e. love of neighbour as active rational benevolence (see ch. 4.2.2). But it seems that from the side of natural inclination-based love (which for Kant is the more paradigmatic type of love) we still get a *residue* or a *supplement*, which informs the kind of emotional state we should aim to approximate when acting from duty: 'To love God means, in this sense, to do what He commands *gladly*; to love one's neighbor means to practice all duties toward him *gladly*.' (C2, 5:83.12–14)[13] The idea of gladness in love for God retains a reference

---

[11] 'Von den Triebfedern der reinen praktischen Vernunft'.
[12] 'Denn es fordert doch als Gebot Achtung für ein Gesetz, das *Liebe befiehlt*, und überläßt es nicht der beliebigen Wahl, sich diese zum Princip zu machen. Aber Liebe zu Gott als Neigung (pathologische Liebe) ist unmöglich; denn er ist kein Gegenstand der Sinne.'
[13] 'Gott lieben, heißt in dieser Bedeutung, seine Gebote *gerne* thun; den Nächsten lieben, heißt, alle Pflicht gegen ihn *gerne* ausüben.'

to inclination-based love in moral action. As noted above, however, there cannot be a direct duty to be glad; rather, gladness is something for which we must strive [*streben*]. The commandment to love God (and one's neighbour) 'presents the moral disposition in its complete perfection' (C2, 5:83.23–24)[14], and were this to be attained, the moral agent would not have any inclinations that run contrary to the moral law. She would be fully inclined to do what morality commands in every situation: she would always be moral *gladly*. Kant calls this ideal end state, which he stresses is *not attainable* (C2, 5:84.1–2; 5:84.15) for finite imperfect creatures like us, love for the law [*Liebe zum Gesetze*] (C2, 5:84.12).[15] Love for God, or the commandment to love God, thus involves recognising all duties as divine commands and striving to approximate love for the moral law by aiming for gladness in the fulfilment of duties. Love for God concerns one's own moral perfection, which includes a glad, cheerful disposition. It prescribes the rational ideal of the highest subjective moral good. But can we say that love for God and love for the moral law are therefore the same thing?

If it is the case that love for God and love for the law are simply the same, and that love for the law is an unattainable ideal, then it would follow that love for God is also unattainable, not only with regard to feeling or inclination-based love but also with regard to moral practice. It might be more charitable to assume that there is a difference between the two notions, such that while love for the law remains unattainable we can still speak of *some kind* of love for God, in any such case where we are able to practice *some* duty gladly – that is, from respect for the moral law but with an accompanying inclination towards the particular action (or its result)[16]. But to answer the question properly, it is necessary to investigate how love for God and love for the law are linked in Kant's works after the second *Critique*. I will do this by investigating the relevant remarks from the *Religion* and the roughly contemporaneous Vigilantius lectures on ethics.

There are two particularly relevant passages in the *Religion* that shed light on this connection. Firstly, in a 'General Comment' [*Allgemeine Anmerkung*] to the third book of the *Religion*, we find a familiar statement: 'The highest goal, however, of the moral perfection of finite creatures – never completely attainable

---

14 'stellt [...] die sittliche Gesinnung in ihrer ganzen Vollkommenheit dar'.
15 Goy (2014, p. 19) is thus correct to note that in the second *Critique* the love commandment results in an unattainable ideal.
16 I leave open here whether the inclination concerns the action itself, the effect of the action, or both. I don't see evidence to warrant any strong response to this question.

for human beings – is love of the law.' (R, 6:145.17–19)[17] The brief remark does not address love for God directly, but it is important to note that Kant here uses the word 'completely' [*völlig*]. Love for the law is not *completely* attainable, and hence it seems possible that it is attainable *to some extent*. But this still does not answer the question about the relationship between love for God and love for the law. Kant moves on in the immediately following paragraph to discuss God's love for human beings: 'In conformity with this idea, the following would be a principle of faith in religion: "God is love"' (R, 6:145.21–22)[18]. This implies that the idea of love for the law is in harmony with the principle of God's being love, or perhaps that the idea of love for the law should be understood in conjunction with the idea that God is love. In either case, this 'conformity' is a relevant finding and will be discussed in the latter half of this chapter.

There are three very strong readings of the above conjunction in the literature. Firstly, Sidney Axinn states that in the above passages of the *Religion*, 'Kant's interpretation of "God is love" is developed in terms of love of the moral law.' (Axinn 1994, p. 119) However, Axinn does not elaborate on this. Taking a similar position to Axinn's, Bernard Reardon seems to hold that Kant equates love of the law with the notion that God is love: 'To express this idea [love of the law] in religious terms is, he thinks, to affirm that "God is love"' (Reardon 1988, p. 143). Reardon correctly points out that God's love is at least partly a response to 'man's efforts to fulfil the holy law' (Reardon 1988, p. 143), but I fail to see how this (at least partial) interdependence of love of the law and the idea that God is love makes it the case that the latter is simply a 'religious expression' of the former. The same objection can be put to Palmquist, who holds that 'the religious equivalent of the idea of "love of the moral law" is the "article of faith,

---

17 'Das höchste, für Menschen nie völlig erreichbare Ziel der moralischen Vollkommenheit endlicher Geschöpfe ist aber die Liebe des Gesetzes.' DiCenso's reading of the passage is in striking contrast with the second *Critique*. According to DiCenso: 'Learning to *love the moral law* means maturing ethically to the point where we do not require external coercion to offset our predilection for maxims based on self-love.' (DiCenso 2012, p. 197) In the second *Critique*, however, loving the moral law is dependent on having a thorough liking for what the moral law commands. The criterion for love of the law in DiCenso's interpretation is significantly less demanding: it suffices that we do not require 'external coercion' for 'offsetting' the maxims of self-love, i.e. in DiCenso's reading the moral agent loves the law if she is mature enough to autonomously override her maxims of self-love (without being forced to do so by others). But in this case she could, by means of her own will (i.e. without external coercion), offset the predilection to self-love but do it *grudgingly*. In my view, following the moral law autonomously but grudgingly would hardly be love for the law (which somehow requires *liking*), and I have not found textual evidence that would support DiCenso's interpretation.
18 'Dieser Idee gemäß würde es in der Religion ein Glaubensprincip sein: "Gott ist die Liebe"'.

'God is love'".' (Palmquist 2000, p. 261)[19] It seems to me that in their readings (which are immanent to the *Religion*) Axinn, Reardon, and Palmquist do not analyse these two notions of love of God, i.e. love *for* God and love *by* God. It seems completely possible, and even probable, that further evidence will show that there is something in human striving for love of the law (or in human love for God) that is not as such contained in God's love, and vice versa, that there is some element in God's love that goes beyond human striving for love of the law. We should not equate the two directions of love without careful and thorough analysis. It should also be remembered that in the second *Critique*, the regulative ideal of loving the law is itself occasioned by the command to love God, and hence the notion of loving the law is grounded in religious vocabulary. It would thus be somewhat odd, in my opinion, to call God's love the 'religious expression' or 'religious equivalent' of love for the law, as love for the law, too, seems very much connected to an interpretation of Christian scripture. While the commentators are right to note that love for the law and God's love are obviously linked (through the notion of conformity), in the light of textual evidence love for the law and love *for* God seem even more tightly connected, as they are both loves where the human being is the subject of love. In love for God and love for the law, the object of love is ideal or 'higher' than human nature, i.e. both of these loves have an 'upward' direction.

The second passage in the *Religion* concerns human love for God, but it also relates implicitly to love for the law. In discussing service to God, Kant distinguishes between two doctrines that can be taught in relation to religion: 'the *doctrine of godliness*' [*Gottseligkeitslehre*][20] and 'the *pure doctrine of virtue*' [*die reine*

---

19 Perhaps we could make Axinn's, Reardon's, and Palmquist's interpretations plausible by appealing to a subtle distinction in Kant's terminology. In the second *Critique*, Kant uses the term 'Liebe *zum* Gesetze', whereas in the *Religion* he speaks of 'Liebe *des* Gesetzes', which translate roughly to love *for* the law and love *of* the law, respectively. In the latter case, we could try to argue that while the law is (ideally) an object of love, it is also somehow the *subject* of love. Then we might understand God's love in terms of love *of* the law. This position would equate God with the moral law, and love of God in general would be subsumed under love flowing *to and from* the moral law. However, I am not convinced by this argument, as it neglects several passages where God and the moral law seem distinct – the argument seems to uncritically synthesise too many things. Moreover, Axinn, Reardon, and Palmquist do not argue anything of the sort. Further, there would still be two directions of love to be accounted for, and their relationship would then be quite unclear.

20 *Gottseligkeit* is not a modern German word, and according to the Adelung Dictionary it means an endeavour [*Bemühung*] or an aptitude [*Fertigkeit*] to place God at the ground of one's entire conduct and to direct one's actions to God's honour [*Ehre*]. I thank Jens Timmermann for drawing my attention to this.

Tugendlehre] (R, 6:182.21–22). The latter should be the starting point of moral and religious instruction, whereas the former serves 'only as a means to strengthen [...] the virtuous attitude' (R, 6:183.15–16)[21]. The doctrine of godliness consists of two moral attitudes – fear of God and love of God: '*Fear* of God is this attitude in compliance with his commands from *obligated* (a subject's) duty, i.e., from respect for the law, but *love* of God is this attitude from one's own *free choice* and liking [*Wohlgefallen*] for the law (from filial duty).' (R, 6:182.27–30)[22]

In this context, love of God [*Liebe Gottes*] is clearly the human being's love for God. It is again distinguished from mere respect for the law and implies (in addition to involving free choice) a 'liking for the law', which is described in terms of *Wohlgefallen*. Further, the passage strongly suggests that insofar as this liking for the law may indeed be interpreted in terms of love for the law (as the common context of love for God implies), this love is love of delight. The doctrine of godliness therefore seems to provide further evidence for the viability of the general division of love in the context of love for God. What is particularly interesting here, moreover, is that there is no mention of the unattainability of this kind of love for God. Rather, in this context it seems possible that we *can* love God by liking the law. If we now read this passage together with the earlier passage from the *Religion* and the first passage from the second *Critique*, what reveals itself is a scaling structure for the conceptual framework of love for God, where love for God comes in degrees and only its highest stage is properly called love for the law (which remains unattainable). Let us call this *the scale of love for God*.

Recall that in the second *Critique* the command to love God prescribed the ideal of practicing all duties gladly, which was unattainable (but there was no claim that *no duties* could be practiced gladly). In the first passage of the *Religion*, love of the law is described as being not *completely* attainable, whereas in the second passage love for God seems quite possible. The scale of love for God thus has two extreme endpoints, between which the actuality of love for God falls. At one end we have *fear* of God (or mere respect for the law), which is the zero-point of love for God (there is no love present). At the other end we have perfect love for God (i.e. love for the law), where all duties are subjectively accompanied by a corresponding inclination. The normative end of progress on this scale is a state where 'dread changes into liking and respect into love' (C2,

---

21 'nur zum Mittel dienen [...] die Tugendgesinnung, zu stärken'.
22 '*Furcht* Gottes ist diese Gesinnung in Befolgung seiner Gebote aus *schuldiger* (Unterthans-) Pflicht, d.i. aus Achtung fürs Gesetz; *Liebe* Gottes aber aus eigener *freier Wahl* und aus Wohlgefallen am Gesetze (aus Kindespflicht).' Pluhar's translation.

5:84.17–19)²³. The actuality of love for God lies between these endpoints.²⁴ We hereby arrive at a subtle distinction between love for God and love for the law: love for God is any instance of liking the law, i.e. of doing one's duty gladly, whereas love for the law is the ideal and unattainable perfection of this disposition. In this way, despite our imperfections, it is nevertheless possible for us to love God practically.²⁵

The Vigilantius notes on ethics appear to corroborate this general picture, even though the criterion for loving the law is described slightly differently:

> §143. Love towards God is the foundation of all inner religion.
> The maxim of gladly following a law is love for the law itself, which presupposes a liberation from the inclinations that hinder us from following it; and hence we do that very unwillingly, so long as such contrary impulses are still to be found in us, representing an obstacle to be overcome. (LE, 27:720.1–7)²⁶

Here, it seems to be the adoption of the maxim (to follow the moral law gladly) that we ought to strive for in our attempt to approximate love for the law. Since the maxim presupposes 'liberation from the inclinations', it is relatively clear that it cannot be adopted perfectly. This finding seems to be consistent with the accounts given in the second *Critique* and the *Religion*. It is also implied a little further down that love of the law will remain an ideal, whereas love for God may be relatively attained by conjoining a corresponding inclination to the representation of particular duties: 'so in love of the law there is no command, and the so-called categorical: *Love God* tells us no more than to base our observance of laws, not merely on obedience […] but on an inclination in conformity with what the law prescribes.' (LE, 27:721.10–14)²⁷ The notion that love of the law is not associated with any command confirms that this ideal

---

23 'verwandelt sich […] die […] Scheu in Zuneigung und Achtung in die Liebe'.
24 This is not to suggest that there is a calculus for love for God in Kant; the idea is merely that we have two idealised ends and a notion of progress that is being prescribed through an interpretation of the love commandment, such that we are able to speak of *less* and *more* within this context.
25 I am grateful to Jens Timmermann for discussions that led me to arrive at this interpretation.
26 '§143. Die Liebe gegen Gott ist das Fundament der ganzen innern Religion. Die Maxime, ein Gesetz gern zu befolgen, ist Liebe fürs Gesetz selbst, welches eine Befreiung von den Neigungen voraussetzt, die die Befolgung des Gesetzes behindern: und daher thut man es so lange überaus ungern, als noch dergleichen Antriebe zum Gegentheil in uns sich finden, die ein zu überwindendes Hinderniß sind.'
27 'es liegt also in der Liebe des Gesetzes kein Gebot: und die sogenannte Categorie / *liebe Gott* heißt nichts weiter als: die Befolgung der Gesetze nicht blos auf Gehorsam, […] sondern auf eine mit der Vorschrift des Gesetzes übereinstimmende Neigung gründen.'

end state involves the absence of inclinations contrary to morality. It is also important to note that in actual love for God there is no reversal of, or threat to, the ground of morality: respect for the moral law remains the actual determining ground of doing one's duty, but in love for God moral action is also supported[28] by an inclination to execute the prescribed action (or achieve its outcome). For example, we love God when we help others from duty *while also* feeling love for them ('love' here meaning the inclination to benefit others or to derive sensible pleasure from their happiness or their existence). But our love here, or our gladness, is merely subjective and not the objective ground of our duty, and the primary function of this love, from a moral philosophical perspective, is to promote the happiness of others and aid humanity with respect to moral progress.

In sum, love for God is the glad practice of duty (in a religious context where duties are viewed as divine commands). Love for God is closely linked (but not identical) to the ideal of love of the law, which is love of delight for all of one's duties (implying the complete absence of contra-moral inclinations). Ideal love for the law is also the equivalent of perfect love for God. The actuality of love for God thus falls between two endpoints: a state with no love and a state of perfect love. Reason demands that the agent strive to make progress on this continuum toward perfect love for God or for the law. The picture of such an ascent can therefore be called *the scale of love for God*.

3.2 God's Love

I now turn to God's love for human beings. My main aim will be to clarify the role of the general division of love in this context. Once this is clarified, it will be easier to assess the relationship between God's love for human beings and human beings' love for God. There are two distinct accounts of God's love in the Kantian corpus, one in the *Religion* and another in *The Metaphysics of Morals* (the latter is corroborated by the Vigilantius notes on ethics). At the outset, it may seem that these accounts have little in common (and Kant does not discuss them in direct conjunction with each other). I will show, however, that these two accounts may in fact be harmonised by using the general division of love as an interpretative tool. In other words, I will show how the accounts are distinct from each other in terms of the general division and that they may therefore be seen to complement

---

28 Based on the *Groundwork* and the second *Critique*, we know that our observance of or compliance with our duties should not be based on inclinations. In this light, the word '*gründen*' (to 'ground' or to 'base') in the Vigilantius passage above (LE, 27:721.10–14) seems simply too strong, even if we think that this grounding is to be understood merely in a subjective sense.

each other, thus yielding an overall picture of God's love in Kant. I shall term the accounts the *end account* of God's love and the *ground account* of God's love.

The rather striking dynamic structure that emerges from this analysis reveals God's love of benevolence as the ground of human love for God (and human love for one's neighbour), such that human love for God is dependent on God's love and aims to reciprocate it by means of the glad fulfilment of duties. At its highest stage, this human striving connects seamlessly with the other aspect of God's love, moral delight, which is something we can only hope for in our morally imperfect state of existence. God's love is therefore both *the ground of* and *a response to* human love for God, in accordance with the general division of love. In other words, with God's love the beginning and the end of an ascending structure of love are marked in terms of the general division of love.

3.2.1 The End Account

The *Religion* is filled with statements asserting or implying that a key element of religion is to aim to become pleasing to God [*Gott wohlgefällig zu werden*] by means of morally good life conduct (see R, 6:47.19; 6:66.21–22; 6:67.15; 6:71.28–29fn.; 6:73.14–15; 6:75.5–6; 6:105.1; 6:116.11–12; 6:117; 6:120.10–12; 6:133.6; 6.159.14; 6:170–175; 6:177–178; 6:193.19; 6:195.35fn.; 6:198.9–10). Kant repeatedly affirms that the primary example or archetype of a human being who is pleasing to God is God's son, Jesus Christ, in whom we encounter a rational model of humanity in its perfection (see R, 6:60.14; 6:61.25; 6:62.3; 6:62.29–30; 6:63.24–25; 6:64.7; 6:119.7; 6:128.18–129.1; see also GW, 408.28–409.9). Given the features of human love for God discussed above, it seems reasonable to assume that from a religious perspective the good life conduct we ought to aim for is precisely love for God. But the real question is whether the pleasure or delight [*Wohlgefallen*] of God to which good conduct hopefully or ideally leads can be cashed out in terms of love. If it can – if good conduct leads to God's loving us with delight – is that the whole picture when it comes to God's love, or is there more to it?

The evidence directly connecting God's delight with the notion of God's love can be found at the end of the third book of the *Religion*, immediately following Kant's assertion that love of the law is the highest (but never completely attainable) goal of human moral striving. God's love is said to be in conformity with what was said about love for the law, and it is discussed in terms of the Trinity:

> In conformity with this idea, the following would be a principle of faith in religion: 'God is Love'; in him one can venerate the loving one (with his love of moral *delight* for human

beings insofar as they are adequate to his holy law), the *Father*; in him, furthermore, insofar as he exhibits himself in his all-preserving idea, humanity's archetype begotten and beloved by him, one can venerate his *Son*; finally also, insofar as he limits this delight to the condition that human beings harmonize with the condition of that love of delight, and thereby proves it to be a love based on wisdom, one can venerate the *Holy Spirit* (R, 145.20–146.1)[29].

This passage clearly confirms the connection between God's love and God's delight. In other words, in conformity with the regulative ideal of love of the law, God's love is to be understood in terms of love of delight. In his analysis, Kant utilises a tripartite structure for God, which at bottom is standard Christian dogma and which he had already briefly mentioned in his own mature framework in the second *Critique*.[30] In the *Religion*, Kant views the three main attributes of God as expressing God's 'moral conduct' [*das moralische Verhalten*] (R, 6:140.2) towards humankind. First, as 'holy lawgiver', God gives humanity the moral laws. Second, as a 'benign ruler', he accounts for the moral constitution of humans and compensates for their moral inabilities. Third, as 'just judge', he limits his compensation with the condition that humans have tried their best to be moral. (R, 6:141.9–25)

In the long passage quoted above, this tripartite structure is mapped onto the names 'Father', 'Son', and 'Holy Spirit'. In harmony with the notion that 'God is love', Kant's discussion assumes that love somehow encompasses all three attributes. First, insofar as human beings are adequate to the holy law/moral law, God is morally pleased with them, i.e. he loves human beings with the love of moral delight. Second, he loves the archetype or the rational ideal of human moral perfection as his 'Son'. Third, as the 'Holy Spirit', he limits his love of moral delight so that human beings must 'harmonize with the condition of that love'. On the face of it, it seems especially difficult to draw a mean-

---

29 'Dieser Idee gemäß würde es in der Religion ein Glaubensprincip sein: "Gott ist die Liebe"; in ihm kann man den Liebenden (mit der Liebe des moralischen *Wohlgefallens* an Menschen, so fern sie seinem heiligen Gesetze adäquat sind), den *Vater*; ferner in ihm, so fern er sich in seiner alles erhaltenden Idee, dem von ihm selbst gezeugten und geliebten Urbilde der Menschheit darstellt, seinen *Sohn*; endlich auch, so fern er dieses Wohlgefallen auf die Bedingung der Übereinstimmung der Menschen mit der Bedingung jener Liebe des Wohlgefallens einschränkt und dadurch als auf Weisheit gegründete Liebe beweist, den *heiligen Geist* verehren'. Pluhar's translation, but rendering *Wohlgefallen* as 'delight' instead of 'pleasure'.
30 In the second *Critique*, Kant mentions in passing the three main attributes of God, which are all moral. He is holy [*heilig*], blessed [*selig*], and wise [*weise*]. In acting from the first attribute, God creates the world and gives the moral law; in acting from the second, he governs and preserves the world with goodness or benignity [*gütigkeit*]; and in acting from the third, he judges human beings (C2, 5:131.32–38; cf. R, 6:139.22–27; see also LE, 27:306).

ingful distinction between the first and the third attributes, but in a long and obscure footnote Kant explains that the judgment of the 'Holy Spirit' is connected to one's conscience (R, 6:146.5–20). As noted by Palmquist, the 'Holy Spirit' brings with it a first-person perspective on measuring up to the condition of God's love (see Palmquist 2000, p. 262). But in the footnote the 'Son' also judges: he judges between people, based on their being capable of morality or being receptive to the possibility of acquiring moral merit (R, 6:145.29–146.4). The details of Kant's account of the Trinity as love are elusive, but fortunately, the success of my argument does not depend on the correct exegetical interpretation concerning these relationships.[31]

What is essential here is that in the *Religion*, the idea that 'God is love' is discussed in terms of love of delight, and this love *by* God for human beings is somehow dependent on the moral striving of humans. This is how 'God is love' is in 'conformity' with love for the law. But God's love for us is not guaranteed. If we interpret God's conditional response of love in the general context of the delight he takes in us, it seems that the condition of this morally approving love, a love we may at best hope for, is our *sincere attempt* to become morally better: 'everyone must do as much as is in his powers in order to become a better human being' (R, 6:52.2–3[32]; see also e.g. 6:66.21–67.12). If we adopt a moral attitude, the adoption of which Kant also describes as a 'change of heart' [*Änderung des Herzens*] (R, 6:47.28), and strive to approximate love for the law, we will be entitled to the hope that this striving will eventually be met with God's morally approving love for us. In other words, God's love for humans, as love of delight, is a conditioned response to the human moral endeavour to approximate love for the law – that is, it is a response to the human attempt to gladly fulfil moral duties (viewed as divine commands).

I therefore call this account of God's love the *end account*, since it is a love that we may hope for in the end, provided we do our best to love God in the

---

31 In *The Conflict of the Faculties* [*Der Streit der Fakultäten*], written slightly after the *Religion* and published in 1798, Kant himself complains in passing that reason cannot keep up with the text of the Bible when it comes to the Trinity (7:23.25–28). He now holds that, as such, the doctrine of the Trinity is devoid of practical significance (7:38.33–34), but it may (or even must) be interpreted through practical reason (7:38.28–32). However, contrary to Samuel Powell (who makes his claim without any textual evidence), the *Religion* makes clear that Kant does not 'dismiss' the doctrine of the Trinity 'as idle' (see Powell 2011, p. 268). It is equally not the case that Kant viewed the Trinity as being 'outside the scope of Christian faith' (O'Regan 2011, p. 254). Rather, Kant is attempting a moral-rational interpretation of the Trinity. For a more optimistic/affirmative discussion on Kant's relationship with the Trinity, see Palmquist (2000, pp. 466–467).

32 'ein jeder so viel, als in seinen Kräften ist, thun müsse, um ein besserer Mensch zu werden'.

meantime. Admittedly, the English word 'end' is ambiguous between a purpose and the last point of a temporal series.[33] For Kant, the relevant terms in this respect are *Zweck* and *Ende*, the first referring to a purpose and the second to a temporal end (see also Pluhar, fn.c, in R, 6:35). I intend the end account of God's love to be taken in both senses. By this I mean that the 'end' under discussion in the context of God's love is his love of moral delight for human beings. This love is both the religious purpose of our moral striving and the (quasi-)temporal end of the temporal series (hopefully) connected to this striving. In general, we know that in Kant morality leads to religion, and the idea of God's love is required for us to hope that the end of the highest good (in the sense of purpose or *Zweck*) will be realised. Insofar as God's love of moral delight is lacking, we clearly have yet to attain the highest good. In religious terms, our end, i.e. our purpose, is that God will love us with the love of moral delight. But this picture is tightly connected to a further meaning of God's love of delight as the (quasi-)temporal end of human moral striving. Despite any possible 'change of heart', in this life our moral striving will remain deficient. We are imperfect by nature and can only gradually approximate moral perfection, which means that at any given point in time we will not have reached the moral ideal of humanity that would be pleasing [*wohlgefällig*] to God (R, 6:66–67). According to Kant, however, God judges the 'heart' (R, 6:48.4–16), or the fundamental 'attitude' [*Gesinnung*] of the human being, as a 'unity of time' [*Zeiteinheit*] that is not divided into time segments (R, 6:70.fn) but is rather a 'perfected whole' [*vollendet Ganze*] (R, 6:67.13). This kind of perspective of eternity is not easy to understand, and Kant acknowledges that the (religious) notion of a temporal 'end of all things' is theoretically incomprehensible (see Kant's essay by the same name in 8:327–339; see also my Conclusion). We can only hope that our moral striving will be met with God's delighted love at the incomprehensible completion of the temporal series, where God will hopefully compensate for our lack of perfection by means of grace (see e.g. R, 6:118–120)[34]. By this I mean that while God's love of moral delight is the purpose of our moral striving from a particular religious perspective, *this same love* is also the hoped-for (temporal) end of the tem-

---

33 I thank Rae Langton for reminding me of this.
34 A very interesting question, but one that cannot be pursued here any more explicitly, is whether Kant's account of *grace* should actually be analysed in terms of *God's love*. My findings certainly seem to point in that direction, or at least in the direction that in the light of textual evidence, it is plausible to assume such a link between God's grace and God's love. However, as Kant is not explicit about this link and does not elaborate on it more than I have shown, it is understandable that the previous commentators on grace don't discuss this connection (see e.g. Vanden Auweele 2014 and Stevenson 2014).

poral series related to moral striving. The reason for this is that in the religious picture, nothing comes after God's perfect love of moral delight for human beings. In this way, God's love of delight can be seen to mark a transition from time to eternity (see 8:327), signifying salvation and eternal bliss. Of course, nothing of this can be known theoretically, but in 'The End of All Things' Kant playfully envisions the heavenly congregation 'as striking up always the same song, their "Alleluia!" [...] by which is indicated the total lack of all change in their state.' (8:335.1–3)[35] According to Kant, at the end of temporal alteration 'the last thought, the last feeling in the thinking subject will then remain forever the same without any change.' (8:334.29–30)[36] If God is love (as the *Religion* suggests), and if the purpose of God's love as moral delight is achieved, the last thought or the last feeling (be it in God or in the human being) can only be the very same love that is achieved. To put it simply, if we sincerely strive to become more moral, we may *hope* for God's love of delight in the sense that 'all's well that ends well' [*Ende gut, alles gut*] (see R, 6:70fn.; 6:77.36).

3.2.2 The Ground Account

In *The Metaphysics of Morals*, we find a distinctly different account of God's love. The main point of the concluding remark of the entire work is that religion lies beyond ethics. Since the idea of God is man-made, our duty toward God is, ethically speaking, 'a duty of a human being to himself [...], for the sake of strengthening the moral incentive in our own lawgiving reason.' (MM, 6:487.22–25)[37] In this context Kant continues his discussion of the moral attributes of God (including God's love):

> The divine end with regard to the human race (in creating and guiding it) can be thought only as proceeding from *love*, that is, as the *happiness* of human beings. [...] To express this in human terms, God has created rational beings from the need, as it were, to have something outside himself which he could love or by which he could also be loved. (MM, 6.488.26–35)[38]

---

35 'immer dasselbe Lied, ihr Hallelujah, [...] anstimmen [...] wodurch der gänzliche Mangel alles Wechsels in ihrem Zustande angezeigt werden soll.'
36 'der letzte Gedanke, das letzte Gefühl bleiben alsdann in dem denkenden Subject stehend und ohne Wechsel immer dieselben.'
37 'Pflicht des Menschen gegen sich selbst, [...] zur Stärkung der moralischen Triebfeder in unserer eigenen gesetzgebenden Vernunft.'
38 'Den göttlichen Zweck in Ansehung des menschlichen Geschlechts (dessen Schöpfung und Leitung) kann man sich nicht anders denken, als nur aus *Liebe*, d.i. daß er die *Glückseligkeit* der

Here, God's love is presented as the ground of the existence of the human race. The divine end related to this love is the happiness of human beings. The connection between God's love and human happiness in this context seems strongly to imply that this love is the love of benevolence, as we know from the cases of self-love and love of neighbour that love of benevolence has precisely the happiness of the object of love as its end. In other words, if we view the ground of creation through the notion that God is love, it makes sense to assume that it is God's love of benevolence that yields the moral commandments, through which God wants us to be happy and wants us to love him back. But the problem with this interpretation is that love of benevolence is not mentioned in this context. It is unclear what kind of love Kant is talking about.

There is another passage at the end of the conclusion that sheds light on this issue. Kant's problem is now how to harmonise God's justice (or right) with his love with regard to the end or purpose of the human race. Basically, if God is omnipotent and the ground of creation is God's love, then in the end all human beings will be happy. But Kant sees this as contradicting some of the deepest commitments of his moral philosophy, namely that happiness can only be morally proportioned according to virtue. There are, Kant thinks, criminals who do not deserve to be happy, in which case God's love and God's justice seem to conflict:[39]

> punitive justice would make the *end* of creation consist not in the creator's *love* (as one must yet think it to be) but rather in the strict observance of his *right* [...]. But since the latter (justice) is only the condition limiting the former (kindness), this seems to contradict principles of practical reason, by which the creation of a world must have been omitted if it would have produced a result so contrary to the intention of its author, which can have only love for its basis. (MM, 6.490.21–491.4)[40]

Menschen sei. [...] Mann könnte sich (nach Menschenart) auch so ausdrücken: Gott hat vernünftige Wesen erschaffen, gleichsam aus dem Bedürfnisse etwas außer sich zu haben, was er lieben könne, oder auch von dem er geliebt werde.'

[39] This is of course one of the classical problems of Christian theology: how can an omnipotent and omnibenevolent God send certain people to hell for eternal damnation and suffering?

[40] 'würde die Strafgerechtigkeit den *Zweck* der Schöpfung nicht in der *Liebe* des Welturhebers (wie man sich doch denken muß), sondern in der strengen Befolgung des *Rechts* setzen [...], welches, da das Letztere (die Gerechtigkeit) nur die einschränkende Bedingung des Ersteren (der Gütigkeit) ist, den Principien der praktischen Vernunft zu widersprechen scheint, nach welchen eine Weltschöpfung hätte unterbleiben müssen, die ein der Absicht ihres Urhebers, die nur Liebe zum Grunde haben kann, so widerstreitendes Product geliefert haben würde.' Translation modified.

From this Kant concludes that in ethics, the moral relation between God and human beings is incomprehensible, and therefore ethics can only concern relations between human beings. (MM, 6:491) There are no duties toward God (see also MM, 6:443–444). This does not mean, however, that Kant renounces the postulate of God. He merely delineates the sphere of ethics so as to keep it clearly separate from religion. God remains a practical postulate that entitles us to hope for the complete highest good, even though just how God can or will help to bring about the highest good cannot be rationally made sense of in ethics. With this said, from my interpretative perspective it now seems clear that in the concluding argument of *The Metaphysics of Morals* Kant does indeed appeal to what can be called the *ground account* of God's love. In the latter passage quoted above, the contradiction between God's punitive justice and his love relies precisely on the idea that God's original intention in creating the world 'can have only love for its basis'. These two passages in *The Metaphysics of Morals*, compared with the discussion in the *Religion*, are enough to warrant the claim that there are two distinct accounts of God's love in Kant's works: the ground account and the end account. But even though they are discernible from each other with respect to the quasi-temporal structure of God's creation, it is still unclear whether they can be distinguished in terms of the general division of love. The end account of God's love in the *Religion* clearly concerns love of delight, but the ground account in *The Metaphysics of Morals* merely implies that the love at issue is perhaps love of benevolence. However, a strong case for this interpretation can be made by using the Vigilantius lecture notes as an auxiliary source.

In the Vigilantius notes, God's love is discussed not in terms of delight (as in the *Religion*) but explicitly in terms of benevolence. Kant's treatment is again intimately connected with love for God and the notion of loving the law. However, unlike in the *Religion*, God's love is presented here not as a response to our moral striving but as a 'necessary presupposition' of our love for God. In the Vigilantius notes, the picture is that by loving God we *return* or *give back* our love in response to God's original love for us: 'If we are to think, morally, that we love God, then it is necessary for us to presuppose His love for us, and His will for our well-being, or His loving-kindness. For no return of love can be elicited there, if the command to that effect does not itself arise from moral love.' (LE 27.720.18–22)[41]

---

[41] 'Sollen wir uns moralisch denken, daß wir Gott lieben, so ist notwendig, daß wir seine Liebe gegen uns und seinen Willen für unser Wohl oder seine Güte voraussetzen. Denn es läßt sich da nicht Gegenliebe erzwingen, wenn das Gebot dazu nicht aus der moralischen Liebe selbst entspringt.'

This looks very much like an elaboration of the idea in *The Metaphysics of Morals*, according to which God created us to have something to love or 'by which he could also be loved' (MM, 6:488.35). In the Vigilantius notes, the idea is that in order for it to be possible for us to love God, the source of the divine command must itself be 'moral love' [*moralische Liebe*]. In other words, the commandment that we love God is here portrayed as being grounded in God's moral love.[42] What is this moral love? Given that God's love for us is described in the *Religion* as love of moral delight, it is safe to say that this love is moral. But there is no mention of *Wohlgefallen* in this context in the Vigilantius lectures, and the source of the moral love now at issue is linked to God's will [*Wille*] for our well-being [*Wohl*][43] and his loving kindness [*Güte*]. The fact that God's moral love is here discussed in terms of God's wanting things to go well for us (implying our happiness as the end of that love) suggests that the love at issue might instead be the love of benevolence. This suspicion is confirmed only a few lines down:

> God's love for us (also expressed by the words: *God is love*) is thus the divine benevolence and kindness toward us, which constitutes the foundation of the potestas legislatoria divina. Now to return that love is the corresponding duty of all His subjects, and constitutes the prime source of any disposition to religion. But this love of God can be known only through our reason (LE, 27:721.1–6)[44].

This both differentiates the account from the one given in the *Religion* and supports the interpretation according to which God's love in *The Metaphysics of Morals* can be viewed as love of benevolence (see also 28:1114). It also shows the two-directionality of love of God: here, love of God is God's love. There is no

---

42 This point is well noted by Moors (2007, pp. 257–259), but he goes so far as to claim that the duty of love is thereby grounded in an 'originating theologico-metaphysical basis' (Moors 2007, p. 259). Moors may not fully appreciate the basic point that for Kant, religion is very much about *viewing* our duties *as* divine commands, and the notion of God is a rational *idea* derived from moral reason. I would thus be wary of talking about a 'theologico-metaphysical basis' of anything in Kant. In the Vigilantius notes, for instance, just before the passage in question, Kant states that '[i]t is easy to see that for man there is no way left, but that of fashioning his own God on the basis of morality.' (LE, 27:719.37–38) / 'Man sieht leicht, daß für den Menschen kein Weg überbleibt, als sich auf dem Grunde der Moral seinen eigenen Gott zu machen.'
43 This must mean our overall moral-physical well-being.
44 'Die Liebe Gottes gegen uns (oder welches man auch ausdrückt: *Gott ist die Liebe*) ist also das göttliche Wohlwollen und Güte gegen uns, die das Fundament der potestatis legislatoriae divinae ausmacht. Die Gegenliebe ist nun die correspondirende Pflicht aller Untergebenen und macht die erste Quelle aller Religionsgesinnung aus. Diese Liebe Gottes kann aber nur durch unsere Vernunft erkannt […] werden.'

question as to the apparent difference in terminology between how God's love is discussed in the *Religion* and in the Vigilantius notes on ethics. In the former, it is love of delight; in the latter, love of benevolence. Indeed, the Vigilantius notes are highly consistent with *The Metaphysics of Morals*. In both texts, God's love for us is viewed as logically prior to our love for God: God's love is seen as the ground of our love for God. As noted above, I don't see any reason for therefore viewing the ground account and the end account as contradictory. Rather, the existence of these accounts suggests that even though Kant didn't analyse the relationship between the two aspects of the general division of love in the context of God, he in fact made use of the division. In the *Religion*, God's love of delight is viewed as a response to our love for God, whereas in the Vigilantius notes God's love of benevolence is viewed as prior to the commandment to love God. In the Vigilantius notes, our love for God is a response to God's love of benevolence. The existence of the end account and the ground account of God's love further corroborates the plausibility of the general division approach to Kant on love.

Thus, the general picture of God's love is that God's love of benevolence is the ground of creation and the ground of the duty to love God by practicing moral duties gladly. God's love of moral delight is the loving response we may hope for in the end if we do our best to be moral gladly, i.e. if we love God and strive to love the law. We may call this general picture *the ascent model of love of God* (see fig. 4). God's benevolent love lies at the basis of the existence of the world, and God's delighted love is hoped for at the end of human moral progress. Actual human love for God takes place between these two aspects of God's love, with the implied prescription to ascend higher through moral striving. Even though questions remain about the relationship between God's love and God's justice, the evidence thus suggests that an unqualified negative claim such as Goy's, that Kant's God 'is not a loving god' (Goy 2014, p. 23), is implausible. Kant's God is indeed a loving God (in harmony with Wood 1970, p. 248).[45]

---

[45] Timmermann has expressed (in private discussion) an interesting worry with respect to love of God: If, as I have shown, love of God includes two-directionality, then maybe there is no such thing as love of God, as it includes two subjects (God and the human being) and two objects (the same two) that are not on par with each other. In one sense God is an object of love, and in another sense he is the subject of love, and the same holds for the human being. Perhaps this means that we should put love of God in scare quotes: 'love of God'. Maybe so, but only if we think that an aspect of love (without scare quotes, that is) cannot be fundamentally ambiguous, and of this point I'm not convinced. We may accept that in a given linguistic community or research framework the ambiguities related to an aspect of love are sufficiently standard or nor-

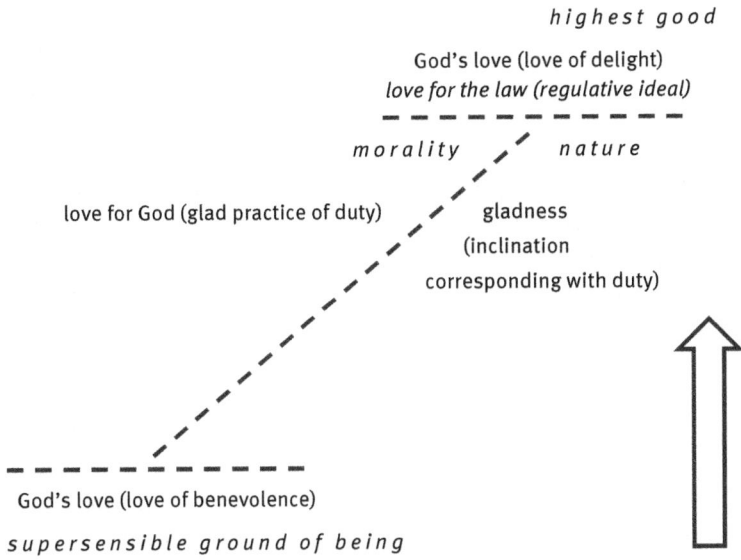

Figure 4. The Ascent Model of Love of God

3.3 Is Love of God Self-Love?

Before concluding this chapter, I would like to address a further question, which has until now been lurking in the background of my discussion. This question concerns the relationship between love of God and the self.

If one takes a panoptic view of the various statements about God in Kant's major writings from the critical period (mainly in the three *Critiques*, the *Religion*,

---

mal to warrant talk of that aspect without inverted commas. We may clarify ambiguities without irony or scepticism with respect to the way a culturally acknowledged aspect of love appears in the writings of a historical philosopher. The dynamic Kantian picture of love of God begins with God's benevolent love creating human beings (and giving them duties), who then return God's love via the glad practice of duties. When God has received his own love back, he loves his creation with delight. Of course, the whole business of love of God becomes morally reduced to ideas that reason gives to itself. But the picture is structurally similar to the reciprocal self-surrender we see in sexual love and love in friendship, where one gives oneself to the other and then gets oneself back through the other's love (see LE, 27:388.23–37; cf. 27:423.37–424.6). Sure, love of God is a special case because it refers to a transcendent being. But we could not see this interesting similarity (with regards to giving oneself or one's love and then being loved back in return) between these aspects of love if we didn't accept love of God as an aspect of love in all its ambiguity.

and *The Metaphysics of Morals*), one gets the impression that there is a certain amount of ambiguity as to the place of God in the logical structure of the Kantian universe. It is clear from the first *Critique* that we may have no theoretical knowledge of God, but that God is nevertheless a morally necessary assumption derived from the practical necessity of the efficacy of moral laws in the world. (C1, A811/B839–A819/B847) In other words, if the moral law is to ultimately have its final effect (virtue accompanied by proportionate happiness) *necessarily*, then we must assume the existence of God as the first cause of the world.[46] For Kant, a perfect effect requires a perfect cause.[47] It is also relatively clear from the second *Critique* and *The Metaphysics of Morals* that the *concept* of God in Kant is derived from or based on moral reason. Or, in the terminology of the third *Critique*: on the basis of the final purpose of the highest good (visible even to 'the commonest reason' [*die gemeinste Menschenvernunft*] (C3, 5:448.30)), God is judged to be the moral cause of the world (C3, 5:450). Again, this argument does not provide us with any theoretical insight into God and ultimately rests on our prior awareness of morality.[48] All in all, Kant clearly holds that if all rational creatures are to become morally happy (as reason dictates), God must be postulated.

What is less clear, however, is whether we are to assume, with the practical postulate of God, that God is something external to our reason or merely a product of our reason. It seems that in order for us to have faith or even hope that God will eventually supplement our imperfections, and thus occasion the complete highest good, we must believe that God is irreducible to our own being, which by definition consists of moral imperfection. On the other hand, toward the

---

[46] In the first *Critique*, Kant thinks that without the assumption of God, moral laws would be 'idle chimeras' [*leere Hirngespinste*] (C1, A811/B839). In the third *Critique*, however, it seems that the moral law is still binding even if God is not assumed to exist – the drawback to not postulating his existence being that we then cannot aim for the complete highest good as the moral happiness of all rational creatures (C3, 5:451).

[47] See e.g. C2, 5:124. This sort of position, I believe, was widely shared among generations of Scholastic philosophers and is clearly visible in Kant's close predecessors, e.g. Descartes (see Russell 1945, p. 567) and Berkeley.

[48] In more elaborate terms, this is close to what Kant means when he speaks of God, or love of God for that matter, in terms of the notion of a *schematism of analogy*. For instance, when we discuss God's love in terms of his sacrifice of his son, we are not expanding theoretical cognition but merely elucidating a concept that is otherwise incomprehensible to our reason. This kind of endeavour takes place for purposes that are ultimately moral. (See R, 6:65fn.) In the technical jargon of the third *Critique*, such a procedure is called 'symbolic hypotyposis' (C3, 5:351), which serves what Kant in that work terms 'ethicotheology' (C3, 5:484–485). I thank Dieter Schönecker for reminding me of the notion of analogy in the context of love of God.

end of Kant's philosophical career we find increasingly strong statements concerning the mind-dependence of God. According to the Vigilantius notes on ethics, human beings can but 'fashion' or make [*machen*] their 'own God on the basis of morality' (LE, 27:719.37–38)[49]. In *The Metaphysics of Morals* the idea of God is something that reason 'makes for itself' (MM, 6:487.11)[50]. And in the *Opus Postumum*, where Kant explicitly asks whether the idea of God 'has reality or whether it is a mere thought-object' (22:117.8)[51], he consistently holds that God is not a substance or a being outside of man (22:52.11–12; 22:55.10–11; 22:60.15–16; 22:123.1) but rather an idea of pure reason (22:53.1–2).[52]

Now I do not wish to make any conclusive interpretative claim as to what Kant thought about the existence of God, but I do think that insofar as God is an idea of reason based on what he must be like in order for the highest good to be possible, we must think that our conceptions of the relations of love between God and human beings are given to us by our reason. There is a sense in which love of God is essentially dependent on and derived from the workings of the human mind. It is this point, I think, that occasions Moors's claim that love of God is actually self-love. I find this idea highly intriguing and wish to consider it carefully.

Moors argues that since love for God involves 'the moral command of gladness', love of God is turned into a love 'one has to have for one's own purified heart' (Moors 2007, p. 256). Moors then picks up the definition of love of delight for oneself from the *Religion* and claims (I take it) that since this love for oneself denotes a contentment following the subordination of one's maxims to the moral law, 'love of God is indeed nothing but this egocentric, rationally sublimated variation of amor complacentiae (a morally sublimated *Liebe des Wohlgefallens an sich selbst*).' (Moors 2007, p. 257) I think we ought to begin by noting that by love of God Moors means love *for* God (his argument doesn't seem to be meant to apply to love of God as two-directional). From this perspective Moors is moving in the right direction but only to the extent that love for God is mainly about our own moral perfection.

---

49 'auf dem Grunde der Moral seinen eigenen Gott zu Machen.'
50 'sie sich selber macht.'
51 'Realität habe oder blos ein Gedankending [...] sey'.
52 It is of course possible to contest the relevance of the *Opus Postumum* as a source. These are posthumously published fragmentary notes from a period when Kant's mental capacity was already waning. Depending on the context, I would argue that we should give the *Opus Postumum* roughly similar weight as the lecture notes. In this case, the Vigilantius notes and the *Opus Postumum* support each other.

Strictly speaking, love for God cannot be equated to moral self-love. The reason for this is that Kant's adverb 'gladly' and the notion of 'contentment' [*Zufriedenheit*], the latter of which is characteristic of moral self-love, do not denote the same thing, which technically excludes the possibility of equating these two loves. The indirect imperative to strive for gladness in the practice of duty seems to imply a liking for the actions or the effects of the actions, whereas *Zufriedenheit* is, I would argue, a state of (negative) self-satisfaction that stems from consciousness of one's ability to override maxims of self-love (maxims of love of benevolence for oneself). It is true that love for God may bring about moral love of delight for oneself (even though Kant himself doubts the relevance of the term 'self-love' in this context in the *Religion*). There is, however, a basic difference between love for God and love of delight for oneself: love for God is very much about *striving* (for gladness in the fulfilment of duties), whereas love of delight for oneself is very much about *contentment* (in respect for the moral law). They are not exactly the same thing, and it is also very important to note that neither notion is 'egocentric', at least in the sense of 'caring too much about yourself and not about other people'[53]. On the contrary, love for God depends on the laborious cultivation of other-regarding attitudes, and moral self-love relies on our capacity to override selfish maxims through respect for the moral law.

3.4 The Ascent of Love of God

In this chapter, I have argued for a *two-directionality thesis* of love of God according to which love of God consists of human beings' love for God on the one hand and God's love for human beings on the other. I pointed out that love for God can be analysed in terms of a *scale*, where fear of God (or mere respect for the moral law) denotes the zero-point of love for God, and love for the moral law is an unattainable endpoint of love for God, prescribed to us via a moral philosophical interpretation of the Christian commandment. The actuality of love for God lies between these endpoints and consists in practicing moral duties (viewed as divine commands) *gladly*.

I also showed that God's love can be analysed in terms of the general division of love. That is, it can be divided into a *ground account* and an *end account*, such that from a religious perspective the ground of creation and moral duties is God's love of benevolence (which also grounds the moral duty to love God). In the end, the sincere agent can hope that her moral striving to love God (and the

---

53 The Merriam-Webster Dictionary.

moral law), understood in terms of a moral *ascent*, will be met with God's love of moral delight.

While the place of God (and its relation to the self) in the Kantian universe remains somewhat ambiguous, it is clear that the idea of God is a product of human reason for the purposes of securing hope for the highest good. It does not follow from this, however, that love of God is to be equated with moral self-love. In sum, the overall analysis yields an *ascent model of love of God*.

4 Love of Neighbour

The aim of this chapter is to analyse the notion of love of neighbour [*Nächstenliebe*] in Kant's moral philosophy, focusing on the published works from the mature period. As was the case with the earlier chapters, although the literature does contain discussions related to this topic, there has not been a detailed examination of what Kant means when he speaks of loving one's neighbour and what kind of role the notion plays in his ethical thought.

Based on the work of previous commentators, we now know that even though the duties of love we have to others may be less fundamental than duties of respect, they are vital for Kantian ethics (Baron & Fahmy 2009, p. 226). Further, it has been shown that Kantian practical love is not reducible to beneficence but involves the cultivation of benevolent attitudes (Fahmy 2010). We are also aware that love in Kant's virtue ethics is (at least in part) a kind of moral emotion that plays a secondary role (Horn 2008, p. 173), and that Kant's account of this moral emotion is developed in conjunction with the biblical commandments (Goy 2014). A part of love of neighbour is a natural predisposition necessary for one's subjective receptivity to duty, and this predisposition is love of delight (Schönecker 2010). Now I think all these accounts are in important ways correct and can well be said to illuminate love of neighbour in Kant. I do not take issue with them, but I think they are incomplete.

What I think is missing from the analyses mentioned above is attention to the underlying general structure of love that is at work behind the various sections and passages that the existing interpretations rely on. This underlying structure can only be grasped through a chronological and fairly detailed exegetical investigation of the notion of love of neighbour *per se*. Perhaps not all will agree with me that there is an underlying general structure, but I aim to show that there is, and to clarify it. This enquiry should also work more generally to draw further attention to the complex relationship between the emotive and moral-rational aspects of human existence in Kant.

Several interpretative problems are particularly tricky in the context of love of neighbour. To begin with: what is the role of the general division of love – to what extent can it be used to capture Kant's idea of love of neighbour? What exactly is practical love, and how does it relate to the feeling of love? Is there a discontinuity between Kant's accounts of love of neighbour in the *Groundwork* and the second *Critique* in comparison with the one presented in *The Metaphysics of Morals*? Why does Kant use a distinction between pathological love and practical love in the two former works – and why does he distinguish between love of delight and love of benevolence only in the latter? Are these two pairs of distinc-

https://doi.org/10.1515/9783110544978-006

tions parallel? In other words, how are pathological love/the feeling of love (these may or may not be the same), practical love, love of delight, and love of benevolence all related to each other?

In what follows, I shall argue for two main positions. First, that love of neighbour is most comprehensively understood in the light of what I have throughout this work called the general division approach to Kant on love. In the context of love of neighbour, the principal feature of the general division approach is its emphasis on the co-existence and interrelatedness of sensory-emotive and rational-moral components in love, captured by Kant's use of the terms love of delight and love of benevolence. Second, I hope to show that the general division approach yields what may be called the *feeling-action-cultivation account*, which can be defended as a viable interpretation of love of neighbour in Kant. Essentially, this account involves the claims that 1) love of neighbour includes feeling or sensation, rationally willed action, and the cultivation of a moral disposition, and that 2) love of neighbour is irreducible to any of its components taken in isolation. I also argue that while the details are sometimes elusive, there is an intricate continuity in Kant's conception of love of neighbour between 1785 and 1797, and the broad outlines of the concept remain consistent throughout the mature period. I therefore take it that the general division approach is indeed robust in outline and supports the feeling-action-cultivation account. My aim here is not to engage in casuistry or debates in normative ethics, but rather to make sense of the broadest conceptual divisions that love of neighbour in Kant entails.

To make my case, I will track down the history and evolution of the concept of love of neighbour in Kant's moral thinking from the 1762–1764 Herder notes onwards. I will also have to recap some evidence already presented in the study to make the argument as transparent as possible. The kind of chronological, dynamic, and cumulative reading I'm about to offer will make it easier to see the changes in Kant's thought between the different works. The concept of love of neighbour indeed varies throughout Kant's writings, but it does not vary randomly, and foundational invariances and subtle evolution can be detected. The conceptual framework becomes more and more complex, more refined, as Kant's thought matures. The task of the interpreter is to understand the differences between the relevant instances and to preserve overall continuity and consistency as far as is rationally possible.

This chapter is divided into two major sections, followed by a concluding summary. In the first section, I discuss love of neighbour prior to *The Metaphysics of Morals*, and in the second section I analyse the notion within *The Metaphysics of Morals* (also using the Vigilantius notes). I will begin by grounding my interpretation in the Herder and the Collins notes on ethics and will then move on to discuss the conceptual divisions of love of neighbour in the *Groundwork of the Metaphysics of Morals* and the *Critique of Practical Reason*, by means of a close comparison of two relevant passages. I then analyse the main distinctions that are relevant to love of neighbour in *The Metaphysics of Morals*, with the aim of harmonising the conception presented in Kant's final moral philosophical treatise with those from the *Groundwork* and the second *Critique*, giving special emphasis to the general division of love and the notion of cultivation. I conclude by outlining the feeling-action-cultivation account of love of neighbour.

4.1 The General Division Prior to *The Metaphysics of Morals*

Recall the basic published evidence for the existence of a general division of love in Kant: 'Like love in general, *self-love* too can be divided into love of *benevolence* and love of *delight* (BENEVOLENTIAE ET COMPLACENTIAE), and both (as is self-evident) must be rational.' (R, 6:45.22–25)[1] Does this apply to the context of love of neighbour? In other words, can love of neighbour also be divided into the loves of benevolence and delight? As we shall see, the general division of love is operative in this context, but to understand just how, and to see the exegetical difficulties that remain, requires a thorough analysis that utilises various moral philosophical resources within Kant's corpus.

The first piece of evidence to note comes from the Herder lectures on ethics from 1762–1764[2]. These early notes refer to 'a system of love of human beings' [*System der Menschenliebe*], the concept of which is divided into two kinds of love of benevolence: 'love of benevolence (of the other's greater welfare) is either active or wishful.' (LE, 27:64.13–14)[3] The wishful love of benevolence is here weak, fanciful, or idle, whereas active love of benevolence is 'practical love' [*Praktische Liebe*]. Practical love relates mainly to helping others, such as when a man of nature, his love uncorrupted by society, saves someone in danger on the basis of instinct (LE, 27:64.20–65.7).[4] From the perspective of the general division of love, what is important to note in the context of the Herder notes is

---

1 'Wie *Liebe* überhaupt, so kann auch *Selbstliebe* in die des *Wohlwollens* und des *Wohlgefallens* (BENEVOLENTIAE ET COMPLACENTIAE) eingetheilt werden, und beide müssen (wie sich von selbst versteht) vernünftig sein.'
2 Note that the reliability of the Herder notes in particular has been questioned by Kant's editors (see Schneewind 1997, p. xiv, esp. n.5).
3 'die Liebe des Wohlwollens (anderer großerer Wohlfart) ist entweder thatig oder wünschend.'
4 Kant's discussion reminds one of Rousseau's admiration of the simple, 'natural' state of human existence (see also Grenberg 2015, pp. 239–244).

that one of the two basic components of the general division is already in place: love of benevolence. But love of delight is not mentioned. Also significant is the fact that active love of benevolence is associated with practical love.

The general division of love is explicitly presented for the first time in the Collins notes on ethics from the late 1770s. These notes are an invaluable resource for interpreting love of neighbour in Kant's later works. I will thus pause here to quote the Collins notes at length. As we now know that the Collins notes in fact predate the *Groundwork*, there is, however, also the danger of reading too much into the notes, or making overly strong interpretations of Kant's later views on their basis. I wish to avoid these dangers, and that's why I find it very important to stress that, at least when it comes to love of neighbour or love of other human beings, the Collins notes should never be used uncritically or on their own, but always only in conjunction with the authoritative published works from the mature period. The distinctions Kant draws in these notes in relation to love seem tentative, like a work in progress, and it is not always clear how what he has said last relates to, or could be harmonised with, what he stated in the preceding paragraph. This said, the foundational components of love of neighbour that Kant continues to use up to *The Metaphysics of Morals* are found here.

At the outset of Kant's discussion of duties to others[5], love is again (as in the Herder notes) defined in terms of benevolence:

> Love is benevolence from inclination. But there can also be kindness on principle. Hence our pleasure and delight in doing good to others may be either an immediate or a mediate pleasure. The immediate pleasure in well-doing towards others is love, the mediate pleasure of beneficence, where we are simultaneously conscious of having done our duty, is well-doing by reason or obligation. (LE, 27:413.18–25)[6]

---

5 In the Collins notes, duties to others are divided into duties of benevolence [*Wohlwollen*] and duties of indebtedness [*Schuldigkeit*], which distinction corresponds roughly with the mature distinction between imperfect and perfect duties to others.

6 'Liebe ist Wohlwollen aus Neygung. Es kann aber auch Gütigkeit statt finden aus Grundsätzen. Demnach ist unser Vergnügen und Wohlgefallen am Wohlthun anderer entweder ein unmittelbares oder ein mittelbares Vergnügen. Das unmittelbare Vergnügen am Wohlthun anderer ist die Liebe, das mittelbare Vergnügen des Wohlthuns, wo wir uns zugleich bewußtsein, unsre Pflicht erfüllet zu haben, ist das Wohlthun nach Verbindlichkeit.' Retaining Heath's translation. The German construction '*Wohlthun anderer*' implies that it is the others who are being beneficent. This is, however, in contrast with how Kant usually speaks of these issues: elsewhere he seems to have in mind the beneficence of the agent. Rendering '*Wohlthun anderer*' as 'beneficence of others' would also introduce a weird shift of perspective at the end of the passage, where the mediate pleasure is clearly about *our* consciousness of having done *our* duty. Timmermann has suggested (in private conversation) that we are probably dealing with a usage of the

The elements of the general division of love are visible, but the division itself is not yet clearly in place. What is implied above is that love is 1) benevolence from inclination or 2) the immediate delight taken in beneficence, which beneficence is apparently based on benevolence from inclination. Here, both benevolence and delight are on the side of inclination, and this inclination-based love is distinguished from kindness [*Gütigkeit*], or beneficence from rational principles. But as Kant's discussion continues for a page or two, the terminology changes, and this change leads up to a new definition of love. First, Kant makes room for two different kinds of benevolence – one from love, and one from obligation: 'Benevolence from love cannot be commanded, though benevolence from obligation can.' (LE, 27:417.10 – 11)[7] Kant explains that practicing beneficence from duty will eventually, through habituation, lead to our being beneficent also from love (LE, 27:417.11 – 19). Immediately after this we get a new definition of love, now a strong statement affirming the general division:

> All love is either love of benevolence or love of delight. Love of benevolence consists in the wish and inclination to promote the happiness of others. Love of delight is the pleasure we take in showing approval of another's perfections. This delight may be either sensuous or intellectual. All such delight, if it is love, must first of all be inclination. The love that is sensuous delight is a delight in the sensuous intuition, due to sensuous inclination [...]. The love based on intellectual delight is already harder to conceive. (LE, 27:417.19 – 30)[8]

This statement explicitly divides 'all love' into the variants of the general division of love found later in the *Religion*. I will return to the distinction between the two kinds of delight (sensuous and intellectual) in the latter part of this chapter.[9]

---

genitive peculiar to 18th-century German, and I thank him for making me aware of this obscure feature of the passage.

7 'Das Wohlwollen aus Liebe kann nicht geboten werden, wohl aber das Wohlwollen aus Verbindlichkeit.'

8 'Alle Liebe ist entweder Liebe des Wohlwollens oder Liebe des Wohlgefallens. Die Liebe des Wohlwollens besteht im Wunsch und in der Neigung das Glück anderer zu befördern. Die Liebe des Wohlgefallens ist das Vergnügen, welches wir haben, den Vollkommenheiten des andern Beyfall zu beweisen. Dieses Wohlgefallen kann sinnlich und intellectual seyn. Alles Wohlgefallen, wenn es Liebe ist, muß doch vorher Neygung seyn. Die Liebe des sinnlichen Wohlgefallens ist ein Gefallen an der sinnlichen Anschauung, aus sinnlicher Neigung [...]. Die Liebe des intellectualen Wohlgefallens ist schon schwerer zu concipiren.' Note that in the Collins notes sexual inclination is classed with sensuous love of delight (LE, 27:417.19 – 30), whereas *The Metaphysics of Morals* rejects this classification (MM, 6:426.26 – 28). This serves as indirect evidence that love of delight in the published work could be *intellectual* love of delight.

9 As such, the framework in the Collins notes is not my main target, and I will discuss these ideas and elaborate on them further to the extent required by my analysis of the mature published works.

After defining 'all love' in the above terms, Kant goes on to make yet another major change to his conception of love for others in the Collins notes. Towards the end of his discussion, Kant begins to allow for talk of love from obligation, whereas at the beginning of the discussion love is defined exclusively in terms of inclination. In this last manoeuvre, he provides an interpretation of Jesus' commandment to love one's neighbour, and now he equates love of benevolence with love from obligation, while love of delight seems to remain closer to inclination: 'If we are told: *Thou shalt love* thy neighbour, how is this to be understood? It is not with love of delight that I am to love him, for with that I can also love the worst of villains; it is with love of benevolence.' (LE, 27:417.34–37)[10]

Again, Kant is clearly appealing to the general division of love in the context of love of neighbour. When it comes to understanding the development of Kant's thinking about this aspect of love from the *Groundwork* onwards, this last passage is particularly important. In the mature period, Kant continually draws a distinction between two kinds of neighbourly love: one that is not commanded, and one that is. This distinction roughly parallels the nature-freedom distinction that lies at the heart of Kant's mature moral theory. The question is: can the mature distinction between different kinds of love for others be interpreted in terms of the distinction between love of benevolence and love of delight? If so, then love of benevolence should most likely be identified with the love that is commanded, and love of delight with the love that is not commanded. These latter passages from the Collins notes, when combined with the *Religion*, certainly suggest that something along these lines might be the case.

I now proceed to the *Groundwork*, where love of neighbour will again be discussed via philosophical interpretation of Jesus' commandment.[11] One of the

---

10 'Wenn es nun heißt: du sollst deinen nächsten lieben, wie ist das zu verstehen? Nicht mit der Liebe des Wohlgefallens soll ich ihn lieben, mit solcher kann ich auch den größten Bösewicht lieben, sondern mit der Liebe des Wohlwollens.' Kant explains that this kind of love of benevolence for the villain will contain the wish that he actually become worthy of happiness (LE 27:417.37–418.4), and apparently it is this that separates the moral love of benevolence here from sensuous delight or from the mere benevolent inclination to promote the material well-being of the villain in question. Note also that in the Collins notes Kant ends up maintaining that even though love of delight cannot be commanded, to love the humanity of the villain with (intellectual) love of delight is still a duty (LE, 27:418).
11 As with love of God, the cultural context is decisively Christian here, and the classical concept of love as *Agape* looms in the background. It is worth mentioning Kant's key references from the New Testament. Jesus articulates his basic idea of love of neighbour when preaching in Jerusalem, in response to a scribe's question about God's first commandment: 'The first is, "Hear, O Israel: The Lord our God, the Lord is one; and you shall love the Lord your God with all your heart, and with all your soul, and with all your mind, and with all your strength."

most basic distinctions of *Groundwork* I is between a good will [*der gute Wille*] and inclinations: these two are profoundly different. A good will must be produced by reason, and in humans it is closely connected to the concept of duty. Inclinations, on the other hand, are based on natural impulses, are not morally commanded, and are often in tension with duty. Inclinations relate to sensations or feelings such as satisfaction, sympathy [*Sympathie*], compassion [*Theilnehmung*], and love (GW, 4:397.28 – 398.36; see Timmermann 2011, p. xiii). It must also be emphasised that in *Groundwork* I, when Kant speaks of love without further qualification (GW, 4:397.28 – 30), he is relating love to inclinations. This is in line with the earlier lecture notes on ethics, where love is often discussed through the notion of inclination. The finding warrants the hypothesis that the love proximal to inclinations is somehow a more paradigmatic type of love.

With this in mind, let us move to the passage concerning love of neighbour. It appears in the context of Kant's famous proposition that beneficent action only has true moral worth if carried out from duty rather than inclination. Kant explains that while beneficence [*Wohltätigkeit*] is a duty, there are compassionate [*theilnehmend gestimmte*] philanthropists [*Menschenfreunde*] who are such that 'even without another motivating ground of vanity, or self-interest, they find an inner gratification in spreading joy around them, and can relish the contentment of others, in so far as it is their work.' (GW, 4:398.9 – 12)[12] Properly speaking, the actions of these philanthropists, which are guided by inclinations, have no moral worth, even though the actions conform with duty and may be considered amiable or worthy of love[13] [*liebenswürdig*].[14] However, if a philanthropist of the

---

The second is this, "You shall love your neighbour as yourself." There is no other commandment greater than these.' (Mark 12:28; similar in Matt. 22:34) In his Sermon on the Mount, Jesus implies that the concept of one's neighbour may even include one's enemies: 'But I say to you, Love your enemies and pray for those who persecute you' (Matt. 5:43; see also Luke 6:27, cf. the Old Testament, Leviticus 19:18, where the concept of one's neighbour does not include one's enemies).

12 'sie auch ohne einen andern Bewegungsgrund der Eitelkeit oder des Eigennutzes ein inneres Vergnügen daran finden, Freude um sich zu verbreiten, und die sich an der Zufriedenheit anderer, so fern sie ihr Werk ist, ergötzen können.'

13 According to the Grimm dictionary, *liebenswürdig* literally means 'worthy of love' but is normally used in a more external sense. Adelung, however, stresses the worthiness aspect: 'der Liebe würdig, würdig geliebt zu werden'.

14 Any reading that affords Kant the view that it would be *bad* or *wrong* to be beneficent from inclination is hence clearly incorrect. In the second *Critique*, doing good from the feeling of love is described as being beautiful. (C2, 5:82.18 – 20) Note also how the feeling of love as a motivational force conditions Kant's widest formulations of self-love in the second *Critique:* all material practical principles belong to self-love/one's own happiness (C2, 5:22.6 – 8). In the widest sense,

above sort is overtaken by sorrow and hence loses 'all compassion for the fate of others' (4:398.21–22)[15] and yet still acts beneficently from duty without inclination, the action is morally worthy. According to Kant, the case is similar when a beneficent agent has little sympathy [wenig Sympathie] to begin with: only actions done from duty have moral worth. These considerations form the moral philosophical context of the passage on love of neighbour. Kant writes:

> It is in this way, no doubt, that we are to understand the passages from Scripture that contain the command to love one's neighbor, even our enemy. For love as an inclination cannot be commanded, but beneficence from duty itself – even if no inclination whatsoever impels us to it, indeed if natural and unconquerable aversion resists – is *practical* and not *pathological* love, which lies in the will and not in the propensity of sensation, in principles of action and not in melting compassion; and only the former can be commanded. (GW, 4:399.27–34)[16]

This looks a lot like the previous passage on the same topic from the Collins notes: love from inclination cannot be commanded, but beneficence from duty can. What is clearly different is that in the *Groundwork* neither love of benevolence nor love of delight is explicitly mentioned. The basic distinction is now between *pathological love* and *practical love*. In *Groundwork* I, practical love relates to the good will, to principles of action, and to duty, whereas pathological love relates to sensation or feeling [*Empfindung*] and to compassion [*Theilnehmung*] and cannot be commanded. While both pathological and practical love can have the happiness of others as their ends, in practical love the motive of duty is primary, whereas in pathological love the agent's interest in the happiness of others is determined by inclination (see Timmermann 2009, p. 55).

If we now tentatively interpret the distinction between pathological love and practical love in the light of the earlier lecture notes, keeping in mind the terminology of the general division of love, we are led to the following observations. First, the Herder notes explicitly appeal to the notion of practical love, and there

---

self-love need not be directly self-interested and may in fact appear as inclination-based beneficent love of neighbour. As Wood puts it, while the self imposes limits on love, an inclination toward the happiness of others is not a mere means to my happiness: 'Love exhibits a kind of second-order self-partiality' (Wood 1999, p. 271).
15 'alle Theilnehmung an anderer Schicksal'.
16 'So sind ohne Zweifel auch die Schriftstellen zu verstehen, darin geboten wird, seinen Nächsten, selbst unsern Feind zu lieben. Denn Liebe als Neigung kann nicht geboten werden, aber Wohlthun aus Pflicht selbst, wenn dazu gleich gar keine Neigung treibt, ja gar natürliche und unbezwingliche Abneigung widersteht, ist *praktische* und nicht *pathologische* Liebe, die im Willen liegt und nicht im Hange der Empfindung, in Grundsätzen der Handlung und nicht schmelzender Theilnehmung; jene aber allein kann geboten werden.'

practical love is active love of benevolence. The Collins notes do not explicitly mention practical love, but they do refer to a love to which there is obligation, and the context there is identical to that in *Groundwork* I (both interpret Jesus' commandment). The love that is obligatory in the Collins notes (in the immediate vicinity of the discussion of Jesus' commandment) is love of benevolence. These findings strongly suggest a tentative identification of practical love with love of benevolence. Also significant is the fact that the identification of pathological (or inclination-based love) in terms of the general division is more difficult. In Herder, love of benevolence is based on inclination or instinct, and in Collins, the love based on inclination can be either love of benevolence or love of delight. But in the particular passage in Collins, the context of which is identical with the context in the *Groundwork*, it is explicitly love of delight that is not commanded (even though just a bit further in Collins Kant says that there is also an obligation to love the humanity of others with love of delight). Furthermore, we have thus far established a relatively clear tentative identification between practical love and love of benevolence. It is therefore plausible to assume that, insofar as we take seriously the statements from the Collins notes and the *Religion* to the effect that all love is either love of benevolence or love of delight, or that love in general is divided into those two, the love that is not commanded in the *Groundwork* (i.e. pathological love) might very well be love of delight. But we do not know this.

However, the above conceptual analysis can already be used to make better exegetical sense of the previously mentioned famous example of the sorrowful philanthropist in *Groundwork* I, who is beneficent without inclination. Wood argues that the way Kant construes the example is due to his aim of setting 'up a derivation of the most formal version of the categorical imperative', and that Kant fails to notice that help given to others 'is not the result of sticking to a principle'[17] (Wood 2008, p. 35). Rather, Wood argues, the philanthropist acts out of the love of human beings [*Menschenliebe*] that Kant describes in 'Introduction XII' in the 'Doctrine of Virtue' as feeling. Wood thinks that this love is a 'feeling produced directly by reason' (Wood 2008, p. 35) – not to be confused with practical love, which Wood reduces to action. Here, I think, Wood misconstrues love's general structure. The love produced directly by reason is itself an obligation; it is love of benevolence or practical love. It is not the same as the feeling of love, which even in the 'Doctrine of Virtue' resides on the side of nature (as we will see later in this chapter). I don't think Kant says or implies anywhere that the feeling

---

[17] Cf. Timmermann (2009, pp. 46, 50), who holds that actions always imply laws, or maxims as subjective principles of action.

of love is produced directly by reason. It is of course possible that the sorrowful philanthropist has neglected the indirect duty of cultivation and that he ought to have more loving feeling, but this is not discussed in the example. If we wish to interpret Kant charitably and respect the premises of his example, acknowledging what we know about the general structure of love while still appealing to the notion of love of human beings, we ought to say that the sorrowful man is acting from the love that is benevolence; that is, he is acting from practical love.[18]

In the second *Critique*, the passage on love of neighbour is found in the third chapter of the analytic of practical reason, where Kant discusses the incentives [*die Triebfedern*] of pure practical reason. While both *Groundwork* I and this chapter deal with the proper motivational ground of moral action, in *Groundwork* I the question concerns the moral worth of actions, whereas here the discussion revolves around how to make respect for the law a reliable determining ground of the will. The closer we get to the passage, the more Kant seems to apply the specific ideas of *Groundwork* I, repeating the basic notion that actions only have moral worth (see C2, 5:81.17–19) when done '*from duty* and from respect for the law, not from love and liking for what the actions are to produce.' (C2, 5:81.23–24)[19] As in *Groundwork* I, the feeling of love in the second *Critique* is not moral as such and does not constitute a proper basis for moral conduct: 'It is very beautiful to do good to human beings from love for them and from sympathetic benevolence; or to be just from love of order; but this is not yet the genuine moral maxim of our conduct' (C2, 5:82.18–20)[20]. Now this remark, which appears just before the principal passage on love of neighbour in the second *Critique*, confirms the division between some sort of love and morality that was clear in the *Groundwork*. Obviously, the love mentioned above cannot be the practical love of the *Groundwork*, because that practical love would have to be related to our duty or to a 'genuinely moral maxim'. If we think of the context of beauty, and the idea that doing good to others from love is beautiful, we

---

18 This will become even clearer as we progress to *The Metaphysics of Morals*. There, love of human beings is discussed in two different places and is given two different principal meanings. In the Introduction to the 'Doctrine of Virtue', love of human beings is equated with love of neighbour (MM, 6:399; cf. 6:401) and discussed as a natural aesthetic predisposition to morality, or even as a 'feeling', as Wood notes. In the doctrine of the elements, however, love of human beings is discussed as practical love (MM, 6:450). In his analysis of the sorrowful philanthropist, Wood is not sensitive to this distinction within the concept of *Menschenliebe* (or *Nächstenliebe*).
19 '*aus Pflicht* und aus Achtung fürs Gesetz, nicht aus Liebe und Zuneigung zu dem, was die Handlungen hervorbringen sollen'.
20 'Es ist sehr schön, aus Liebe zu Menschen und theilnehmendem Wohlwollen ihnen Gutes zu thun, oder aus Liebe zur Ordnung gerecht zu sein, aber das ist noch nicht die ächte moralische Maxime unsers Verhaltens'.

are closer to love of delight than practical love of benevolence. However, the passage also refers to 'sympathetic benevolence' [*theilnehmendes Wohlwollen*], which is not properly moral. I think this must now be understood in the light of the earlier lecture notes, where it was possible to have benevolence for others either from inclination or from obligation.

Quite clearly, in the second *Critique* Kant continues to rely on the distinction between pathological love and practical love familiar from *Groundwork* I. The issue is now how to make respect for the law the incentive of action. As in the *Groundwork*, Kant sees our relation to the moral law as analogous to – or more precisely, as agreeing with [*stimmt Hiemit*] – Jesus' commandment to love God above all and one's neighbour as oneself (C2, 5:83.3). Kant explains first that, as a transcendent being, God cannot be loved pathologically, and while pathological love towards other humans is possible, it cannot be commanded. Jesus' dictum therefore concerns only practical love:

> It is, therefore, only *practical love*, that is understood in that kernel of all laws. To love God means, in this sense, to do what he commands gladly; to love one's neighbor means to practice all duties toward him *gladly*. But the command that makes this a rule cannot command us to *have* this disposition in dutiful actions but only to *strive* for it. (C2, 5:83.11–16)[21]

The idea is familiar from *Groundwork* I, but Kant's conception of love of neighbour does indeed vary from the *Groundwork* to the second *Critique*. In the *Groundwork*, Kant argues that Jesus' commandment concerns practical love and not the feeling of love, period. Here he argues that while Jesus' commandment concerns practical love and pathological love cannot be commanded, what is commanded is nevertheless love, and so the commandment brings with it a duty to strive for a glad disposition in practical love.[22] How is this obvious difference between the passages of the *Groundwork* and the second *Critique* to be explained?

---

[21] 'Also ist es bloß die *praktische Liebe*, die in jenem Kern aller Gesetze verstanden wird. Gott lieben, heißt in dieser Bedeutung, seine Gebote *gerne* thun; den Nächsten lieben, heißt: alle Pflicht gegen ihn gerne ausüben. Das Gebot aber, das dieses zur Regel macht, kann auch nicht diese Gesinnung in pflichtmäßigen Handlungen zu *haben*, sondern bloß darnach zu *streben* gebieten.'

[22] The idea of doing what God commands *gladly* can already be found in Kant's lectures on ethics. It appears all over the Collins notes (LE, 27:274.15; 27:300.8–9; 27:322.32–33; 27:335.35–36), and given that these notes are morally precritical, it is not the case that Kant came up with this idea somewhere between the *Groundwork* and the second *Critique*. For more discussion, see ch. 3.1 above.

It has been noted that what is at stake in the *Groundwork* is the establishment of the supreme principle of morality, and what Kant most wants to steer clear of is the naturalist empiricism of Hutcheson and Hume, which grounds morality in natural passions (e. g. Baron 1995, p. 204). This explains, at least in part, why Kant excludes feelings from the sphere of duty in the *Groundwork*, but I think there is more to be said about the apparent shift between the conceptions presented in these two works. It is significant that in the second *Critique*, Kant considers not only the ground of morality but also its ends. The second *Critique* passage appears in the middle of a discussion that pertains to the impossibility of achieving holiness (a perfectly moral disposition), the attainment of which would mean that we no longer had any inclinations against morality and could speak of a love for the law (C2, 5:84).[23] Love for the law remains impossible for imperfect creatures, but it seems that one way to approach it is by striving for gladness in loving one's neighbour practically. This interpretation relies on an idea according to which increasing the amount of glad practical love from duty in our lives will consequently diminish the power that (contra-moral) inclinations generally have over us (see ch. 1.3). It can at least be said that whenever we practice love for our neighbours *gladly* – that is, with an accompanying inclination for the moral action or its end – we do not *at the same time* struggle with contra-moral inclinations. Optimistically, approaching love for the law through glad practical neighbourly love corresponds with Kant's assertion that love from duty will actually lead to love from inclination (MM, 6:402.14 – 21; LE, 27:419.4 – 7). In any case, the *Groundwork* passage discusses the ground of moral action in the good will, whereas the second *Critique* passage prescribes the end of subjective moral perfection.

Another way of making a nearly equivalent point is to note a basic difference in how the *Groundwork* and the second *Critique* present the notion of the highest good. In the *Groundwork*, the highest good is used in the sense of the good will

---

23 With regard to love of God, Kant's treatment of the command to love God shifts the object of love from God to the moral law, such that love for the law becomes the unattainable object of one's moral striving. I discuss this point in ch. 3.1. What is interesting here, however, is that while the notion of cultivation is already present in Collins (LE, 27:317.35 – 38), there would appear to be no mention of the ideal of loving the law in the context of loving God prior to the second *Critique*, even though the term comes up in Mrongovius II (but there in the context of rewards) (see LE, 29:639.39). I think this can be explained simply by the fact that only after the *Groundwork* had established and solidified the status of the moral law was Kant able to view loving the moral law as analogous or parallel to loving God, as the second *Critique* shows. This hypothesis is consistent with the later Vigilantius notes, where love towards God *is* discussed in terms of loving the law (LE, 27:720.1ff.).

(GW, 4:396.25) or God[24] (GW, 4:408.37–409.1), so that in the latter case, the concept of the highest good is derived 'from the *idea* of moral perfection' (GW, 4:409.1–3)[25]. Unlike in the second *Critique*, in the *Groundwork* the notion of the highest good is not developed in terms of a subjective process of striving to approach it. Further, the component of happiness is not mentioned in connection with the highest good in the *Groundwork*, which again implies simply that the focus there is on the ground of morality. In the second *Critique*, however, the highest good has morality as its supreme condition (C2, 5:119) and the happiness of the rational moral agent as its end; only the perfectly virtuous agent is worthy of perfect happiness. Following my interpretation of the relation between love for the law and glad practical love of neighbour presented above, we may take it that as love for the law denotes a subjectively perfect virtuous condition, it is a partial description or an element of the complete highest good. Hence, glad practical love of neighbour can be plausibly viewed as a regulative guideline for striving to approach the highest good in the subjective sense. By marking this difference regarding the usage of the highest good in the two works, I'm not implying any kind of worry about contradiction or inconsistency. I'm merely noting that in the *Groundwork* passage on love of neighbour this sort of 'end-notion' of the highest good is not at issue, and thus the contexts of the two passages are clearly different: the one concerns the ground of morality, the other its end.

With respect to their ground, the conceptions of love of neighbour in the *Groundwork* and the second *Critique* are therefore similar and consistent since both divide love of neighbour into practical and pathological love and hold that only practical love can be commanded. Unlike the passage in the *Groundwork*, the passage in the second *Critique* includes a duty to strive for a glad disposition in practical love for the end of one's moral perfection, and in this respect the two conceptions are different. As the following will show, the second account anticipates *The Metaphysics of Morals*, where the duty of love and the sensible side of love will still be seen as distinct, but even more intertwined. It should also be kept in mind that in both the *Groundwork* (GW, 4:421.31–33) and the second *Critique* (C2, 5:8.15–23), Kant explicitly reserves the systematic division or classification of duties for a future work, which, as implied in the second *Critique*, might further include a special reference to human nature.

But the problem concerning the relationship between love of neighbour and the general division of love still remains. In the Collins notes on ethics and in the *Religion*, Kant claims that all love, or love in general, can be divided into love of

---

24 As such, associating God with the highest good is of course traditional for Christianity.
25 'aus der *Idee* [...] von sittlicher Vollkommenheit'.

benevolence and love of delight. The Collins notes explicitly rely on this distinction in the context of love of neighbour or love of other human beings. In the *Groundwork* and in the second *Critique*, however, the terms of the general division are not applied to the context of neighbourly love. Instead, both works distinguish between practical love and pathological love. In light of Herder and Collins, it is plausible to interpret practical love as love of benevolence, but the status of pathological love in terms of the general division remains unclear. Even though indirect evidence indicates that pathological love for others is most likely love of delight, this is by no means certain, and pathological love might actually refer to *both* pathological love of delight *and* love of benevolence from inclination. I will now move on to analyse love of neighbour in *The Metaphysics of Morals*, which will corroborate my tentative identifications concerning the general division of love in this context. However, the picture will again become different and even more complex than one might have assumed based on the previous works.

4.2 Love of Neighbour in *The Metaphysics of Morals*

I have now established that despite their obvious differences, Kant's discussions on love of neighbour in both the *Groundwork* and the second *Critique* contain a distinction between pathological love and practical love – a distinction that it makes sense tentatively to interpret in terms of love's general division. In *The Metaphysics of Morals* we find love of neighbour addressed in two specific places within the 'Doctrine of Virtue'. It first appears in 'Introduction XII' and then in the 'Elements'. I will now analyse the basic divisions of the concept of love in these contexts to demonstrate that the way Kant organises his discussion explicitly relies on the general division of love found in his earlier works. This analysis will show that the *broad outline* of Kant's conception of love of neighbour remains consistent throughout the mature period, even though its treatment in the 'Doctrine of Virtue' is much more nuanced and detailed, and hence exegetically more cumbersome, than the passages found in the *Groundwork* and the second *Critique*. Compared to the *Groundwork* in particular, which focuses on the ground of morality, the 'Doctrine of Virtue' proposes a more or less systematic division of duties from the perspective of the ends of morality, while placing more emphasis on the fact that besides reason, the human being is also endowed with specific natural qualities or dispositions that may not just be morally indifferent or work against morality, but may also serve the realisation of moral ends, or even lie at the subjective bases of becoming moral. We will see an obvious distinction between a feeling or sensation of love (love of delight) and practical love (love of benevolence), but the feeling or the aesthetic predisposition of neighbourly love as described in the 'Doctrine of Virtue' is not necessarily merely pathological but may in fact be closer to what Kant in the Collins notes termed *intellectual* love of delight (as Schönecker (2010, pp. 155–157) has shown). Lastly, I take a look at the conceptual distinctions related to the more specific duties of practical love in order to establish the basic system of the feeling-action-cultivation-account of love of neighbour.

4.2.1 On the Feeling[26] of Love

In Section XII of the Introduction to the 'Doctrine of Virtue', Kant distinguishes between four '[a]esthetic preconditions of the mind's receptivity to concepts of duty as such' (MM, 6:399.2–3; Guyer 2010)[27]. These are 'natural predispositions of the mind' (MM, 6:399.11)[28] or '*subjective* conditions of receptiveness to the concept of duty' (MM, 6:399.8–10)[29]. According to Kant, '[t]o have these predispositions cannot be considered a duty; rather, every human being has them, and it is by virtue of them that he can be put under obligation.' (MM, 6:399.12–14)[30] Subjectively, they 'lie at the basis of morality', but they are not morality's 'objective conditions' (MM, 6:399.9–10)[31]. As such, the predispositions seem to have received little attention in the literature (see Guyer 2010; Schönecker 2010), and their function is somewhat unclear. At face value, they might seem to suggest some sort of departure from Kant's previous premises in the a priori groundings

---

26 I use the English word 'feeling' here broadly, somewhat like Gregor does in her translation of 'Introduction XII' in the 'Doctrine of Virtue'. This is not implausible as I'm trying to cover with it those variants of love of neighbour that are not presented as a duty in Kant's mature published works. The English word 'feeling' can refer to bodily sensations, emotional states, and thoughts of wanting to help others (Merriam-Webster Dictionary). These aspects of 'feeling' correspond roughly to Kant's usage of *Empfindungen, Gefühle,* and *(wohlwollende) Neigungen.* These are all close to each other in Kant, and generally on the side of nature in contrast with pure practical reason. The technical term for specific emotional 'feelings' in Kant is *Gefühle*, and I indicate these more subtle distinctions in my discussion whenever necessary.
27 'Ästhetische Vorbegriffe der Empfänglichkeit des Gemüths für Pflichtbegriffe überhaupt.' Following Guyer's translation in 'Moral feelings in the *Metaphysics of Morals*'. Note also the mistake in footnote 'f' of Gregor's translation (MM, p. 528fn.*f*). The German should read as above, not '*Ästhetische Vorbegriffe der Empfänglichkeit des Gemüts Achtung*'.
28 'natürliche Gemüthsanlagen'.
29 '*subjective* Bedingungen der Empfänglichkeit für den Pflichtbegriff'.
30 'welche Anlagen zu haben nicht als Pflicht angesehen werden kann, sondern die jeder Mensch hat und kraft deren er verpflichtet werden kann.'
31 'der Moralität zum Grunde liegen' / 'objective Bedingungen'.

of moral philosophy, as he now holds that there are some sorts of specific natural sensory conditions which make duty subjectively possible. My aim here is not to provide a detailed interpretation of the function or meaning of these predispositions in general, nor to make any strong claim as regards their overall status, but merely to analyse the conceptual outlines of love of neighbour from the perspective of love's general division in this context. I do take it that, against the backdrop of the previous works I've discussed in this chapter, we are slowly arriving at a more nuanced, more comprehensive picture of the relationship between human nature and morality, just as Kant indicates in the second *Critique* (C2, 5:8.15–23). By making further assumptions about the natural side of the cognitive make-up of the agent, the moral grounding of the concept of duty is not thereby inverted. I think that Kant's basic moral philosophical positions stand, and we are just witnessing a further step in the gradual unfolding of his attempt to make sense of human existence. Even if I am mistaken about this more general point, my specific exegetical analysis of the conceptual outline of love can still be viable.

The four aesthetic predispositions that Kant lists are moral feeling, conscience, love of neighbour or love of human beings, and self-respect. There is one previous exegetical account of the aesthetic predisposition of love for one's neighbour. Schönecker (2010) argues that this predisposition, as presented in 'Introduction XII', cannot be practical love and must instead be understood as love of delight. I believe Schönecker is correct, and I adopt the main results of his reading and will merely make a very similar systematic point from the perspective of love's general division. I do think that as Schönecker is not ultimately grounding his analysis in the distinction between love of delight and love of benevolence, the overall results my reading yields regarding love of neighbour are more general (even if less detailed) than the ones arrived at by Schönecker.

Before looking at the passages on love of neighbour in more detail, I would like to say something about the conceptual relationship between love of neighbour [*Nächstenliebe, die Liebe des Nächsten*] and love of human beings [*Menschenliebe*] in *The Metaphysics of Morals*.[32] Based on the division of 'Introduction

---

32 From a strictly historical and etymological perspective, Dagobert de Levie (1963) shows, interestingly, that the German word *Menschenliebe* only emerged during the 18th century. It was derived from the Christian principle of love, and could even be identified with *Nächstenliebe* (de Levie 1963, p. 301). *Menschenliebe* was used both in religious contexts and as a secularised Enlightenment version of the Christian principle (de Levie 1963, pp. 301ff.). Even though *Nächstenliebe* and *Menschenliebe* are nearly equivalent in Kant, I am emphasising *Nächstenliebe* to acknowledge the importance of the cultural context of Christianity, in which Kant's discussions of love take place, as well as to highlight the interrelatedness of love of neighbour, self-love,

XII', love of neighbour and love of human beings would seem to be the same. In the first preliminary instance, Kant lists *die Liebe des Nächsten* as one of the four natural predispositions (MM, 6:399.6–7) and then groups his discussion under the title 'On the Love of Human Beings' [*Von der Menschenliebe*] (MM, 6:399.22). In the 'Elements', where love of neighbour is discussed from the point of view of duty or practical love, Kant uses the general heading 'On the Duty of Love to Other Human Beings' [*Von der Liebespflicht gegen andere Menschen*] (MM, 6:448.7). In both 'Introduction XII' and the 'Elements', a large part of Kant's treatment revolves around interpretation of the biblical commandment to love one's neighbour, and in this sense there is clear continuity from the *Groundwork* and the second *Critique* to *The Metaphysics of Morals*. There is a general sense in which Kant seems to equate love of human beings or love of other human beings with love of neighbour (see MM, 6:402.17; cf. 6:448.16–17; cf. 6:450.3; cf. 6:450.16; cf. 6:450.33–34). He also speaks of universal love of human beings [*allgemeine Menschenliebe*] in terms of love of neighbour [*Nächstenliebe*] (MM, 6:451.21; cf. 6:451.29), but from this perspective a distinction in the extensions of love of neighbour and love of human beings can be drawn. Kant's conceptual work on love of neighbour (or love of other human beings) involves an account of morally conditioned self-benevolence in the love of all human beings towards one another. If the maxim of benevolence is to hold universally as a duty, I must include myself in the set of 'all others' as an object of benevolence, which inclusion makes self-benevolence permitted on the condition that one is benevolent towards others as well (MM, 6:450.30–451.19; see ch. 1.3 above). So there seems to be a sense in which love of human beings in general can be interpreted to be extensionally a slightly broader concept than love of neighbour. While love of human beings might be thought to include a type of morally conditioned self-love, in the second *Critique* Kant clearly rejects any interpretation of the biblical commandment that would reduce love of God or love of neighbour to self-love (C2, 5:83fn.33–36; *pace* Moors 2007, pp. 256, 269). Love of neighbour therefore equates to love of human beings in the Introduction to the 'Doctrine of Virtue' (see also MM, 6:458.1–19), and generally to love of other human beings.

The Introduction account of love of neighbour is reminiscent of the *Groundwork* and the second *Critique*:

> *Love* is a matter of *sensation*, not of willing, and I cannot love because I *will* to, still less because I *ought* to (I cannot be constrained to love); so a *duty to love* is an absurdity.

---

and love of God, which interrelatedness is essential both for Christianity and for the 'enlightened' Kantian concept of love.

But *benevolence* (AMOR BENEVOLENTIAE), as conduct, can be subject to a law of duty. (MM, 6:401.24 – 28)[33]

This passage aligns especially nicely with the *Groundwork*, and the general division terminology is clearly in operation (benevolence is termed *amor benevolentiae*). This suggests that the love at issue here is not something completely new, of which Kant has not spoken previously; instead, we are getting an account of the natural side of love of neighbour, as mentioned previously in the *Groundwork* and the second *Critique*, but now developed differently, as a natural sensory predisposition for subjective receptivity to duty. Even though the parallel with the previous works is clear and love is here a natural sensation distinct from the love of benevolence, it is not clear that this aesthetic predisposition is merely *pathological*. The above distinction is similar to those from the *Groundwork* and the second *Critique*, but it's not exactly the same. Further on, we also learn that it is inappropriate to call benevolence love (MM, 6:401.28 – 29), and we should read this claim as saying that benevolence cannot be called love in the context of sensation, or that it cannot be called love without qualification. Since we know that having the aesthetic predisposition cannot be a duty, and since the passage on love of neighbour here begins specifically by identifying love with sensation [*Empfindung*] rather than willing, it is clear that the love at issue here cannot be the practical love of benevolence (practical love implies duty and willing).

But can the aesthetic predisposition of neighbourly love be identified with love of delight, as Schönecker claims? Once again, Kant refers to the biblical commandment of love, and once again his discussion introduces new logical relationships between the different notions of love at play in that context:

> *Beneficence* is a duty. If someone practices it often and succeeds in realizing his beneficent intention, he eventually comes actually to love the person he has helped. So the saying 'you ought to *love* your neighbor as yourself' does not mean that you ought immediately (first) to love him and (afterwards) by means of this love do good to him. It means, rather, *do good* to your fellow human beings, and your beneficence will produce love of them in you (as an aptitude of the inclination to beneficence in general).
>
> Hence only the love that is *delight* (AMOR COMPLACENTIAE) is direct. But to have a duty to this (which is a pleasure joined immediately to the representation of an object's ex-

---

[33] '*Liebe* ist eine Sache der *Empfindung*, nicht des Wollens, und ich kann nicht lieben, weil ich *will*, noch weniger aber weil ich *soll* (zur Liebe genöthigt werden); mithin ist eine *Pflicht zu lieben* ein Unding. *Wohlwollen* (AMOR BENEVOLENTIAE) aber kann als ein Thun einem Pflichtgesetz unterworfen sein.' Translation modified.

istence), that is, to have to be constrained to take pleasure in something, is a contradiction. (MM, 6:402.14–21)[34]

Guyer calls this discussion 'limited and disappointing' (Guyer 2010, p. 145). According to Guyer, 'Kant actually claims that feelings of love towards (specific) others are a consequence or effect of beneficence, not an aesthetic precondition or cause thereof.' (Guyer 2010, p. 145) Guyer's view is understandable, but he does not really analyse the passage or problematise the love at issue in 'Introduction XII'. So what is going on in the above quotation? In harmony with Schönecker's results, we can note, first, that the love Kant discusses as the object of Jesus' love commandment cannot be the aesthetic predisposition. This is because Jesus' commandment concerns practical love, and as I've shown above the identification of practical love with the aesthetic predisposition of love is already ruled out in the first sentence of Kant's discussion of the aesthetic predisposition of love of neighbour. Second, along the lines of his thinking in the Collins notes (LE, 27:417.11–19; 27:419.4–7), Kant continues to hold that beneficence from duty will produce an inclination of love in the beneficent subject. In the 'Doctrine of Virtue', the love that results from beneficence is defined as 'an aptitude of the inclination to beneficence in general' (MM, 6:402.20–21). Building on the Collins notes, we can identify this derivative love as love of benevolence from inclination. It is the supposed identification of this derivative love with the aesthetic predisposition of neighbourly love that disappoints Guyer. But as Schönecker (2010, pp. 152, 154) has shown, the point is precisely that because the aesthetic predisposition of love is 'antecedent' [*vorhergehend*] and 'lies' subjectively 'at the foundation' [*zum Grunde liegen*] of morality, the aesthetic predisposition *cannot* be identified with the love that results from beneficence – a point that Guyer does not consider. What we are left with is the last sentence of the long quotation above, where Kant defines love of delight, and love of delight 'alone' [*allein*], as direct or immediate pleasure in the presentation of an object's existence – a

---

34 '*Wohlthun* ist pflicht. Wer diese oft ausübt, und es gelingt ihm mit seiner wohlthätigen Absicht, kommt endlich wohl gar dahin, den, welchem er wohl gethan hat, wirklich zu lieben. Wenn es also heißt: du sollst deinen Nächsten *lieben* als sich selbst, so heißt das nicht: du sollst unmittelbar (zuerst) lieben und vermittelst dieser Liebe (nachher) wohlthun, sondern: *thue* deinem Nebenmenschen *wohl*, und dieses Wohlthun wird Menschenliebe (als Fertigkeit der Neigung zum Wohlthun überhaupt) in dir bewirken!

Die Liebe des *Wohlgefallens* (AMOR COMPLACENTIAE) würde also allein direct sein. Zu dieser aber (als einer unmittelbar mit der Vorstellung der Existenz eines Gegenstandes verbundenen Lust) eine Pflicht zu haben, d. i. zur Lust woran genöthigt werden zu müssen, ist ein Widerspruch.'

pleasure that it is not a duty to have. This love of delight matches the general characteristics of the aesthetic predispositions and is the only logical option left when it comes to identifying the aesthetic predisposition of love of neighbour, given the conceptual resources of love generally at our disposal.

By building on Schönecker's analysis, I believe I have shown that the elements of the general division of love are clearly at work in 'Introduction XII' and that the aesthetic predisposition of love of neighbour can only be identified with love of delight. Strictly speaking, this would be enough for the argument I wish to make in this context, but I think just a bit more should be said about the kind of love of delight at play here. Recall that the basic division in the *Groundwork* and the second *Critique* is between pathological love and practical love (the latter being love of benevolence from duty). As love in 'Introduction XII' is distinguished precisely from benevolence, which is a matter of duty, it may be tempting to identify the aesthetic predisposition with *pathological* love of delight, because this would introduce a very smooth continuity to the natural side of the concept of love of neighbour among all the main moral philosophical works from the mature period. But how could a pathological sensation lie at the subjective basis of receptivity to concepts of duty? Furthermore, regarding the predispositions in general, Kant holds that: 'Consciousness of them is not of empirical origin; it can, instead, only follow from a consciousness of a moral law, as the effect this has on the mind.' (MM, 6:399.14–16)[35] If love of delight is merely pathological, how can consciousness of it depend on one's consciousness of the moral law?

Fortunately, the Collins notes provide the resources to identify the love of delight here as *intellectual*, which means that the object of the antecedent predisposition to love one's neighbour is an immediate delight in the *humanity* (or the rational nature) of another person (see LE, 27:418). Again, I owe this point to Schönecker (2010, pp. 156–157). The actual feeling of delight will vary according to the moral perfection of the actual other in question, but Kant does not really spell this out in much detail, and he never draws a clear distinction between the aesthetic predisposition (or the capacity) of the feeling of love and the actual feeling of love. Perhaps it is still possible that the love of delight in question is *both* pathological *and* intellectual, but my argument does not depend on the answer to this question.[36] For my purposes, the context-specific existence of the general division of love is enough.

---

35 'Das Bewußtsein derselben ist nicht empirischen Ursprungs, sondern kann nur auf das eines moralischen Gesetzes, als Wirkung desselben aufs Gemüth, folgen.'
36 For further discussion of the attributes of love of delight in this context, see Schönecker (2010, pp. 158 ff.).

4.2.2 On Practical Love

I now turn to love of neighbour in the 'Elements' of the 'Doctrine of Virtue'. The basic division here is that between duties to oneself and duties to others. Duties to others are further divided into duties of love and duties of respect.[37] Based on Kant's previous accounts in the *Groundwork*, the second *Critique*, and 'Introduction XII', which all hold that only practical love can be a duty, we should now assume that in the light of love's general division the love that is primarily at issue in Kant's overall discussion in 'On the Duty of Love to Other Human Beings' (MM, 6:448.7)[38] is not love of delight but practical love. And so it is:

> In this context, however, LOVE is not to be understood as *feeling* (aesthetic), that is, as pleasure in the perfection of others; love is not to be understood as *delight* in them (since others cannot put one under obligation to have feelings). It must rather be thought as the maxim of *benevolence* (practical love), which results in beneficence. (MM, 6:449.17–22)[39]

The basic premise of practical love in *The Metaphysics of Morals* is therefore very much consistent with the *Groundwork* and the second *Critique* (see also MM, 6:450.16–19). Practical love is once again distinguished from the feeling of love to which there is no duty (here explicitly delight or *Wohlgefallen*) and is now identified as the maxim of benevolence resulting in beneficence. The duty of practical love is further divided into three distinct duties: beneficence [*Wohltätigkeit*], gratitude [*Dankbarkeit*], and sympathetic participation[40] [*Theilnehmung*] (MM, 6:452.11–12). Next, I shall discuss each of these in turn to

---

[37] The basic division of duties in general in the Vigilantius lecture notes from 1793 is between duties of right and duties of love (LE, 27:600.12–19; 27:604.5–6), which suggests that Kant was still working out the final form of the divisions of the moral system around the time of the publication of *The Metaphysics of Morals*.

[38] 'Von der Liebespflicht gegen andere Menschen.'

[39] 'Die LIEBE wird hier aber nicht als *Gefühl* (ästhetisch), d.i. als Lust an der Vollkommenheit anderer Menschen, nicht als Liebe des *Wohlgefallens*, verstanden (den Gefühle zu haben, dazu kann es keine Verpflichtung durch Andere geben), sondern muß als Maxime des *Wohlwollens* (als praktisch) gedacht werden, welche das Wohlthun zur Folge hat.' Translation modified. Gregor translates both *Gefühl* and *Empfindung* as 'feeling', even though for *Empfindung*, 'sensation' could be used. However, it is difficult to make out a consistent technical distinction between the two terms in Kant. Note how both *Gefühl* and *Empfindung* (MM, 6:401.24–28) are related to the aesthetic or the sensory, which, in the context of love of neighbour, seems to confirm yet again the parallelism between the general division of love and the nature-freedom division. *Gefühl* and *Empfindung* are terms of nature.

[40] Following Fahmy's (2009) suggestion in translating *Theilnehmung*.

show that the general division approach and the feeling-action-cultivation account of love of neighbour are indeed robust. Again, rather than providing an interpretation of each of these duties, I aim primarily to trace the conceptual outlines of my general account of love of neighbour in Kant's writings. That is, I hope to show that Kant's discussions continue to rely on a distinction between feeling and reason-based action, or between affective and rational elements in the cognitive apparatus of the agent, and that the notion of cultivation is operative when it comes to the duties of practical love.

A) Beneficence

Given my foundational aim of systematising the general outlines of a Kant immanent conceptual framework, with regard to beneficence it suffices to make sense of the logical relationship between beneficence and benevolence and how this distinction relates to love of neighbour through notions of practical love and cultivation. It should now be basically clear that Kantian *amor benevolentiae* involves at least goodwill, maxims of action, and actual beneficence. In the 'Elements', the general duty of love for one's neighbour [*Nächstenliebe*] is further characterised 'as the duty to make others' *ends* my own (provided only that these are not immoral)' (MM, 6:450.4–5)[41], which would make *amor benevolentiae* the duty to adopt maxims that further the ends of others, according to their concepts of happiness (see MM, 6:454.18–20). In the specific discussion on beneficence, however, we are given new definitions of benevolence and beneficence: 'Benevolence is satisfaction in the happiness (well-being) of others; but beneficence is the maxim of making others' happiness one's end' (MM, 6:452.26–28)[42]. Here, benevolence is defined as satisfaction, beneficence as the maxim.

At face value, this seems confused, but I think the new definitions must be understood in the light of the immediately preceding paragraph, where Kant discusses degrees of benevolence and explains that 'the benevolence present in love for all human beings is indeed the greatest in its *extent*, but the smallest in its *degree*' (MM, 6:451.21–22)[43]. This is 'benevolence in wishes' [*das Wohlwollen des Wunsches*] (MM, 6:452.1; cf. LE, 27:64.13–14), which borders on indiffer-

---

[41] 'die Pflicht Anderer ihre *Zwecke* (so fern diese nur nicht unsittlich sind) zu den meinen zu machen'.
[42] 'Wohlwollen ist das Vergnügen an der Glückseligkeit (dem Wohlsein) Anderer; Wohlthun aber die Maxime, sich dasselbe zum Zweck zu machen'.
[43] 'Das Wohlwollen in der allgemeinen Menschenliebe ist nun zwar dem *Umfange* nach das größte, dem *Grade* nach aber das kleinste'.

ence. According to Kant, this weak, universal benevolence is a rather passive delight [*Wohlgefallen*] in the well-being of others (MM, 6:452.2–3), and we see Kant actually using the *Wohlgefallen* terminology to describe this form of well-wishing. The weak benevolence is distinguished from practical love, which is 'active, practical benevolence (beneficence), making the well-being and happiness of others my end.' (MM, 6:452.4–5)[44] The seemingly confused passage ceases to be confused: we should take the 'satisfaction definition' of benevolence as referring to weak, universal benevolence and the 'maxim definition' of beneficence as referring to active benevolence. Certain cases of rational benevolence are therefore merely wishful and do not lead to actual beneficence, which means that rational benevolence and beneficence can be viewed as logically distinct. Kant allows that acts of beneficence in general can be limited by beneficence toward individuals closer to oneself. For Kant, in terms of the Christian commandment, loving the other 'as oneself' refers to the rational ground of universal benevolence, whereas in acting I am allowed to love those further away from me to a lesser degree and may love those closer to me more, perhaps even 'as myself', in the closest of cases (see §28, MM, 6:451–452). It is therefore possible that beneficence toward, say, one's parents, may effectively inhibit the actualisation of beneficence toward someone further away. In the inefficient case, too, rational benevolence as the ground of obligation remains in place and may at least in some cases be experienced as what Timmermann calls 'subjective regret'. (See Timmermann 2013, esp. pp. 47 ff.) Once again, rational benevolence is not exactly the same as beneficence.[45] Given the above, it should now be clear that Kantian practical love involves *both* benevolence *and* beneficence.

This finding is relevant to the current exegetical debate, as is made clear when we consider a recent take on practical love in the literature. In her article 'Kantian Practical Love', Fahmy (2010) argues that practical love is best understood through what she calls the 'cultivation account', according to which '[t]he duty of practical love is the duty to cultivate a benevolent disposition toward other human beings as well as practical beneficent desires.' (Fahmy 2010, p. 321) In particular, and correctly, I would argue, Fahmy refuses to reduce

---

[44] 'ein thätiges, praktisches Wohlwollen, sich das Wohl und Heil des Anderen zum *Zweck* zu machen, (das Wohlthun)'.
[45] Kant does not specify how much is required from us in terms of beneficence, and it is not my aim here to discuss Kant's take on the normative issue of demandingness (see e.g. van Ackeren & Sticker 2015). At a minimum, one should not be so beneficent as to come to need the beneficence of others (MM, 6:454).

practical love to respect or beneficence.[46] The division between love and respect is a grounding dualism in the 'Doctrine of Virtue', and benevolence and beneficence, while sometimes nearly equivalent, remain logically distinct. I also agree that throughout the 'Doctrine of Virtue' Kant emphasises our duty to cultivate a moral disposition, including our natural feelings.

What does it mean to cultivate something in Kant's moral philosophy? As Fahmy (2010, pp. 319–322) has shown, it is essential to keep in mind that one of the most foundational claims in the 'Doctrine of Virtue' is that there are two ends that are also duties: one's own perfection and the happiness of others (MM, 6:385–388). Pursuing these is necessarily an ongoing process, in which an agent cultivates herself by increasing her fitness or capacity for pursuing these ends: '*Natural* perfection is the *cultivation* of any *capacities* whatever for furthering ends set forth by reason.' (MM, 6:391.29–31[47]; see also 6:418fn.) As regards morality, cultivation aims at the perfection of doing one's duty *from* duty (MM, 6:392), which involves a cheerful heart in carrying out one's duties with the thought of duty in mind (MM, 6:484–485). I think we can say generally that the kind of cultivation that is ethically required of us with regard to the ends that are also duties is striving to harmonise our emotive or affective faculties with what duty commands, in order to remove cognitive hindrances that make it more difficult for us to do our duty.

In the case of beneficence, Kant consistently holds, from the Collins notes onwards, that beneficent action from duty produces a feeling or an inclination of love in the virtuous subject, which feeling is in turn prone to yield more beneficence (LE, 27:417.11–19; 27:419.4–7; MM, 6:402.14–21). This would be an instance of cultivating neighbourly love. However, I fear that in correctly distancing herself from the reductive action account, Fahmy risks undermining the action component of practical love. She not only holds that practical love is distinct from beneficence but claims, further, that practical love is one of four distinct duties of love *alongside* beneficence, gratitude, and sympathetic participation (Fahmy 2010, p. 327). From a systematic exegetical perspective, this view is difficult to maintain. In my opinion, it fails to acknowledge the general consistency in love's division throughout the *Groundwork*, the second *Critique*, and *The Metaphysics of Morals*, according to which love of neighbour divides into

---

[46] I will therefore not use any further resources to discuss the possibility that in Kant's ethics practical love might be reducible to respect or to mere beneficent action. These kinds of ideas are not in line with the text. For more detailed debate, see Fahmy (2010); cf. e.g. Johnson (1997).

[47] '*Physische, d. i. Cultur* aller *Vermögen* überhaupt zu Beförderung der durch die Vernunft vorgelegten Zwecke.' Gregor picks the word 'perfection' [*Vollkommenheit*] from the subheading immediately above the German quote to make the English smoother.

the feeling of love and the duty of love, the latter being everywhere practical love. We also saw above how in Kant's text beneficence was a part of the definition of practical love. Further, in the 'Elements' the duty of love is generally identified with practical love twice in the preliminary main clauses (MM, 6:449.17–22; 6:450.16–19), and the duties of love are then explicitly divided into *three* specific duties further along: 'They are duties of A) *beneficence*, B) *gratitude*, and C) *sympathetic participation*.' (MM, 6:452.11–12)[48] In my opinion, the charitable view, which does not assume a significant gap or a radical change in Kant's ideas within the critical period, and which is also exegetically consistent with the letter of Kant's text, is to see beneficence, gratitude, and sympathy as falling within the division of practical love.

B) Gratitude

What role does love play in the duty of gratitude? According to Kant, '[g]ratitude consists in *honoring* a person because of a benefit he has rendered us. The feeling connected with this judgment is respect for the benefactor (who puts one under obligation), whereas the benefactor is viewed as only in a relation of love toward the recipient.' (MM, 6:454.31–455.1)[49] On the face of it, gratitude as such involves not the feeling of love on the part of the grateful agent but rather respect as a response to received beneficence. In relation to practical love, then, it would seem to be a duty specifying how we ought to *react* to love.[50]

We then learn that gratitude may be divided into 'active' [*thätige*] and 'affective' [*affectionelle*] variants, implying that mere benevolence 'without physical results' occasions affective gratitude (MM, 6:455.1–4)[51]. Such benevolence is 'already a basis of obligation to gratitude', in which case the grateful disposition is called 'appreciativeness' [*Erkenntlichkeit*] (MM, 6:455.22–24)[52]. However, Kant does not explicitly elaborate the division further, and interpretations of his position vary. Some, like Baron and Fahmy, seem to reduce active gratitude to the cultivation of affective gratitude (Baron & Fahmy 2009, p. 224), somewhat ne-

---

48 'Sie sind: A) Pflichten der *Wohltätigkeit*, B) der *Dankbarkeit*, C) der *Theilnehmung*.' Translation modified.
49 '*Dankbarkeit* ist die *Verehrung* einer Person wegen einer uns erwiesenen Wohlthat. Das Gefühl, was mit dieser Beurtheilung verbunden ist, ist das der Achtung gegen den (ihn verpflichtenden) Wohlthäter, da hingegen dieser gegen den Empfänger nur als im Verhältnis der Liebe betrachtet wird.'
50 I wish to thank Jens Timmermann for bringing this to my attention.
51 'ohne physische Folgen'.
52 'schon Grund der Verpflichtung zur Dankbarkeit'.

glecting those passages that emphasise action in gratitude. Others, such as Smit and Timmons (2011) and Gudrun von Tevenar (2006), construe gratitude as having no necessary connection to feeling (Smit & Timmons 2011, p. 304; Tevenar 2006), but they tend to somewhat neglect the active-affective distinction (Smit & Simmons, Tevenar) or end up arguing that Kantian gratitude is primarily about discharging the duty (Tevenar). Given these varied interpretations, I think that a more balanced view of active and affective gratitude is required in order to appreciate what I see as the gist of Kant's discussion from love's perspective.

In the first place, Kant asserts that gratitude is a sacred duty, by which he means that 'it cannot be discharged completely by any act in keeping with it (so that one who is under obligation always remains under obligation).' (MM, 6:455.16–17)[53] Second, Kant does seem to hold that affective gratitude is a duty, which at face value presents an interpretative problem since we know that it cannot be a duty to have a feeling. The duty of affective gratitude might be understood as an indirect duty to cultivate the moral feeling, which is dependent on reason-induced respect for the moral law. This would be consistent with Kant's account of the moral feeling in 'Introduction XII' (see MM, 6:399.32–400.1), but I do not want to force this interpretation and will leave the question open. Active gratitude is also a duty, however, for Kant maintains that '[t]he least degree[54] [of gratitude] is to render *equal* services to the benefactor if he can receive them (if he is still living) or, if he cannot, to render them to others' (MM, 6:456.6–8)[55]. This is clearly a demand for action that is missed by Baron and Fahmy, and if the cultivation account of active gratitude is to make sense, the action component should be unambiguously incorporated *as action*.[56] The idea, then, is that gratitude cultivates love. Rather than 'regarding a kindness received as a burden one would gladly be rid of' (MM, 6:456.8–11)[57], we should actively seek out opportunities to be grateful:

---

[53] 'die [...] durch keinen ihr gemäßen Act völlig getilgt werden kann (wobei der Verpflichtete immer noch verpflichtet bleibt).' Tevenar (2006, p. 181) mentions this passage at the beginning of her reading but does not wish to incorporate it in her interpretation of Kant's actual position.
[54] The German text gives the impression that what is under discussion in the last paragraph on gratitude is the *least degree* of gratitude. This seems somewhat peculiar, if only because Kant gives no account whatsoever of other degrees of gratitude.
[55] 'Der mindeste Grad ist, *gleiche* Dienstleistungen dem Wohlthäter, der dieser empfänglich (noch lebend) ist, und, wenn er es nicht ist, Anderen zu erweisen'.
[56] The implications of gratitude as action have been analysed in some detail by Smit and Timmons (2011).
[57] 'eine empfangene Wohlthat [...] wie eine Last, deren man gern überhoben sein möchte, [...] anzusehen'.

> taking even the occasion for gratitude as a moral blessing, that is, as an opportunity given one to unite this duty of love of human beings, which combines the *cordiality* of a benevolent disposition with *sensitivity* to benevolence (attentiveness to the smallest degree of this disposition in one's thought of duty), and so to cultivate love of human beings. (MM, 6:456.11–16)[58]

Kant's discussion thus ends with an emphasis on sensitivity, which, since beneficence is not mentioned or implied here, should be taken as related to affective gratitude or the feeling of respect occasioned by even the most minor instances of benevolence. We may interpret the passage such that respecting benevolence in other human beings strengthens their incentive to it[59] and hence cultivates love of human beings, which in this context can only be viewed as benevolent love from others. It can therefore be argued that Kantian gratitude, as a sacred duty of practical love to other human beings, involves the feeling of respect for one's benefactor, the active rendering of equal services where possible, and, through affective sensitivity to benevolence, the cultivation of love of benevolence (see fig. 5).

C) Sympathetic Participation

Finally, let us turn to the problem of sympathetic participation [*die Theilnehmung*]. Like gratitude, the duty of *Theilnehmung* has often been viewed as an adjunct to beneficence. In recent years, however, this picture has started to shatter,

---

[58] 'selbst die Veranlassung dazu als moralische Wohlthat aufzunehmen, d.i. als gegebene Gelegenheit, diese Tugend der Menschenliebe, welche mit der *Innigkeit* der wohlwollenden Gesinnung zugleich *Zärtlichkeit* des Wohlwollens (Aufmerksamkeit auf den kleinsten Grad derselben in der Pflichtvorstellung) ist, zu verbinden und so die Menschenliebe zu cultiviren.' Translation modified. The syntax of this passage is fairly difficult to follow. While I take it to be relatively clear that *dazu* refers to gratitude, just what is meant to be combined or united with *zu verbinden* is far less clear. Gregor takes it that gratitude is united *with* love of human beings, but the German syntax does not imply this. I believe we should read *zu verbinden* according to sense 5 in the Grimm dictionary – *der begriff des bandes, der bei allen bisherigen bedeutungen hervortrat*, as the concept of the ties by which all meanings thus far surface – in which case *verbinden* does not grammatically require that something is combined *with something else* and may instead refer to a sort of inner unification. I translate *Wohlthat* as 'blessing' to emphasise the sacredness of the duty, following sense 2 of *Wohltat* in *Grimm*, where the meaning shifts from the action to the effect of the action and *Wohlthat* is related to *Geschenk*, or 'gift'. I wish to thank Martin Sticker for his help with the linguistic difficulties of the passage.

[59] I owe this point to Smit and Timmons, although they make it in terms of beneficence: 'having a grateful disposition that is manifested in acts of sincere gratitude tends to encourage further acts of beneficence' (Smit & Timmons 2011, p. 318).

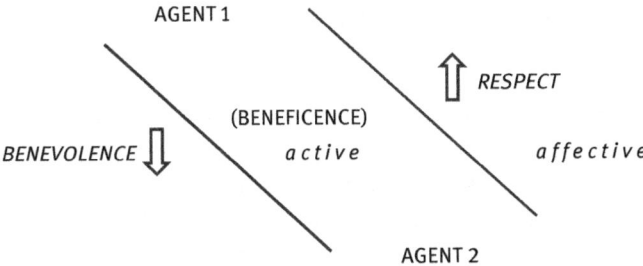

Figure 5. Gratitude

with interpreters like Wood (2008, pp. 176–177)[60] and Fahmy (2009) pointing out that in Kant, there is a sense in which *Theilnehmung* is a direct duty in its own right. However, the exegetical details of Sections 34 and 35 remain under discussion. I will not attempt a general interpretation of these passages; adopting the basic results of Fahmy's reading in particular,[61] my aim is to consider the way in

---

60 Even though Wood problematically conflates beneficence and practical love (Wood 2008, p. 176; cf. Fahmy 2010). As I have shown, the consistent way of reading Kant in the light of the general division of love involves viewing beneficence, gratitude, and sympathy as the division of practical love (admittedly, beneficence seems to be the paradigm case).
61 My only real exegetical disagreement with Fahmy's interpretation relates to the translation of the title of Kant's discussion: '*Theilnehmende Empfindung ist überhaupt Pflicht*' (MM, 6:456.18), which Gregor translates as 'Sympathetic feeling is generally a duty'. As Fahmy (2009, p. 34) notes, the title presents a problem since we know that in Kant, it cannot be a duty to have a feeling. Fahmy suggests that the title refers to cultivated sympathetic feeling (Fahmy 2009, p. 46), in which case I think it would read something like 'cultivated sympathetic feeling is generally a duty'. Fahmy herself still finds 'the title somewhat odd' (Fahmy 2009, p. 50fn.23), and I agree, for it seems to imply that to have the cultivated feeling is generally a duty, as opposed to the idea that to cultivate sympathetic feeling is (only) an indirect duty. According to Fahmy (2009, p. 49fn.4), Timmermann has suggested that it might be better to translate *überhaupt* as *as such*, but this move doesn't help to solve this particular issue. I do believe, however, that a different translation of *überhaupt* will. While it is clear that the basic abstract meaning of *überhaupt* (literally, *overhead*) refers to generality (as opposed to particularity), the Grimm and Adelung dictionaries show that, at least in 18th-century German, *überhaupt* often carries the meaning of 'in sum', 'in all', or 'all things considered'. It refers to something along the lines of the endpoint of a calculation or consideration. Grimm B.1 reads: *eine mehrheit von gegenständen zusammenfassend* – the majority of objects summarised or attached together. Adelung 1. reads: *In allem, alles zusammen genommen* – in all, all taken together. This would make good sense in relation to Kant's accounts (e.g. GW, 4:399.27–34; MM, 6:457.24–25), which hold that sympathetic feeling is not a duty: all in all, when not just the ground of morality but also the final ends of humanity are taken into account, together with the fact that human beings are natural creatures with feelings, on which their happiness largely relies, there is an important sense in which sym-

which the feeling-action division is yet again repeated in the duty of *Theilnehmung* and how cultivation figures in this division from the perspective of the concept of love.

Kant's basic distinction here is between *humanitas practica* and *humanitas aesthetica*. *Humanitas aesthetica* is a natural receptivity to 'joy for others and pity (SYMPATHIA MORALIS)', which are 'sensuous feelings of (what should therefore be called aesthetic) pleasure or displeasure at the state of gratification as well as pain of others' (MM, 6:456.20 – 22)[62]. According to Kant, 'to use them as a means to the advancement of active and rational benevolence is still a particular, if only conditional, duty under the name of *humaneness* (HUMANITAS).' (MM, 6:456.24 – 27)[63] In other words, at the beginning of Section 34, 'humaneness' [*Menschlichkeit*] is a conditional duty to use *humanitas aesthetica* or our natural receptivity to the feelings of others to promote active benevolence, which might make the duty of humaneness an adjunct to beneficence. As Wood and Fahmy have argued, however, a closer look at how Kant elaborates the notion of 'humaneness' (see also C2, 155fn.) seems to reveal the existence of another, independent direct duty:

> Now, it can be seen either as the *capacity* and *will* to *communicate* with one another with regard to one's *feelings* (HUMANITAS PRACTICA), or merely as the *receptivity*, given by Nature herself, to the feeling of gratification or pain we share with others (HUMANITAS AESTHETICA). The first is *free* and is therefore called *participating sympathetically* (COMMUNIO SENTIENDI LIBERALIS), and is founded on practical reason. The second is *unfree* (COMMUNIO SENTIENDI ILLIBERALIS, SERVILIS) and can be called *communicable* (like that of heat or of contagious diseases) and also compassivity, because it spreads naturally among human beings living side by side. There is obligation only to the first. (MM, 6:456.28 – 457.5)[64]

---

pathetic feeling is after all a duty, if only an indirect duty of cultivation. I therefore propose what I call the 'all-in-all' intepretation of *überhaupt:* the title should be translated as 'All in all, sympathetic feeling is a duty'.
62 'Mitfreude und Mitleid (SYMPATHIA MORALIS)' / 'sinnliche Gefühle einer (darum ästhetisch zu nennenden) Lust oder Unlust an dem Zustande des Vergügens sowohl als Schmerzens Anderer'. Timmermann's (privately communicated) translation.
63 'diese als Mittel zu Beförderung des thätigen und vernünftigen Wohlwollens zu gebrauchen, ist noch eine besondere, obzwar nur bedingte Pflicht unter dem Namen der *Menschlichkeit* (HUMANITAS)'. Timmermann's (privately communicated) translation.
64 'Diese kann nun in dem *Vermögen* und *Willen*, sich einander in Ansehung seiner *Gefühle mitzutheilen* (HUMANITAS PRACTICA), oder blos in der *Empfänglichkeit* für das gemeinsame Gefühl des Vergnügens oder Schmerzens (HUMANITAS AESTHETICA), was die Natur selbst giebt, gesetzt werden. Das erstere ist *frei* und wird daher *theilnehmend* genannt (COMMUNIO SENTIENDI LIBERALIS) und gründet sich auf praktische Vernunft: das zweite ist *unfrei* (COMMUNIO SENTIENDI ILLIBERALIS, SERVILIS) und kann *mittheilend* (wie die der Wärme oder ansteckender

4.2 Love of Neighbour in *The Metaphysics of Morals* — 139

Above, Kant states that there is obligation [*Verbindlichkeit*] only to *humanitas practica*. It therefore appears that the direct duty of *Theilnehmung* based on *humanitas practica* should not be confused with the duty of humaneness in the earlier sense. *Humanitas practica* occasions a direct participatory duty of human beings to communicate their feelings to each other or to incorporate their feelings in their communication (see Fahmy 2009, pp. 35–36, 42). In comparison with gratitude, we may note that, whereas gratitude includes asymmetrical subject positions in a respectful reaction to beneficence or benevolence, the direct duty of *Theilnehmung* as *Mittheilung* is symmetrically reciprocal (see fig. 6).[65]

Kant provides one further description of the relationship between these two duties of sympathy:

> But while pity (and thus also joy) for others is not in itself one's duty, active sympathetic participation in their fate is; and to this end it is thus indirectly one's duty to cultivate the natural (aesthetic) feelings of pity in us, and to use them as so many means to sympathetic participation from moral principles and [from] the feeling that conforms to them. (MM, 457:24–29)[66]

Krankheiten), auch Mitleidenschaft heißen: weil sie sich unter nebeneinander lebenden Menschen natürlicher Weise verbreitet. Nur zu dem ersteren giebts Verbindlichkeit.' Timmermann's (privately communicated) translation. As Fahmy correctly points out, the verb *mittheilen* involves giving something to another (Fahmy 2009, p. 35). In fact, according to Grimm, communication is but one of its instances, and the general meaning is something like 'imparting'; it hovers close to the notions of gift [*das Geschenk*], active favour [*die Wohlthat*], and even blessing [*die Gnade*], bringing its meaning in intimate proximity to beneficence. The English word 'compassivity' [*Mitleidenschaft*] is an archaic word for compassion, which Timmermann uses to emphasise the 'passive' nature of this mechanical sympathy (on '*Mitleidenschaft*', see Timmermann 2016b; AP, 7:179.15–24).

65 Tyler Paytas (2015) has proposed a 'patient-centred' account of Kant's duty of sympathy. I sympathise with Paytas's careful and emotionally astute argumentation and agree fully that the needs of others have a subjectively grounding moral significance. However, I worry that the term 'patient-centred' risks obscuring the basic idea of reciprocity in the direct duty of *Theilnehmung*: it is a duty that human beings owe *to each other*. Paytas's position is indeed sensible, but because he uses Gregor's translation as his sole source, he cannot see that her translation does not preserve the construction *sich einandern mitzutheilen*. It seems that Paytas is talking more about the duty of cultivation or the role of feelings in beneficence to others.

66 'Obzwar aber Mitleid (und so auch Mitfreude) mit Anderen zu haben an sich selbst nicht Pflicht ist, so ist es doch thätige Theilnehmung an ihrem Schicksale und zu dem Ende also indirecte Pflicht, die mitleidige natürliche (ästhetische) Gefühle in uns zu cultiviren und sie als so viele Mittel zur Theilnehmung aus moralischen Grundsätzen und dem ihnen gemäßen Gefühl zu benutzen.' Timmermann's (privately communicated) translation. Note that the last instance of '*Gefühl*' is singular and governed by '*aus*' (not '*zur*') (cf. Fahmy 2009, p. 37). It is very likely that Kant means to suggest that we take the singular feeling as conforming to the moral principles rather than aesthetic feelings.

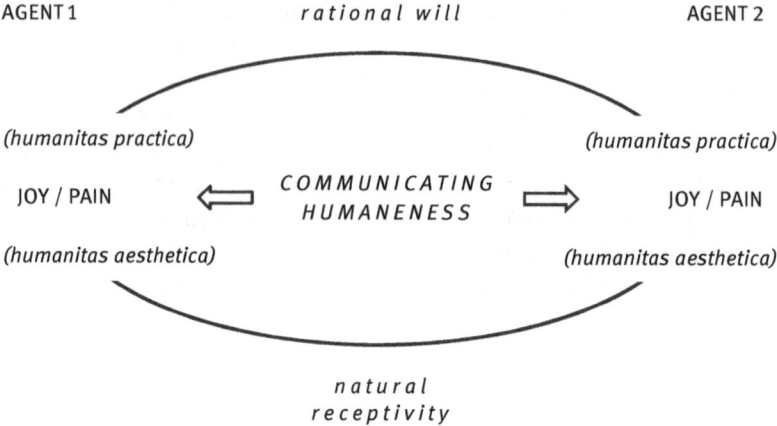

Figure 6. Sympathy

In this passage, it seems that active participation in the fate [*das Schicksal*] of others is a duty of *humanitas practica*, and one might well argue that this includes, besides communication with regard to feelings, actual beneficence (this is indeed how the passage is often read). It is reasonable to suppose that *humanitas practica* is a direct duty of communication [*mittheilen*] with regard to feelings and hence distinct from beneficence. On a broader interpretation, it may perhaps even be thought to include beneficence in such a way that it is then beneficence *with* feelings. This interpretation would unite Fahmy's approach with the previous consensus view.

On the other hand, the cultivation of feelings is here clearly supplementary to the duty of active sympathetic participation. The indirect duty should hence be understood as the cultivation of compassionate natural feelings that may be of use *both* in communication with regard to our feelings *and* in active benevolence or beneficence. But the passage implies further that compassionate feelings should be used as a means to sympathetic participation *from* [*aus*] the feeling that conforms to the moral principles of *humanitas practica*. We can say that *humanitas practica* resides in the free rational will and belongs to practical love, but what the 'feeling' and the 'moral principles' here actually refer to is less clear. The feeling appropriate to moral principles could very well be respect for the moral law. But if the moral principles in question are principles of love of benevolence (as we are, after all, immersed in the rubric of practical love), the feeling could also be love of delight. We know that generally, love and respect are the two feelings that relate to the performance of duties of virtue to others (MM, 6:448.14–15). The idea might be that while the duty of sympathetic participation (as communication) is grounded in pure practical reason, this communication necessarily requires love of benevolence and is profoundly facilitated by love of delight as the feeling of love, for which our mechanical receptivity to the feelings of others serves as a further aid. But this is speculation, and the conservative view would be to say that Kant is talking about respect. I do not know whether the feeling referred to in this last instance is love or respect, and I am happy to leave it open. Remaining at the level of conceptual outline, my point is that we do encounter the notion of cultivation in this context, and that it is relatively important.[67]

In Sections 34 and 35 of the 'Doctrine of Virtue', there is thus a direct duty of sympathetic participation (reciprocal communication with regard to feelings), as well as an indirect duty to cultivate natural sympathetic joy and pity, to be used as means to active rational benevolence and to sympathetic participation from moral principles and the feeling of love or respect. Quite clearly, the duty of sympathy (or *Theilnehmung*) includes feelings, the reciprocal action of communication, and the cultivation of feelings.

4.3 The Feeling-Action-Cultivation Account

To my knowledge, the most general previous account of neighbourly love in Kant's moral philosophy is that proposed by Christoph Horn (2008). I believe I'm now in a position to evaluate what I take to be his main proposition. In 'The Concept of Love in Kant's Virtue Ethics', Horn offers a rich reading of love in several of Kant's works, focusing on *The Metaphysics of Morals*. If I interpret Horn correctly, he ends up viewing love as one of our moral feelings, sug-

---

67 Baron (1995, p. 213) has wondered whether *humanitas aesthetica* is the same as love of neighbour or whether it is 'somewhat narrower'. I believe I can now answer Baron's question. *Humanitas aesthetica* is clearly narrower than love of neighbour in the sense that, systematically, it belongs to love of neighbour through belonging to the duty of *Theilnehmung*, which in turn belongs to practical love – which, alongside the feeling of love, is a primary subset of love of neighbour. On the other hand, since *humanitas aesthetica* is defined in natural, emotive terms, it bears a special relation to the sensory-emotive side of love of neighbour. With this said, *Humanitas aesthetica* is identical neither with inclination-based love of benevolence nor with love of delight; the former is an inclination to benefit the other, and the latter is a particular positive feeling of delight or immediate pleasure occasioned by the other's perfections or humanity (perhaps regardless of whether the other feels any love for us or not), or it is a natural predisposition to have such a feeling. *Humanitas aesthetica* seems to be a more general capacity of receptiveness to the positive and negative feelings of others, such that through *humanitas aesthetica* the feelings of others may occasion similar feelings in us.

gesting that Kant 'admits only an indirect or secondary role for love and other moral feelings.' (Horn 2008, p. 173) I think Horn's proposition is true in the sense that Kant would never accept that morality is objectively grounded in the feeling of love. To equate love with a moral feeling, however, is possible only if we begin by reading 'love' in the unqualified sense (as feeling). Admittedly, there is evidence in support of this interpretation. But in the light of the division between the feeling of love and practical love, which Kant uses throughout his published main works in moral philosophy, Horn's conclusion cannot be considered plausible, since practical love belongs to love as part of the division of love of neighbour. The love of practical love involves goodwill that results in beneficence and hence cannot be reduced to a moral feeling. In other words, systematically, practical love of benevolence cannot be reduced to (even if moral) love of delight. Too much is left out if practical love is omitted from the concept of love.

Before concluding, there is still one final taxonomical worry that I have yet to discuss. Indeed, it is possible that I have misconstrued the taxonomy of love of neighbour altogether, at the foundational level of the basic divisions.[68] For is it not the case that when Kant is talking about love of neighbour he is most often referring to Jesus' love commandment? And doesn't he explicitly say that, unlike practical love from duty, the feeling of love cannot be commanded? And if this is the case, then shouldn't we say that love of neighbour actually consists only of practical love and does not include the feeling of love at all? If Kant's position in the context of neighbourly love were indeed reducible to affirming practical love, this would be the case. In other words, if Kant's position on love of neighbour were identical to his interpretation of Jesus' position, the feeling of love might actually be ruled out of the framework.[69] I do not think, however, that the text warrants this kind of reductivist reading, which would equate love of neighbour with practical love. First, in 'Introduction XII' in the 'Doctrine of Virtue', Kant does use the term *die Liebe des Nächsten* (MM, 6:399.6) to refer to love as a feeling, or more precisely, love as 'a matter of sensation' [*eine Sache der Empfindung*] (MM, 6:401.24), and thus there is direct textual evidence that he does use the term 'love of neighbour' more broadly.[70] Another point is that when Kant speaks

---

[68] I thank Günter Zöller for attacking my position from this perspective at a workshop at the University of Luxembourg in 2015.
[69] This is the position held by Streich, who speaks of 'love of neighbour without love' [*Nächstenliebe ohne Liebe*] (Streich 1924, pp. 29, 39).
[70] Schönecker's position is here similar to those of Zöller and Streich, and Schönecker calls Kant's use of the term *die Liebe des Nächsten* in 'Introduction XII' 'misleading' [*irreführend*]

of love of neighbour, he usually refers to the distinction between pathological love and practical love, or between the feeling of love and practical love, and the text seems always to affirm that it is possible to love others from inclination or with feeling (even though this is not commanded). Thus it is only if we try to narrow Kant's account of love of neighbour down to the love that is commanded that we encounter this taxonomical worry. But if we think that love of neighbour means the same thing as love of other human beings, it is clear that Kant's taxonomy is broader than mere practical love. The third thing is that even if we try to reduce love of neighbour to practical love, in order to appreciate how practical love actually works in Kant's ethics and to account for the notion of cultivation we must still make sense of how the feelings of love operate within this conceptual framework. If love of neighbour includes practical love and practical love produces an inclination of love in the beneficent subject, and if the aesthetic predisposition of the feeling of love is, to begin with, a subjectively necessary precondition of practical love, then shouldn't we say that the feeling of love *somehow* belongs to love of neighbour? I take it that Kant's account of love of neighbour is *not identical* to what Jesus said, and that Kant's framework of love of neighbour does include feeling, action, and cultivation. (For basic divisions, see fig. 7.)

In this chapter, I have argued that love of neighbour is best understood in the light of a general division approach to love in Kant, and that this general division gives support to a new interpretation of love of neighbour in Kant, which I call the feeling-action-cultivation account.

I began by grounding the general division of love in Kant's earlier works, and I problematised it in the *Groundwork* and the second *Critique* from the perspective of love of neighbour. I then showed the existence of the general division of love in the 'Doctrine of Virtue' of *The Metaphysics of Morals*. A comparison of the *Groundwork*, the second *Critique*, and *The Metaphysics of Morals* revealed that while Kant's account of love of neighbour is constantly in flux, some basic elements remain consistent throughout the mature period. If the earlier lectures on ethics are included, it is possible to detect inclination-based love of benevolence, active rational love of benevolence, sensuous love of delight, and intellectual love of delight as all appearing in terms of love of neighbour. Despite all the complexity, in the most general terms of the published main works, love of neighbour divides into the natural feeling or sensation of love (love of delight) and the duty of practical love (love of benevolence). Hence, the general division

---

(Schönecker 2010, p. 153). For a view more like mine, which accepts emotive elements as belonging to love of neighbour, see Green (1992, pp. 276–277).

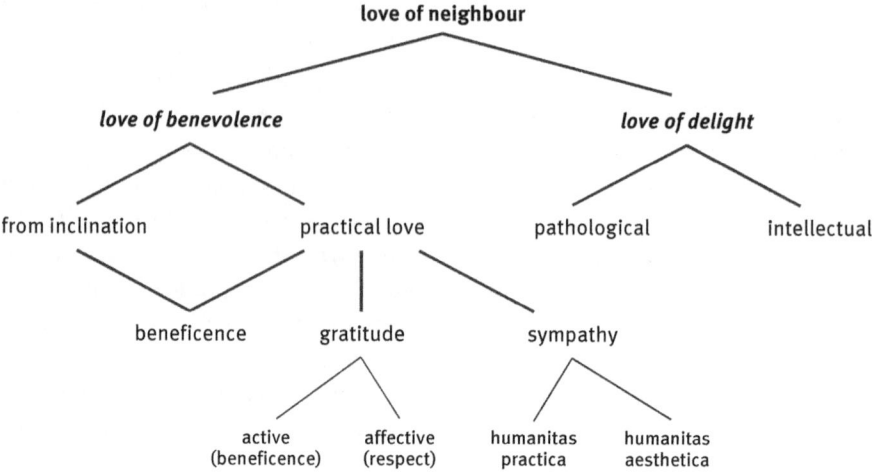

Figure 7. Basic Divisions of Love of Neighbour

of love in love of neighbour consists of a natural, sensory-emotive component and a rational-moral component that emphasises action in furthering the ends of others. I have also analysed how feeling, action, and cultivation figure in the duties of beneficence, gratitude, and sympathy, and in this way I have shown that love of neighbour includes the moral cultivation of the sensory-emotive aspects of our cognitive apparatus. I have thus provided a conceptual outline for the feeling-action-cultivation account of love of neighbour.

5 Love in Friendship

In this final chapter, I discuss love in friendship. Over the past twenty years or so, a fair amount of discussion has gradually accumulated around the notion of friendship in Kant. In the previous treatments, three basic propositions concerning love may be detected. First, some hold that friendship in Kant is always based on the feeling of love (Wood 2015, pp. 12, 16). Second, the majority of scholars take the view that for Kant, friendship essentially or ideally includes a union, or a balance, between love and respect (Paton 1993, p. 137; Denis 2001b, p. 4; Filippaki 2012, p. 35; Moran 2012, p. 170; Baron 2013, p. 381; Wood 2015, p. 4). And third, there are those who posit that for Kant, love is even opposed to the concept of friendship, or at least bracketed from what Kant calls 'moral friendship' (Marcucci 1999, p. 440; Van Impe 2011, p. 137).

What is common to the previous approaches is that they tend not to offer a very detailed or systematic account of how the word 'love' actually operates within the framework of friendship.[1] In particular, there is relatively little uniformity in the literature concerning the logical relations that obtain between the basic components of love's general division within this context, that is, relations between love of benevolence and love of delight. Some accounts leave the love at issue in friendship relatively unspecified (Marcucci 1999; Moran 2012; Van Impe 2011; Baron 2013)[2], some equate love with benevolence (Denis 2001b, p. 7; Moran 2012, p. 173), and some equate it with both benevolence and delight (Paton 1993, p. 138; Wood 1999, pp. 278, 280; Wood 2015, pp. 12–15). Some view the love at issue as practical love (Denis 2001b, p. 7), whereas others see it as the feeling of love (Moran 2012, pp. 197–198; Wood 2015, p. 16).

In what follows, I will offer a systematic reconstruction of Kant's mature philosophy of friendship from the perspective of the concept of love. The basic question to be asked is simply: what does it mean to love one's friends, according to Kant – or how does love function in the context of Kantian friendship? Against the backdrop of the previous discussions, a number of more specific problems must be highlighted: what is the relationship between love and respect in friend-

---

[1] With the possible exception of Wood (1999; 2015), whose account nevertheless has some problems, to which I will return below.
[2] Marcucci and Baron do not discuss the components of the general division. Kate Moran notes that mere 'well-wishing love' in the Vigilantius notes seems weaker than the love at issue in friendship in *The Metaphysics of Morals* (Moran 2012, p. 173), but she doesn't connect this to delight in terms of love (see Moran 2012, pp. 197–198). Van Impe recognises the distinctions between different types of love in the Vigilantius notes but does not analyse their connection to love in friendship in *The Metaphysics of Morals*.

ship? Is friendship based on love or rather on respect, or does it rest equally on both? What role does the general division of love play in loving friendship? Is the love at issue in friendship love of benevolence, love of delight, or both? Is love opposed to the concept of friendship, or at least somehow bracketed in some kinds of friendship? And finally, what is the role of love and friendship in humanity's ascent toward the ideal ethical community?

In general, I will argue that if the systematic or architectonic role of friendship in Kant's philosophy is taken into account and an exegetical interpretation of how the word 'love' operates within the context of friendship is provided, it becomes clear that love (conditioned by respect) marks the path towards the highest good in equal and reciprocal human relationships. Kant is not out to deny the relevance of love but views both love and respect as the necessary conditions of friendship (even though respect has a morally grounding function). Together, love and respect form the relatively sufficient condition of friendship. In friendship we cultivate benevolence (*Liebe des Wohlwollens*) and openheartedness while enjoying each other intellectually (*Liebe des Wohlgefallens*) and respecting appropriate distance. Friendship also serves a mediating role in humanity's ascent toward the ideal moral community (see Wood 2015, p. 6): by cultivating personal friendships, and as friends of humanity in general, we strive to bring about a cosmopolitan community of love and respect. I call this overall interpretation (for which I am indebted to Moran and Wood) *the ascent view of love in Kantian friendship*. When taken alongside analysis of the general division of love in friendship and the previous chapters of the study, the ascent view of love in Kantian friendship serves to corroborate the main claim of this study as a whole: that the general division approach and the ascent view of love are plausible and defensible general notions regarding Kant on love.

I will begin by summarising Kant's discussion of love in friendship prior to *The Metaphysics of Morals*. I will then reconstruct the 'official' mature position in the 'Doctrine of Virtue', paying special attention to the distinction between love and respect and the question of how to interpret the general division of love in this light. Finally, I show how an ascent towards a community of 'cosmopolitan love' may be detected in Kant's accounts of friendship.

5.1 Love in Friendship Prior to *The Metaphysics of Morals*

Depending on which textual source one emphasises, there is more than one possible way to construct the basic taxonomy of friendship in Kant. The three main sources that scholars commonly use in this context are the Collins/Kaehler notes on ethics, the Vigilantius notes on ethics, and the section on friendship at the end of the 'Doctrine of Virtue' of *The Metaphysics of Morals*. I think it is very important to note that the discussion in the 'Doctrine of Virtue' is the only published account of Kant's conception of friendship. Admittedly, the lecture notes give a much richer and more nuanced picture of the topic, and it is not at all surprising that scholars have been keen to draw interpretations on their basis. However, I believe that for an accurate 'official' account of Kant's mature position, one has to emphasise the 'Doctrine of Virtue', even though one should also use the lectures as auxiliary tools for interpretation insofar as they can be harmonised with the published work. I will begin my discussion by considering how the notion of love works in the lecture notes on friendship, before turning to *The Metaphysics of Morals*.

In the Collins notes' discussion of friendship, the basic distinction is between the motives of self-love and morality. Friendship is about overcoming the motive of self-love: it is chosen on moral grounds and involves an inter-individual, reciprocal mode of caring about another's happiness (LE, 27:422–423). In the idea of friendship, 'self-love is swallowed up in the idea of generous mutual love.' (LE, 27:423.8–9)[3] Kant makes clear that friendship is an unattainable idea or ideal that marks 'the maximum of mutual love' [*Das Maximum der Wechselliebe*] (LE, 27:423.37–38), which is a state where one loves the other as oneself.[4]

He divides friendship into three forms or types: those of 'need' [*Bedürfniß*], 'taste' [*Geschmack*], and 'disposition' [*Gesinnung*] (LE, 27:424.38–39). The friendship of need is the 'lowest' or most rudimentary form of friendship and is about mutual help in the satisfaction of material needs. It occurs, for instance, 'when savages go hunting' (LE, 27:425.5)[5]. Every friendship presupposes the friendship of need, which means that friends can rely on each other's help if necessary, even though they should avoid asking for help, because this would threaten the equality of the relationship (LE, 27:425.27–426.21). The friendship of taste is not real friendship but its 'analogue' [*Analogon*] and occurs when persons of different occupations (e.g. a scholar and a soldier) take pleasure in each other's company, perhaps without a view to each other's happiness (LE,

---

3 'die Selbstliebe verschlungen ist in der Idee der großmüthigen Wechselliebe.'
4 The ideal nature of the idea of friendship remains consistent throughout Kant's discussions. For analysis of the idea/ideal distinction in the 'Doctrine of Virtue', see Baron (2013, p. 375). Victoria Wike (2014) provides a helpful account of the notion of 'practical idea' in this context. For my purposes, it is sufficient to note that for Kant, moral or practical ideas come with regulative ideals for action and the cultivation of character, and the idea of friendship means just that: that friendship has an ideal nature we ought to strive to approximate in practice or in some actual human relationships.
5 'Wenn daher Wilde auf die Jagd gehn'.

27:426.21–37). The third form is the friendship of disposition or sentiment [*Sentiment*]. Friendship of disposition is based on the human need to communicate thoughts and feelings to others. In society, our prudential mistrust of others places constraints on the openness of communication, and the friendship of disposition is about establishing the trust required for confiding in another individual, in order to be 'fully in companionship' (LE, 27:427.13)[6]. This sort of friendship is only possible with one or two people (LE, 27:427.20–21), but it may help to open our hearts more generally (LE, 27:428.12–23). It is about 'dispositions of feelings, and not those of actual service.' (LE, 27:426.39–427.1)[7] A condition for the possibility of this 'highest' form of friendship is that the friends share a similar moral outlook: 'They need to have the same principles of understanding and morality, and then they can fully understand each other' (LE, 27:429.6–7)[8].

This brief summary of Kant's early account reveals the unwavering importance of love in Kantian friendship. Friendship is contrasted with self-love, and the idea of friendship is defined as the maximum of mutual love. In a tone reminiscent of Kant's approach to (moral) sexual love in the same lectures, in the idea of friendship one gives oneself (or one's love) to the other and gets oneself back through the other's love. In this way, one may love one's friend 'as oneself', or as much as oneself. (LE, 27:423.37–424.6; cf. 27:388.23–37; see ch. 2.2.3; Korsgaard 1996, p. 195; Langton 2009, pp. 319, 363) The account in Collins also brings with it certain questions that are useful to keep in mind as we proceed towards Kant's later discussions. While the general division of love is already given a formulation in the Collins notes (LE, 27:417–418), Kant does not elaborate on the 'mutual love' [*Wechselliebe*] referred to in the context of friendship in terms of the general division. Indirect evidence suggests that in Collins, the love at issue in friendship is at least love of benevolence, for with regard to the extension of friendships Kant states: 'People do not favour everyone with their benevolence, but would sooner confine themselves, in that respect, to a small circle.' (LE, 27:427.37–39)[9] But I don't see anything to exclude the possibility that friendship in Collins could also include love of delight. Recall that in Col-

---

[6] 'gänzlich in Gesellschaft.' Translation modified. The German *Gesellschaft* is ambiguous between society at large and more restricted companionship or company. Kant might be implying that by harbouring close special bonds we are also better able to participate in society in general (see ch. 5.3).
[7] 'Gesinnungen der Empfindung und nicht der wirklichen Dienstleistungen.'
[8] 'Sie Müssen gleiche Principia des Verstandes und der Moralität haben, denn können sie sich complet verstehn'.
[9] 'Die Menschen machen sich nicht allgemein mit ihrem Wohlwollen, sondern mögen sich gern darin restringiren auf einen kleinen Zirkel.'

lins, *intellectual* love of delight for another's humanity is defined as a duty (see LE, 27:418), and in the 'Doctrine of Virtue', love of delight is a necessary natural predisposition for receptivity to duty (see ch. 4.2.1), and further, one may feel pathological delight in response to the physical perfections of one's friend. Another interesting fact in comparison with Kant's later treatments is that the notion of respect is a lot less prevalent in Collins than in Vigilantius or the 'Doctrine of Virtue'. This is explained at least in part by the fact that Kant's theory of moral autonomy, which relies largely on the notion of respect for the moral law, is not yet in place. We do find the notion of respect in Collins[10], and regarding friendship in particular Kant proposes: 'The name of friendship should inspire respect, and even if our friend has somehow become an enemy, we must still venerate the previous friendship' (LE, 27:429:27–29)[11]. This is an isolated instance of *Achtung*, however, and in the Collins notes friendship is defined nearly exclusively in terms of love.

The Vigilantius notes from 1793–1794 explicitly anticipate the publication of *The Metaphysics of Morals*, and they are particularly interesting when it comes to figuring out the details of Kant's mature conception of love in friendship. As in Collins, the notion of friendship in Vigilantius still involves an ideal that we cannot realise and can only strive for and approach (LE, 27:680.34–35). However, the previous threefold distinction (between friendships of need, taste, and disposition) is no longer explicitly visible, and it is somewhat unclear whether Kant still relies on the previous taxonomy. What is clear is that in Vigilantius friendship is defined explicitly in terms of the general division of love, and the notion of respect now plays a much more important role than it did in Collins. The basic (ideal) definition of friendship in Vigilantius is: 'A complete love of benevolence and delight among equals, in regard to their moral disposition and inclinations.' (LE, 27:680.28–30)[12]

As in Collins, the basic definition of the concept of friendship is here given exclusively in terms of love. It is striking that the ideal of friendship in Vigilantius unites the two aspects of love's general division in a relationship between equal persons. Kant explains that the concept of friendship actually involves five elements, which are combined in the (ideal) definition of friendship: 1) recip-

---

10 See e.g. LE, 27:302.33–34, where pure ethics involves respect.
11 'Man muß Achtung vor vor dem Namen der Freundschaft haben, und wenn auch unser Freund wodurch Feind geworden ist, so müßen wir doch die vorige Freundschaft veneriren'.
12 'eine vollständige Liebe des Wohlwollens und Wohlgefallens gleicher Personen in Ansehung ihrer moralischen Gesinnung und Neigungen.'

rocal love of benevolence; 2) equality; 3) reciprocal possession of each other; 4) reciprocal enjoyment of each other's humanity; and 5) reciprocal love of delight.

Kant describes love of benevolence, the first component of friendship, in a way that is similar to how he depicts it in the context of love of neighbour in *The Metaphysics of Morals*. It is 'the universal duty of love, which we owe to every human being' (LE, 27:675.36–37)[13]. Kant also notes that in comparison with love of delight, this love is 'more closely and strictly coupled with the idea of friendship' (LE, 27:676.10)[14]. Interpreted in terms of the official account of love of benevolence in the 'Doctrine of Virtue', this love would have to be practical love, as it is defined as a duty. But there are interesting differences between Vigilantius and *The Metaphysics of Morals* in terms of how Kant elaborates on the duty. In Vigilantius, 'we must absolutely make it our maxim to promote goodness in others.' (LE, 27:675.38–39)[15] In the 'Doctrine of Virtue', however, love of benevolence is directed to promoting the happiness of others, not their goodness. In the context of friendship, we can understand this in terms of Kant's idea that it is a duty in friendship to point out our friends' flaws, even though this is always risky and must be done cautiously, without loss of respect (MM, 6:470.21–28; LE, 27:685.4–19). In general, benevolence in the intimacy of friendship also involves promoting the moral progress of the other.

The second ideal component says that the friends must be equally capable of promoting each other's well-being in terms of 'powers' [*Kräfte*], 'wealth' [*Reichtum*], and 'influence' [*Einfluß*] (LE, 27:676.29–31). Third, the friends possess each other intellectually or morally, which means that 'each mutually shares in every situation of the other, as if it were encountered by himself' (LE, 27:677.13–14)[16]. Interestingly, Kant here explicitly compares this mutual possession with marriage, but unlike marriage, where the foundation of the union is sexual love, in friendship the 'reciprocal possession is founded [...] on moral principles and a mutual love derived from that' (LE, 27:677.4–5)[17]. This suggests that the sharing and sympathetic concern [*teilnehmen*] are based on rational love of be-

---

[13] 'die allgemeine Pflicht der Liebe, die wir jedem Menschen schuldig sind.'
[14] 'Näher aber und stricte verbindet sich mit der Idee der Freundschaft'.
[15] 'wir das Gute in andern zu befördern uns schlechthin zur Maxime Machen müssen.'
[16] 'wechselseitig an jeder Lage des andern teilnehmen, so als wenn es ihm selbst wiederfahren wäre'.
[17] 'wechselseitige Besitz ist aber auf moralische Grundsätze und eine daher abgeleitete Wechselliebe gegründet'. Another obvious difference in comparison with marriage is that according to Kant (in Vigilantius), the marriage relation is not equal and is instead a relation of '*superioris erga inferiorem*' (LE, 27:683.9), such that the husband is superior to the wife (see ch. 2.2.3). For an elaborated list of six differences between friendship and marriage in Kant, see Denis (2001b, pp. 13–16).

nevolence or intellectual love of delight. The fourth component is 'the reciprocal enjoyment of their humanity' (LE, 27:677.23)[18], which occurs through openhearted communication [*Mitteilung*], where the friends 'communicate not only their feelings and sensations to one another, but also their thoughts.' (LE, 27:677.26–27)[19] It is thus clear that the friends enjoy each other through both the sensory-aesthetic and the rational parts of their humanity. That is, the communication that brings about this enjoyment involves both *humanitas practica* and *humanitas aesthetica* (see MM, 6:456–457; ch. 4.2.2.C) and relates both to rational and to inclination-based loves in accordance with the general division. Kant points out, however, that our friends might become our enemies in the future, and in contrast to the ideal he expresses a significant amount of prudential caution with regard to actually opening up one's heart to another: 'Trust him with caution only, and disclose to him nothing which he might be able to misuse, to the detriment of your respect.' (LE, 27:679.11–13)[20]

The fifth component is 'love for mutual delight' (LE, 27:680.22)[21]. The description of this component is very brief. In the definition, we are told only that it 'lies solely in the intellectual disposition of the friends, engendered through the material of reciprocal esteem, and on this rests the intellectual need for friendship.' (LE, 27:680.23–25)[22] The notion that the love of delight belongs exclusively to 'the intellectual disposition of the friends' must clearly be understood in terms of the Collins notes distinction between sensuous and intellectual delight: 'The love of delight is the pleasure we take in showing approval of another's perfections. This liking may be either sensuous or intellectual.' (LE, 27:417.21–24)[23] I think what is ruled out in Vigilantius is (ideal) friendship's being based on, for instance, sexual inclination, or more generally a delight in the physical perfections of another (since we are, however, dealing with a 'complete love' also with respect to inclinations, the possibility of sensuous delight is not ruled out of the framework altogether – it might be irrelevant, but it is not 'prohibited'). The 'intellectual need' [*das intellectuelle Bedürfnis*] seems to refer to a

---

18 'Der wechselseitige Genuß ihrer Humanität'.
19 'sich nicht allein ihre Gefühle und Empfindungen, sondern auch ihre Gedanken einander mitzuteilen.'
20 'Traue ihm nur mit Vorsicht, entdecke ihm nichts, wovon er mit Nachteil deiner Achtung Misbrauch machen könnte.'
21 'Die Liebe zu dem wechselseitigen Wohlgefallen.' Translation modified.
22 'liegt aber blos in der intellectuellen Gesinnung der Freunde, durch den Stoff wechselseitiger Werthschätzung erzeugt, und darauf beruht das intellectuelle Bedürfnis zur Freundschaft.'
23 'Die Liebe des Wohlgefallens ist das Vergnügen, welches wir haben, den Vollkommenheiten des andern Beyfall zu beweisen. Dieses Wohlgefallen kann sinnlich und intellectual seyn.' See ch. 4.1.

special kind of reciprocal desire to take delight in the moral perfections or the humanity of another. This moral love of delight is not mere respect, for the effect does not seem to be described as essentially humbling, and Kant's use of the word 'need' implies the idea of approaching each other or coming together in communion. Recall that in Collins, the object of intellectual love of delight is at bottom the sheer humanity of another human being (see LE, 27:418.19–20; ch. 4.1). We may thus take it that in friendship 1) reciprocal intellectual love of delight has the humanity of the other person as its object. And, since the definition of love of delight includes pleasure or satisfaction [*Vergnügen*] in the perfections of another (MM, 6:449.17–20; LE, 27:417.21–24), 2) there can be a greater or a lesser amount of intellectual love of delight, depending on the actual moral dispositions of the agents involved.

It seems that this is exactly what Kant has in mind when he speaks of intellectual love of delight in the context of friendship in the Vigilantius notes. The above considerations map very closely onto the fourth ideal component of friendship, where the reciprocal enjoyment of the friends' humanity is brought about by comprehensive communication. In other words, when, as friends, we come to appreciate each other's moral standing or disposition through various acts of communication, we love each other by approving of each other's humanity. The more morally perfect we become, the more complete our intellectual love of delight for each other.[24] In this sense, we may speak of an ascent of love in this context. Our moral ascent has a correlate in the love we experience when we observe each other's moral attributes as unifying through sympathetic communication:

> So when friendship demands a reciprocal love, in that it is based on unity of the moral disposition, this is not a natural inclination, but rather an intellectual unification of the feelings and thoughts of the parties, and the well-being that springs from this constitutes reciprocal love. (LE, 27:682.16–20)[25]

---

[24] Wood goes so far as to say that mutual love of delight 'is the characteristic of friendship that makes it the final end of morality.' (Wood 2015, p. 15) I think Wood is right, if we can take the Vigilantius notes as truly capturing Kant's final position. The reciprocal delight human beings would take in view of each other's moral disposition in the state of the perfect moral community is perhaps best expressive of what Kant might mean by 'moral happiness' as an ideal cosmopolitan notion. (See also Korsgaard 1996, pp. 193–194.)

[25] 'Daher wenn die Freundschaft eine wechselseitige Liebe erfordert, indem sie sich auf Einheit der moralischen Gesinnung stützt, so ist dies nicht natürliche Zuneigung, sondern es ist dies eine intellectuelle Vereinigung ihrer gefühle und Gedanken; und das daraus entsprießende Wohlbefinden macht die Wechselliebe.'

Here, the reciprocal love must be love of delight since the love at issue is defined as well-being that is an effect of intellectual communion. In the context of friendship, love of delight is thus intellectual pleasure rooted in the friends' reciprocal openhearted moral approval of each other (this cannot be directly commanded, since it cannot be a direct duty to be delighted by another's existence).

In the Vigilantius notes, Kant clearly makes use of love's general division, which now lies at the heart of his concept of friendship. Whether Kant still implicitly relies on the threefold taxonomy found in Collins is not clear (nor is it essential to my argument), but it seems that what Kant is mainly talking about in Vigilantius is a kind of 'moral friendship' that matches roughly what in Collins is called 'the friendship of disposition'.[26] In contrast to the Collins notes, respect is now also given a fundamental role. Kant emphasises that in friendship, mutual love must be accompanied by 'mutual respect for humanity in the person of the friend' (LE, 27:683.23–24)[27], and hence respect must restrict reciprocal love. This means that we should not force ourselves on our friends, neither in terms of our beneficence nor in terms of our needy demands, since this will always pose a threat to the equality of the friendship.

5.2 Love in Friendship in *The Metaphysics of Morals*

I will now move on to investigate love and friendship in Kant's mature moral philosophical work. This discussion appears as the 'Conclusion of the elements of ethics' (MM, 6:469.13)[28], and, as mentioned above, it is the only published source for Kant's conception of friendship. I will try to understand the relation between love and respect by first aiming to identify the love at issue in Kant's official account and then taking a careful look at the claims made by Silvestro Marcucci (1999) and Stijn Van Impe (2011), according to whom love is in fact opposed to the concept of friendship, or at least bracketed from what Kant calls 'moral friendship'. The section will show 1) that the love now at issue in friendship is (at least) love of benevolence, and 2) that love is not opposed to the concept of friendship. In fact, the available evidence does not even seem to support the claim that love is bracketed from (any kind of) friendship.

---

26 This link seems to be taken for granted by Moran (2012, p. 170) and Wood (2015, p. 7).
27 'wechselseitiger Achtung für die Menschheit des andern'.
28 'Beschluß der Elementarlehre'.

5.2.1 Identifying the Love at Issue

In the Collins and Vigilantius notes, (ideal) friendship is defined solely in terms of love. In Collins, it is 'the maximum of mutual love' (27:423.37–38); in Vigilantius, 'the complete love of benevolence and delight among equals' (27:680.28–30). In the 'Doctrine of Virtue', the definition is different to the extent that it now explicitly includes respect. First, the heading of Kant's discussion is 'On the Most Intimate Union of Love with Respect in Friendship' (MM, 6:469.14–15)[29]. The definition given immediately under the heading is: '*Friendship* (considered in its perfection) is the union of two persons through equal mutual love and respect.' (MM, 6:469.17–18)[30]

To understand what love Kant is now talking about, it will be helpful to take a closer look at what he says generally about the interplay of love and respect in the 'Doctrine of Virtue'. In the introductory section on the duty of love, Kant explains that the laws of duty are analogous to the laws of physical nature. This nature is governed by the Newtonian forces of attraction and repulsion, and by analogy similar forces operate in the moral realm, where love functions as attraction and respect as repulsion[31]:

> The principle of MUTUAL LOVE admonishes them constantly to come *closer* to one another; that of the RESPECT they owe one another, to keep themselves at a *distance* from one another; and should one of these great moral forces fail, 'then nothingness (immorality), with

---

[29] 'Von der innigsten Vereinigung der Liebe mit der Achtung in der Freundschaft.'
[30] '*Freundschaft* (in ihrer Vollkommenheit betrachtet) ist die Vereinigung zweier Personen durch gleiche wechselseitige Liebe und Achtung.'
[31] For more detailed analysis of the relation between Kant's natural philosophy and moral theory with regard to these Newtonian commitments, see Filippaki (2012). Note that Filippaki correctly distinguishes between the duty of love and the feeling of love. But then she divides the feeling of love into 'aesthetic' and 'moral'; she apparently thinks that the 'aesthetic' feeling of love is love of delight, whereas the 'moral' feeling of love is the natural predisposition to love one's neighbour as described in 'Introduction XII' in the 'Doctrine of Virtue' (Filippaki 2012, pp. 31–32). But in 'Introduction XII', the latter (Filippaki's 'moral love') is explicitly defined as aesthetic. There, love of neighbour is one of the *Ästhetische Vorbegriffe*. A logically less cumbersome interpretation is that 'Introduction XII' speaks of love of delight as an aesthetic predisposition to be subjectively affected by the duty of love (even though Kant's distinction between the feeling of love and the aesthetic capacity (of love) to be affected by duty is not clear). A position similar to mine, which identifies the love in 'Introduction XII' as love of delight, is held by Schönecker (2010; see ch. 4.2.1 above). In the broadest sense, the 'feeling' [*Empfindung, Gefühl, Neigung*] of love can refer at least to 1) the sexual impulse, 2) love of benevolence from inclination, 3) sensuous love of delight, and 4) intellectual or moral love of delight, which includes both the aesthetic predisposition and the actual feeling.

gaping throat, would drink up the whole kingdom of (moral) beings like a drop of water' (if I may use *Haller's* words, but in a different reference). (MM, 6:449.8–15)[32]

The next paragraph goes on to explain that the mutual love now at issue is the duty of love (or practical love) and not the feeling of love. On this basis, it is safe to say that when Kant speaks of love as a moral force (which brings human beings closer to each other) and contrasts this love with respect, the love he is talking about is love of benevolence. The general point is the same as that found in Vigilantius: although we should approach each other through active rational benevolence, our actions must be limited by respect, by means of which we are (ideally) able to secure proper limits of intimacy and to preserve the equality of the relationship. This point is made explicitly in the section on friendship in the 'Doctrine of Virtue': 'For love can be regarded as attraction and respect as repulsion, and if the principle of love bids friends to draw closer, the principle of respect requires them to stay at a proper distance from each other.' (MM, 6:470.4–7)[33] Connecting these two passages in the 'Doctrine of Virtue', we are now in a position to identify the love that is contrasted with respect in the context of friendship as the practical love of benevolence. At issue is the 'principle' [*Princip*] of love. Now I do not want to claim that this is the complete picture of love in friendship, and feelings of love do figure in the framework, but the finding does have consequences with regard to previous research.

Wood holds both that love of benevolence is a feeling and that friendship is based on the feeling of love: 'But friendship is nevertheless based on love as feeling. The feeling of love as benevolence or well-wishing takes the form of friendship when it is reciprocal' (Wood 2015, p. 13). Wood bases his interpretation on the Collins and the Vigilantius notes. When he reaffirms that '[t]he basis of friendship is always love as feeling' (Wood 2015, p. 16), I think he is not sensitive enough to the fact that in the *Groundwork* (GW, 4:399.27–34), the second *Critique* (C2, 5:83.3–12), and *The Metaphysics of Morals* (MM, 6:449.17–22), the practical

---

[32] 'Vermöge des Princips der WECHSELLIEBE sind sie angewiesen sich einander beständig zu nähern, durch das der ACHTUNG, die sie einander schuldig sind, sich im *Abstande* von einander zu erhalten; und sollte eine dieser großen sittlichen Kräfte sinken, "so würde dann das Nichts (der Immoralität) mit aufgesperrtem Schlund der (moralischen) Wesen ganzes Reich wie einen Tropfen Wasser trinken" (wenn ich mich hier der Worte *Hallers*, nur in einer andern Beziehung, bedienen darf).'
[33] 'Denn man kann jene [Liebe] als Anziehung, diese [Achtung] als Abstoßung betrachten, und wenn das Princip der ersteren Annäherung gebietet, das der zweiten sich einander in geziemendem Abstande zu halten fordert'.

love of benevolence is consistently distinguished precisely from love as feeling.[34] Perhaps Wood thinks that practical love is also a feeling, but he doesn't argue for this controversial position (what seems to be missing from Wood's discussion is a distinction between love of benevolence from inclination and love of benevolence as practical love, which distinction can only be grasped by careful comparative analysis of the earlier lectures and the mature published works; see ch. 4). Korsgaard, too, thinks that Kant's discussion of friendship in the 'Doctrine of Virtue' is about feelings (Korsgaard 1996, p. 191), and, like Wood, she does not take into account that the *principle* of love can only be rational love of benevolence (as distinguished from love as feeling). In possible contrast with Wood and Korsgaard, Denis (2001b, p. 4) holds that the love at issue in friendship is indeed practical love, but she does not problematise this view.

The basic difficulty in establishing the operation of the general division of love in the context of friendship in the 'Doctrine of Virtue' is that in the published work, love of delight is not directly mentioned even once. But Kant does (at least indirectly) speak about the feeling of love in this context. He notes that one reason for the unattainability of the ideal of friendship is that it is difficult to account for 'what relation there is in the same person between the feeling from one duty and that from the other (the feeling from benevolence and that from respect)' (MM, 6:469.32–34)[35]. In this passage, benevolence is clearly viewed as a duty, so if it is love of benevolence, it must be practical love. The syntax makes clear that the feeling connected with the duty cannot be identified with the duty: it is a feeling *from* [*aus*] benevolence. We also know that, in effect, practical love (as benevolence leading to beneficence) will also bring about the feeling of love in the broad sense, which can be identified as either love of benevolence from inclination or the pleasure of love of delight (see MM, 6:402.14–21; cf. LE, 27:417.11–19; 27:419.4–7). So it is perhaps implied that love

---

34 See ch. 4.1; cf. ch. 4.2.2. One reason for Wood's seemingly odd view might be that he thinks that love of benevolence is caused by love of delight (Wood 2015, p. 4). It is difficult to make out what Wood bases this claim on since the passages he refers to (LE, 27:416; C3, 5:276; MM, 6:449) do not contain any such idea. The evidence we do have suggests that the feeling of love or inclination-based love can at least sometimes be brought about by practical love (love of benevolence) (MM, 6:402.14–21; cf. LE, 27:419.4–7), even though love of delight is indeed the aesthetic predisposition for the subjective receptivity to the duty of love (MM, 6:399–402). It is also the case that there is such a thing as love of benevolence from inclination (which is not moral). As I have just shown above, however, the love in friendship in the 'Doctrine of Virtue' must be identified at base as practical moral love of benevolence.
35 'noch mehr aber, welches Verhältniß das Gefühl aus der einen Pflicht zu dem aus der andern (z. B. das aus dem Wohlwollen zu dem aus der Achtung) in derselben Person habe'.

of delight also figures in friendship, but in the mature work this love does not seem to be the basis of friendship.

Kant also explicitly denies that the love in friendship could be an 'affect' (MM, 6:471.22–24), but we know from elsewhere that affects are particularly rash emotional states that arise suddenly, drastically hindering one's reflective capacities, and then die out quickly (MM, 6:407.29 ff.; AP, 7:252–253). Kant's rejection of love as affect cannot be taken to imply a general rejection of love as feeling in the context of friendship.

One further place to look for the feeling of love in the 'Doctrine of Virtue' account of friendship stems from Kant's distinction between 'moral' friendship and 'aesthetic' or 'pragmatic' friendship[36]: 'But that (pragmatic) friendship, which burdens itself with the ends of others, although out of love, can have neither the purity nor the completeness requisite for a precisely determinant maxim; it is an ideal of one's wishes[37]' (MM, 6:472.27–30)[38]. Here, the love cannot be the moral love of benevolence since that belongs to moral friendship. But since the love 'burdens itself with the ends of others', it is very likely love of benevolence from inclination. The probable interpretation is that the pragmatic friendship here is roughly equivalent to the earlier friendship of need, but this

---

[36] It is not entirely clear whether 'aesthetic friendship' and 'pragmatic friendship' are the same, but I would argue that they are. The clue comes from Wood, who takes it for granted that 'pragmatic friendship' corresponds to the friendship of need (Wood 2015, p. 7). We must remember that in Kant's original formulation in the Collins notes, the friendship of taste is only an analogue of friendship, whereas the 'friendship of need' is presupposed in every friendship (LE, 27:425.27–28), and the 'friendship of disposition' is very close to his later discussions of moral friendship. So there are actually only two friendships in the original classification, and in the mature philosophy this arguably maps onto the phenomenal-moral or the nature-freedom dualism. If we then look at the distinctions in the 'Doctrine of Virtue' – first between 'moral friendship' and 'aesthetic friendship', and only a moment later between 'moral friendship' and 'pragmatic friendship' – we may plausibly conjecture that 'pragmatic friendship' and 'aesthetic friendship' mean the same thing and that the distinction between 'aesthetic-pragmatic friendship' and 'moral friendship' corresponds roughly to the previous distinction between 'friendship of need' and 'friendship of disposition'. This merely assumes that 'aesthetic' is here read in the sense of 'pertaining to' or 'arising from' natural sensory experience. My identification of 'aesthetic' with 'pragmatic' friendship is highly conjectural and very uncertain, and the main points of the chapter stand or fall regardless of its success.

[37] The fact that pragmatic friendship is defined as an ideal of one's wishes shows (perhaps) that the ideal of friendship includes not only moral perfection and an idealised balance between the dispositions of the friends and all the moral components of the friendship but also a kind of maximum of the sensory-aesthetic elements of friendship.

[38] 'jene aber mit den Zwecken anderer Menschen sich, obzwar aus Liebe, belästigende (pragmatische) kann weder die Lauterkeit, noch die verlangte Vollständigkeit haben, die zu einer genau bestimmenden Maxime erforderlich ist, und ist ein Ideal des Wunsches'.

is uncertain. My point is merely that we do find at least some kind of notion of the feeling of love or pathological love in Kant's official account of friendship, but it seems that this cannot be the proper basis of moral friendship. Of course, the aesthetic predisposition of love of neighbour as love of delight must still be assumed to be generally operative as the *subjective* ground for receptivity to the moral benevolence required for friendship (even though the predisposition is not the *objective* ground of moral benevolence; see ch. 4.2.1).

We are now in a position to make the general claim that if one accepts the Vigilantius notes as a reliable source, the general division of love is strongly present in friendship, such that love of benevolence (as active rational benevolence) is the primary basis of friendship in terms of love, and intellectual love of delight is pleasurable moral approval, which is brought about by intimate sympathetic sharing and communication of feelings and thoughts. But if only the published work is accepted as a source, the existence of love of delight in this specific context looks doubtful, and it is fairly clear that the love which ought to unite with respect in friendship is rational love of benevolence (and not so much love as feeling, though we know generally that the feelings of love are related to, and will also be brought about by, rational love of benevolence).

5.2.2 Can We Bracket Love from Friendship?

Given that Kant's general definitions of friendship always include the word 'love', it is somewhat difficult to understand how love could be 'opposed' to friendship, or 'bracketed' from moral friendship. However, precisely these claims have been made in the literature, and since the claims have not yet been discussed critically by other interpreters, I think it is important to analyse them here (Marcucci 1999; Van Impe 2011). Doing so will also clarify the logical relationship between love and respect in friendship in light of *The Metaphysics of Morals* and the Vigilantius notes.

In the 'Doctrine of Virtue', Kant's emphasis on what he calls 'moral friendship' becomes increasingly clear. As already mentioned, the 'Doctrine of Virtue' contains a division between 'moral' friendship and 'aesthetic' friendship [*ästhetischen*] or 'pragmatic' friendship. Here, Kant defines moral friendship as 'the complete confidence of two persons in revealing their secret judgments and feelings to each other, as far as such disclosures are consistent with mutual respect.' (MM, 6:471.27–29)[39]

It is the above notion of moral friendship that supposedly warrants Marcucci's claim, according to which respect becomes 'very important' and 'love is put between brackets' (Marcucci 1999, p. 440). First, Marcucci seems to think that this is obvious given the definition of moral friendship. Supposedly, if love is not mentioned in the definition of moral friendship, then it does not belong to the concept. But if we unpack the definition, three elements can be recognised within it: 1) complete confidence or trust [*das völlige Vertrauen*]; 2) revealing intimate thoughts and feelings; and 3) respect. Now if we understand moral friendship as a special relationship between individuals, a relationship that does not automatically obtain between all human beings, we must also ask how such a relation is possible – that is, how it can occur. What can it be that draws some individuals closer to each other in such a way that they are able to form this special bond? It might be self-love, but then the relationship would not be moral at heart. Even though Kant does not mention love in the definition cited by Marcucci, he is very clear that there are two forces operative in the moral sphere: respect and love. Now the basis for trusting one another, and sharing intimate thoughts and feelings, might well be respect rather than love. As Kant explains, however, in the moral sphere between individuals respect is a force of *repulsion:* respect keeps individuals at a distance from each other. It seems that on this definition of the moral forces as analogous to Newtonian natural forces, respect cannot be responsible for bringing individuals into an intimate union with each other. But (moral) love as *attraction* establishes just that: 'The principle of MUTUAL LOVE admonishes them constantly to come *closer* to one another' (MM, 6:449.8–10[40]; see 6:470.4–5). Without love, there is no intimate relation to begin with, as the principle that draws individuals closer together is lacking. I do not see anything in the definition of moral friendship that would make it the case that love of benevolence is no longer a necessary condition of friendship. Further, revealing intimate thoughts and feelings and being responsive to our friend's disclosures are dependent on a kind of principled empathy, which Kant elsewhere discusses in terms of 'sympathetic participation' or 'communication' [*Teilnehmung, Mitteilung*]. According to Kant, this 'sympathetic participation' is actually a duty of love, and thus it systematically belongs to the concept of love (see MM, 6:456–457; ch. 4.2.2.C). It can also be argued that the

---

39 'das völlige Vertrauen zweier Personen in wechselseitiger Eröffnung ihrer geheimen Urtheile und Empfindungen, so weit sie mit beiderseitiger Achtung gegen einander bestehen kann.'
40 'Vermöge des Princips der WECHSELLIEBE sind sie angewiesen sich einander beständig zu nähern'.

trust or confidence required for moral friendship gradually comes about via the pleasure taken in mutual moral approval, which in the Vigilantius notes is discussed by Kant in terms of love of delight. It does not follow from the mere fact that love is not mentioned in the definition of moral friendship that love is bracketed from its concept, since the conceptual components of moral friendship (excluding respect) seem to assume or presuppose the presence of love. However, if the notion of love is qualified to mean merely the pathological feeling of love, then one may say that love is bracketed from moral friendship – but Marcucci does not analyse the divisions of love.[41]

Marcucci's second point is that 'Kant even opposes love to the concept of friendship itself' (Marcucci 1999, p. 440). How does he argue for this? As evidence for his point, Marcucci quotes the following passage from the 'Doctrine of Virtue': '"the relation between the protector as benefactor, and the protected, as obligated to gratitude, is [...] *a relation of mutual love, but not of friendship*, because their mutual respect is not the same in both parties."' (Marcucci 1999, p. 440; citing MM, 6:473.5 – 8; Marcucci's italics) Unfortunately, other than citing the passage, Marcucci does not elaborate on the rationale for his conclusion. Kant's point in the passage is that a friend of human beings [*Freund der Menschen*][42] not only loves human beings but also takes into account 'the *equality* among them' [*der Gleichheit unter Menschen*] (MM, 6:473.1 – 2). The reason for this is that the relationship between a mere benefactor and the person being protected is not one of friendship, since even though love is present, respect is not equal. It appears to me that Marcucci's argument is a *non sequitur:* from the premises that 1) equal respect is a necessary condition of friendship and 2) not all relations of love are relations of friendship, it does not follow that 3) love is opposed to the concept of friendship.

More recently, Marcucci's arguments have been repeated by Van Impe (2011). Van Impe derives the bulk of his discussion on love in friendship directly from Marcucci's article, and the only new consideration that he adds is the claim that 'Kant already seemed to consider this bracketing of love in the late *Lectures on Ethics* by arguing that "only a reciprocal love *based on* [*gebaut*][43] respect can secure a lasting friendship"' (Van Impe 2011, p. 137; citing LE, 27:683.16 – 18; Van Impe's italics). Even though Van Impe does not say it, I gather that he thinks that

---

41 He is especially unaware of the existence of love of benevolence and its operation in friendship.
42 I discuss the notion of a 'friend of human beings' in more detail in ch. 5.3.
43 The verb Kant uses to describe the relationship between love and respect in that passage is *bauen*, to build, and thus a more appropriate translation might be 'a reciprocal love built on respect'.

if love were somehow reducible to respect or based on respect, then love would be bracketed, and friendship would essentially be about respect. The context of the passage cited by Van Impe is Kant's idea that friendship is similar to marriage because both involve a unity of persons, but that unlike marriage, where the wife respects the husband more than the husband respects the wife, in friendship the parties are obligated to equally 'preserve the other's respect' (LE, 27:683.15)[44]. From this the passage quoted by Van Impe above follows as a conclusion. But does it follow from the passages that love is a mere effect of respect or that we should think that love is ultimately only about respect?

Elsewhere in Vigilantius Kant describes the appropriate relationship between love and respect by noting that love must be 'coupled' with or 'tied to' [*verbunden seyn*] respect (LE, 27:682.24–25), or that respect must impose a 'restriction' [*Einschränkung*] on love (LE, 27:682.35). It is also the case that intellectual love of delight is grounded in a moral 'esteem' [*Schätzung*] (see 27:680.23–25) for another person's characteristics. Further, in 'The End of All Things', Kant holds that respect is a necessary condition of 'true love' [*wahre Liebe*] (8:337.33–34; see Wood 2015, p. 4). Thus it is indeed the case that, for Kant, respect plays a crucial and fundamental role in any kind of moral love. From a moral perspective, respect (for the moral law, for the humanity of the other) forms the ground level on which subsequent moral relations are then built. But if we think of the basic distinction between (moral) love and respect in *The Metaphysics of Morals*, we see that love is still *attraction* and respect is still *repulsion:* the two are clearly different. We must also remember that through the aesthetic predisposition of love of delight, even the duty of love retains a special connection to love as a sensory-aesthetic phenomenon: the bond between love of benevolence and love of delight is close and complicated, and the interrelations between the elements of the general division of love cannot be thought of in terms of mere respect. It therefore seems to me that even though respect is morally primary (as Wood (2015, p. 4) correctly notes), love cannot be reduced to respect. The identification or equation of love with respect would go against one of the most fundamental distinctions of Kant's moral philosophy. Therefore, love cannot be bracketed this way.

The last thing to remember is that during Kant's mature period, the basic definitions of friendship are 'the complete love of benevolence and delight among equals' (LE, 27:680.28–30) and 'the union of two persons through equal mutual love and respect.' (MM, 6:469.17–18) If Kant thought that love (in general) was opposed to the concept of friendship or bracketed from some

---

44 'des Andern Achtung zu erhalten'.

kind of friendship, this would introduce a fairly dramatic contradiction between Kant's definitions and his actual position.[45] As I have shown, the evidence does not support this interpretation. The exegetical stance favours the view that in Kant's philosophy of friendship, love and respect must be balanced.

5.3 Cosmopolitan Friendship: Love's Ascent Toward the Ideal Moral Community

Throughout his discussions, Kant makes clear that friendship is an intimate and special bond between a very limited number of individuals: friendship is usually held between two people. In such relationships, the friends embark on a joint journey of moral progress, sharing their personhood, correcting each other's faults cautiously (through love of benevolence limited by respect), and taking intellectual pleasure (love of delight) in each other's improving moral attributes. They help each other to cultivate virtue and to approach moral happiness in an openhearted union (see Moran 2012, pp. 168 ff.). As they become more virtuous, their active rational benevolence (*Liebe des Wohlwollens*) for each other grows stronger and more consistent, and the more virtuous they are, the greater the delight (*Liebe des Wohlgefallens*) they take in their friendship. In this way, friendship, and the love that grows as the friends make progress, marks a path towards the highest good between two people (see Moran 2012, p. 203). We may therefore speak of an *ascent of love in friendship*, which means that by attending to the duty of friendship, the friends' love becomes greater and more perfect.

But there is another notion closely interwoven with friendship that is more general and that points towards an ascent of love as a more communal or even cosmopolitan notion. This is the notion of being a friend of human beings [*Menschenfreund*], not in an intimate relationship with someone in particular but with regard to humanity as a whole. I will end my discussion with an investigation of what it means to be a friend of human beings from the perspective of love.

In the Collins notes, Kant points out that as society arises from natural crudity or 'savagery' to civilisation, people tend to have fewer intimate friendships: 'The more civilized men become, the more universal their outlook, and the smaller the incidence of special friendships. The civilized man seeks a general friend-

---

[45] Neither Marcucci nor Van Impe addresses this point.

ship and amenity, without having special ties.' (LE, 27:428.30 – 33)[46] This sort of 'universal friendship' [*Die allgemeine Freundschaft*] does not mean that the civilised person would be friends with everyone, but rather concerns a capacity for establishing friendship with anyone. Such people are few in number: they are optimistic and possess benevolence, good-heartedness, understanding, and taste. Kant calls them 'world citizens' [*Weltbürger*]. (LE, 27:430.11– 27)

In the Vigilantius notes, Kant's attitude toward universal concern or affection is more ambivalent. Here he warns that 'the friend to all humanity [...] cannot fail to dissipate his inclination through its excessive generality, and quite loses any adherence to individual persons, [...] though there is no denying that the great value of human love rests in the general love of humanity as such.' (LE, 27:673.25 – 31)[47] So while we should aim for a generalised attitude of love, in doing so we risk losing proper sight of particular individual relationships. Kant explains further that in contrast to intimate reciprocal friendship, which involves *amor bilateralis*, being everyone's friend is a unilateral disposition of love: *amor unilateralis*. This unilateral love, which we ought to cultivate, is here clearly love of benevolence: 'being everyone's friend; it does no more than formulate the duty to harbor love of benevolence for the happiness of others, and is quite different from the term: to *make friends* with everyone.' (LE, 27:676.19 – 22)[48]

Kant's definitive account of what it is to be a friend of human beings is given at the very end of his discussion of friendship in the 'Doctrine of Virtue'. This brief discussion serves as important evidence for Kant's cosmopolitan outlook as a part of his philosophy of love. On this basic definition, a friend of human beings [*Menschenfreund*] is 'one who takes an affective[49] interest in the well-being of all human beings (rejoices with them)' (MM, 6:472.34 – 35)[50]. Kant

---

46 'Je mehr die Menschen gesittet werden, desto allgemeiner werden sie, und desto weniger finden die besondern Freundschaften statt. Der Gesittete sucht eine allgemeine Freundschaft und Annehmlichkeit, ohne besondre Verbindung zu haben.'
47 'der Weltliebhaber [...], da es nicht fehlen kann, daß er seine Neigung durch die zu große Allgemeinheit zerstreut und eine einzelne persönliche Anhänglichkeit ganz verliert, [...] obgleich nicht zu leugnen ist, daß der große Wert der Menschenliebe in der allgemeinen Menschenliebe als solcher beruht.' Note that the word Kant uses in this passage is not *Menschenfreund* but *Weltliebhaber*.
48 'jedermanns Freund seyn: er drückt nichts mehr, als die Pflicht aus, Liebe des Wohlwollens für anderer Menschen Glück zu hegen, und ist ganz verschieden von dem Ausdruck: mit jedermann *Freundschaft stiften*.'
49 Translating *ästhetisch* as affective with Baron, who follows Gregor's 1991 translation (Baron 2013, p. 366). Note that Gregor's Cambridge translation contains a typo: she uses 'effective' for *ästhetisch* when she clearly means 'affective'.
50 'der, welcher an dem Wohl aller Menschen ästhetischen Antheil (der Mitfreude) nimmt'.

then introduces a distinction between being a *Menschenfreund* and a *Freund der Menschen* (both of which translate to 'friend of human beings'), such that being a friend of human beings [*Freund der Menschen*] also involves 'thought and consideration for the *equality* among them' (MM, 6.473.1–2; see 6:450,19–22)[51]. It is this concern for equality that in the 'Doctrine of Virtue' prevents us from equating a friend of human beings with someone who merely possesses love of benevolence.[52] The beneficence of a friend of human beings [*Freund der Menschen*] includes 'a necessary humbling of oneself' [*eine nothwendige Herablassung*] (MM, 6:473.8–9). It is also noteworthy that the interest described is affective or sensory-aesthetic, which might include love of benevolence from inclination or even pathological love of delight in the love of the friend of human beings.[53]

In an appendix immediately following the discussion on being a friend of human beings, Kant explicitly connects the cosmopolitan outlook with the cultivation of virtue in reciprocal relationships, suggesting that, indirectly, this cultivation of reciprocity will lead to what is best for the world. I wish to quote this passage at length:

> It is a duty to oneself as well as to others not to *isolate* oneself [...] but to use one's moral perfections in social intercourse [...]. While making oneself a fixed center of one's principles, one ought to regard this circle drawn around one as also forming part of an all-inclusive circle of those who, in their disposition, are citizens of the world – not exactly to promote as the end what is best for the world but only to cultivate what leads indirectly to this end: to cultivate a disposition of reciprocity – agreeableness, tolerance, mutual love and respect [...]. (MM, 6:473.16–24)[54]

---

51 'die Vorstellung und Beherzigung der *Gleichheit* unter Menschen'.
52 The notion of *Menschenfreund* is similar in the *Groundwork*, in that in the first instance the interest the *Menschenfreund* has for the well-being of others is aesthetic – or to be precise, based on inclination (GW, 4:398.20–34). It is unclear whether the concept of *Menschenfreund* in the *Groundwork* is also supposed to cover the case where the agent lacks sympathy but is nonetheless beneficent from duty (see GW, 4:398.32–399.2).
53 The references to *Menschenfreund* in the *Groundwork* point in this direction (GW, 4:398.20–34).
54 'Es ist Pflicht sowohl gegen sich selbst, als auch gegen Andere, mit seinen sittlichen Vollkommenheiten unter einander Verkehr zu treiben [...], sich nicht zu *isoliren* [...]; zwar sich einen unbeweglichen Mittelpunkt seiner Grundsätze zu machen, aber diesen um sich gezogenen Kreis doch auch als einen, den den Theil von einem allbefassenden der weltbürgerlichen Gesinnung ausmacht, anzusehen; nicht eben um das Weltbeste als Zweck zu befördern, sondern nur die wechselseitige, die indirect dahin führt, die Annehmlichkeit in derselben, die Verträglichkeit, die wechselseitige Liebe und Achtung'.

5.3 Cosmopolitan Friendship: Love's Ascent Toward the Ideal Moral Community — 165

The passage contains a sweeping vision from the narrowly circled individual to 'what is best for the world' [*das Weltbeste*]. Since Kant obviously thinks that the highest good is what is best, I take it that his notion of 'what is best for the world' can here be identified as the complete highest good (moral happiness of all rational beings) with regard to humans. However, Kant seems to think that this communal notion of 'what is best for the world' can only be approached indirectly, through social intercourse. The basic components of friendship are explicitly operative in this cultivation of sociality: reciprocity as disposition and mutual love and respect (alongside agreeableness and tolerance). It seems that by cherishing and cultivating love and respect in friendships, and by gradually opening our 'narrower circles' to people who are not yet our friends, we ascend towards the ideal ethical community. As Langton reminds us, friendship unlocks 'the "prison" of the self' (Langton 2009, p. 319; see MM, 6:472.12–13). Its concept provides us with an ideal model of what human relationships in general ought to be like. Wood suggests that it is friendship 'that is ultimately to encompass the entire human race' (Wood 1999, p. 316). Of course, cosmopolitan friendship will not contain the level of intimacy characteristic of certain exclusive relationships, but we may say that close to the end of the 'Doctrine of Virtue', Kant clearly gives the elements of friendship a decisive role when describing the ascent to what is best for the world. In the words of Moran, friendship is crucial for 'our progress toward the highest good' (Moran 2012, p. 203).[55]

We are now in a position to appreciate the place of love in friendship in the overall structure of love in Kant's philosophy. We have come far from the crude natural impulses of self-love and have temporarily bracketed love of God because we are now considering human moral relations. We now know that love of neighbour alone is not able to bring about the highest communal good – since love of neighbour as such is not necessarily properly conditioned by respect. Only the profound acknowledgment of the equality of all human beings can make one a friend of human beings – one in whom the disposition of love towards the whole race is conditioned by respect for the humanity of all. By becoming friends of human beings, we gradually ascend toward a cosmopolitan community of love and respect. But most of us may only become friends of

---

[55] At this stage, I do not feel a need to distance myself from the basic positions formulated by Wood and Moran with respect to the relationship between friendship and the highest good. I don't feel the urge for 'scientific dissensus'. I take it that their generic propositions are viable and can be adopted by my ascent account of love in friendship. What remains novel in my approach is the relatively detailed analysis of the concept of love in this context, as well as the more general ascent model of love, to which the ascent of love in cosmopolitan friendship belongs – as the final element of the general model.

human beings by engaging in particular friendships, where we approach moral happiness by cultivating intimate love of benevolence conditioned by intimate respect. In order to ascend toward the highest communal good, we must gradually open up our love and extend it to those who are not yet our friends. This we can only learn to do while loving our friends and by striving to love people around us more wisely.

Conclusion

In the Preface to the first edition of the *Religion*, Kant explains that while the foundation of morality abstracts from the presentation of ends altogether, it is still impossible for humans to *act* without conceiving of ends. Because human beings naturally desire happiness, morality leads to the presentation of the final regulative end as the highest good, which is perfect happiness proportionate to perfect virtue. With regard to this highest purpose, Kant writes in a footnote: 'Now in this end human beings seek something that they can *love*, even though it [*the end*] is being proposed to them through reason alone.' (R, 6:7.26–28fn.)[1] What is this love that human beings seek in the highest good? And how should one understand the connection between love and the highest good anyway?

I believe there is no simple answer to this question, and Kant does not spell out what he means by love in the above quotation.[2] There are passages in 'The End of All Things' (1794) that seem somewhat parallel to the above. In that essay, Kant explains that while respect is morally primary and a necessary condition of 'true love' [*wahre Liebe*], love, 'as a free assumption of the will of another into one's maxims, is an indispensable complement to the imperfection of human nature' (8:338.3–5)[3]. Given the context, Kant is probably talking about incorporating the will of God (see ch. 3.1), but he might also be talking about love more generally. In human terms, I take the quotation to mean that love makes us attentive to the ends of others in a way that goes beyond mere acknowledgement of their autonomy. Furthermore, Kant tells us in 'The End of All Things', without love we will not be moral gladly [*gern*]. Without love, our moral actions will be scanty [*kärglich*], and we will be prone to evade what duty commands. (LE, 8:338.6–7) Based on what Kant says above and elsewhere, it appears that love, too, is essential for the moral lives of imperfect rational creatures like us.

---

1 'An diesem Zwecke nun, wenn er gleich durch die bloße Vernunft ihm vorgelegt wird, sucht der Mensch etwas, was er *lieben* kann'.
2 David Sussman thinks this love is close to 'pathological love', by which he means 'a love that fully integrates our feelings, our imagination, and our attention around a particular object of concern' (Sussman 2010, p. 143). While Sussman's understanding of 'pathological love' seems to be broader than what we find in Kant's texts, and while I would not rule out practical love as quickly as Sussman does (especially given that the object of love here is proposed 'through reason alone'), I nevertheless think that from a broader, non-exegetical perspective, Sussman is on the right track.
3 'als freie Aufnahme des Willens eines Andern unter seine Maximen, ein unentbehrliches Ergänzungsstück der Unvollkommenheit der menschlichen Natur'.

Respect is fundamental, but mere respect for the law will not account for our loving God or furthering the happiness of other human beings. By itself, respect can never make us happy. Without love, the path toward the highest good will not be open.

But what love are we *now* talking about? In 'The End of All Things', Kant explains further that there is something loveable or loveworthy [*liebenswürdig*] about the Christian religion, which stems from Christianity's 'liberal way of thinking' [*die liberale Denkungsart*] (8:338.23). Apparently, it is the freedom one feels in the choice of making the highest good one's ultimate end that occasions love in this context. In 'The End of All Things', this love is ultimately connected to God's benevolent disposition towards humanity. It seems that the ideas of God's benevolence and kindness [*Gütigkeit*] are what make Christianity loveable (8:338.23–339.19; cf. C2, 5:131.10–19). But can we interpret the love that human beings seek in the highest good as reducible to rational Christian love of God? Given the ambiguous nature of the highest good (see ch. 1.3), and given the results of my investigations of love in the five chapters of this study, this kind of reduction would be an oversimplification of Kant's position.

At least if we emphasise striving towards the highest good in this life and infinite, intergenerational, species-level progress, and if we put less weight on speculations regarding what the supposedly incorporeal afterlife is like, then we should understand the love that we ultimately seek as a more holistic notion, as the regulative, rational ideality that all the different aspects of love bring with them in their own contexts. In this way, the love we seek is the ideal union of the different kinds of love that condition our lives. In self-love, we seek happiness and love from others; in sexual love, a moral union of two people to procreate and enjoy each other's sexual attributes. In love of God, we strive to practice our duties to others *gladly*, with a benevolent disposition pleasing to God, which disposition at its ideal endpoint could also be called *love for the law*. In love of neighbour, we take delight in the humanity of others and aim to love them practically with active rational benevolence, adopting their ends as our own. In love in friendship, we strive to cultivate benevolence and delight in intimate, equal, and reciprocal human relationships while seeking to open up this love so that one day we might all be able to call each other friends as members of the human race.

In this study, I have provided the first systematic, exegetical, and comprehensive account of the concept of love as it appears in the philosophy of Kant. In particular, I have formulated and defended two major claims: 1) The *general division of love* in Kant is a key to understanding love in Kant; and 2) the *ascent model of love* is a plausible general model of love in Kant. I have not claimed that my approach and results are flawless, absolutely comprehensive, or all-encom-

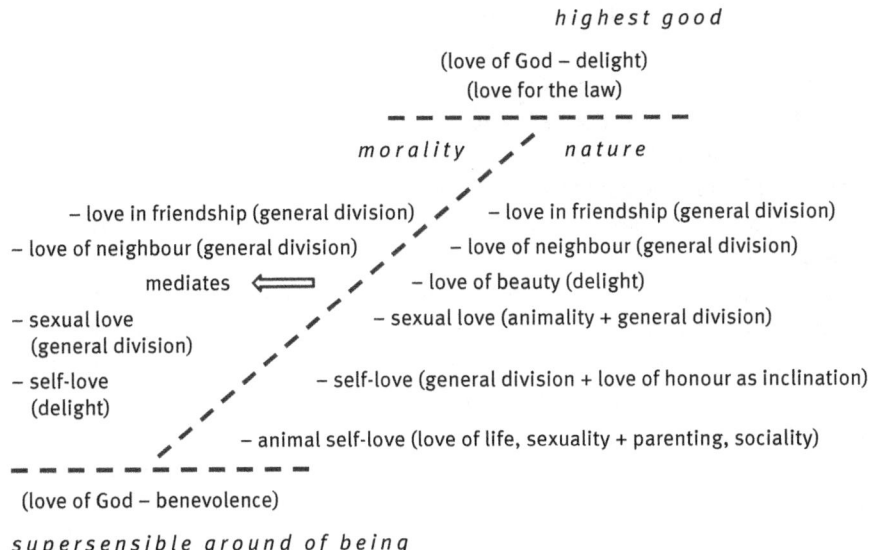

Figure 8. Love's Ascent in Kant

passing, and that no more work remains to be done within this field of enquiry. I am also not saying that the conceptual framework of love in Kant cannot be construed otherwise. In future research on this topic, further historical considerations might be added, so that Kant's conceptions can be situated within a broader framework of love in the history of Western philosophy. On the other hand, Kant's multifaceted concept could be used to formulate a post-Kantian philosophy of love – with a view to contemporary developments, for instance in evolutionary philosophy or analytical metaphysics and ethics. In this work, I am saying merely that the general division of love does provide a key to understanding love in Kant, that the aspects I discuss do exist in Kant's philosophy, and that, taken together, it is rational to view these aspects in terms of an ascent from crude natural impulses to the highest moral-physical good in cosmopolitan friendship. (See fig. 8; see also Appendix.)

I want to conclude by noting the existence of an aspect of love that underlies the whole conceptual framework presented here. This is the foundational method that necessarily connects my approach with that of Kant's. The research object and the method of the study are both in themselves instances of *love of wisdom* – that is, philosophy. Historically, it was the philosophical method that brought about rational enquiry into love in the first place. Sure, people of the distant past experienced love, worshipped love, and so on. But it was Empedocles who first introduced the notion of love in a post-Milesian naturalist framework, in order to make sense of love's place in *physis*, or nature. The status of love as an object of rational enquiry was solidified by Plato. I feel that even though we now have a concept of love in Kant, we must still ask: what is Kant's conception of *love of wisdom*? Surely, if we are after a Kantian philosophy of love, the aspects of love and the ascent model must be understood in this context. But does Kant even speak of love of wisdom? And can we say that 'philosophy' itself is a kind of love, for Kant, if he does not use the word '*Liebe*' in the immediate vicinity of '*Philosophie*'?

Kant's references to 'philosophy' in his writings are abundant, and a proper account of the various connotations would be a topic for another volume. However, the notion of love of wisdom comes up only once in the published works, and an analysis of this passage will be the final task of the present study. The passage appears in the second *Critique,* close to the beginning of the 'Dialectic of Pure Practical Reason'. The issue is once again the highest good, and more precisely how to determine its idea practically. Here, Kant calls this determination the 'doctrine of wisdom' [*Weisheitslehre*], or the science of 'philosophy' in the 'ancient sense':

> We would do well to leave this word [*philosophy*] in its ancient sense, as a *doctrine of the highest good* so far as reason strives to bring it to *science*. For, on the one hand the restrictive condition attached would suit the Greek expression (which signifies love of *wisdom*) while yet sufficing to embrace under the name of philosophy love of *science* and so of all speculative rational cognition insofar as it is serviceable to reason for that concept as well as for the practical determining ground, without letting us lose sight of the chief end on account of which alone it can be called doctrine of wisdom. (C2, 5:108.18–28)[4]

What to make of this somewhat obscure passage and the place of love within it? In general, we know from elsewhere that Kant understands philosophy as the system of rational cognition from[5] concepts (see e.g. C1, A713/B741; A732/B760; A838/B866; C3, 5:171) and that philosophy divides into theoretical and practical

---

4 'Es wäre gut, wenn wir dieses Wort bei seiner alten Bedeutung ließen, als eine *Lehre vom höchsten Gut*, so fern die Vernunft bestrebt ist, es darin zur *Wissenschaft* zu bringen. Denn einestheils würde die angehängte einschränkende Bedingung dem griechischen Ausdrucke (welcher Liebe zur *Weisheit* bedeutet) angemessen und doch zugleich hinreichend sein, die Liebe zur *Wissenschaft*, mithin aller speculativen Erkenntniß der Vernunft, so fern sie ihr sowohl zu jenem Begriffe, als auch dem praktischen Bestimmungsgrunde dienlich ist, unter dem Namen der Philosophie mit zu befassen, und doch den Hauptzweck, um dessentwillen sie allein Weisheitslehre genannt werden kann, nicht aus den Augen verlieren lassen.'
5 I do not wish to debate the correctness of this English preposition. In different places, Kant uses at least the German prepositions *aus, nach,* and *durch* to describe how rational cognition pertains to concepts in terms of philosophy.

philosophy, where theoretical philosophy concerns what *is* and practical philosophy what *ought to be* (e.g. C3, 5:171; C1, A840/B868; see also A850/B878).⁶ In the first *Critique* he states: 'Philosophy refers everything to [the goal of] wisdom. But it does so by the path of science' (C1, A850/B878)⁷. Often when Kant speaks of wisdom or being wise, he connects it with the idea of God. We view the world as if it were the product of a wise author or supreme wisdom, organised purposively with regard to the highest good (see e.g. C1, A628/B656; A687/B715; A699/B727; A826/B854; C2, 5:130–131; C3, 5:444). Sometimes wisdom is discussed as the union of benevolence and justice (C3, 5:444; see 8:257 ff.), and for humans, wisdom is an ideal (C1, A569/B597). In terms of these divisions, the main point that Kant seems to be making with regard to love of wisdom in the second *Critique* is that there are two different kinds of components in the doctrine of wisdom and the way it relates to the highest good: there is a theoretical or scientific aspect and a practical aspect. In the second *Critique*, wisdom is given a twofold definition explicitly in terms of the theoretical/practical distinction: '*wisdom* considered theoretically signifies *cognition of the highest good*, and practically *the fitness of the will for the highest good*' (C2, 5:130.36–131.1⁸; see also 8:256fn.; cf. 8:336.5–7). And at the very end of the conclusion of the second *Critique*:

> In a word, science (critically sought and methodically directed) is the narrow gate that leads to the *doctrine of wisdom*, if by this is understood not merely what one ought *to do* but what ought to serve *teachers* as a guide to prepare well and clearly the path to wisdom which everyone should travel (C2, 5:163.27–31)⁹.

If we now interpret the passage on love of wisdom in the light of the above reflections, the theoretical and practical components of the doctrine of wisdom within the passage are brought to the fore, which helps to clarify the word 'love' in that context. First, the 'restrictive condition' [*einschränkende Bedingung*] must refer to science: the doctrine of wisdom must be scientific. However, this is

---

6 Kant also uses 'transcendental philosophy', 'speculative philosophy', and 'philosophy of nature' to refer to the theoretical approach, and 'moral philosophy' to refer to practical philosophy. As I have already mentioned, however, fine-grained analysis of these taxonomies is beyond my current aims.
7 'Diese [Philosophie] bezieht alles auf Weisheit, aber durch den Weg der Wissenschaft'.
8 '*Weisheit*, theoretisch betrachtet, *die Erkenntniß des höchsten Guts* und praktisch *die Angemessenheit des Willens zum höchsten Gute* bedeutet'.
9 'Mit einem Worte: Wissenschaft (kritisch gesucht und methodisch eingeleitet) ist die enge Pforte, die zur *Weisheitslehre* führt, wenn unter dieser nicht blos verstanden wird, was man *thun*, sondern was *Lehrern* zur Richtschnur dienen soll, um den Weg zur Weisheit, den jedermann gehen soll, gut und kenntlich zu bahnen'.

merely *love of science* if the practical determining ground [*praktische Bestimmungsgrund*] is not included. The context implies that the 'chief end' [*Hauptzweck*] is the end of the highest good, and so we can say that it is *love of science*, together with the practical determining ground (both taken with reference to the highest good) that warrants the term 'love of wisdom'. Immediately following this passage Kant continues to explain that, from another perspective, wisdom can be understood ideally as an object of striving in the sense that its completion is an objective rational idea, 'whereas subjectively, for a person, it is only the goal of his unceasing endeavors' (C2, 5:109.2–3)[10].

This, I think, is connected to how Kant uses the word 'love' in the context of 'love for the law'. In these two cases (love for the law and love of wisdom), love seems to denote an ideal object of striving. The object is, at least to a certain extent, a product of our reason; it is in a sense 'higher' than us, something the completion of which we lack. This reminds one of how *Eros* is discussed in the *Symposium*. Kant's love of wisdom seems to denote precisely this relation of lack, of pursuit, of strenuous ascent towards what we do not yet possess. It therefore seems that, in addition to the most paradigmatic cases of love, where the object of love is a person and the love relation is described directly in terms of the general division of love, there is another category of objects, where the object of love is a rational ideal that one desires and for which one strives. In comparison with animality, these ideals are at the other end of the spectrum of desire (cf. ch. 1.1). The ideal cases are not paradigm examples of love in Kant precisely for the reason that they lack an explicit connection to the general division, but they cannot be glossed as mere anomalies, because the links or the structural similarities to the historical tradition of the concept of love, especially in the case of love of wisdom, are strong and obvious. If we think of Kant's discussions of God as divine wisdom or as possessing supreme wisdom, we can venture one step further and say, in terms of the general division, that there is no wisdom without love of benevolence, which in religious terms is the ground of creation. In general, love of wisdom signifies the unity of theoretical cognition and practical cognition in the pursuit of the highest good.

In summary, the aim of this book was to provide the first relatively detailed analysis of the concept of love in Kant's philosophy. Utilising a novel general division approach, I have pointed out how love permeates human existence from the strongest impulses of nature to the highest ideals of moral happiness. Overall, my analysis has yielded a new ascent model of love in Kant. More generally, I be-

---

[10] 'subjectiv aber, für die Person, nur das Ziel seiner unaufhörlichen Bestrebung ist'.

lieve that I have shown that a comprehensive understanding of Kantian ethical life is not possible without acknowledging the multidimensional presence of love.

To step outside of the exegetical framework, I wish to say, as a person and a philosopher, that love is a very complicated concept, and concepts in general are not the kinds of things one grasps in the blink of an eye. Concepts are *propositional worlds*, worlds one needs to explore without rushing, in peace and quiet, if one is to come to terms with them – even though it all happens in the midst of life. The acquisition, construction, or comprehension of a concept is very much about *coming to inhabit relatively stable propositional structures with one's mind*. We study reality, strive to understand it, and place our sentences under its rubric. A concept as broad and complex as love can only be approached gradually, and when one has understood *something*, it does not imply a complete comprehension of the phenomenon. Love is a concept with both theoretical and practical elements. We can formulate descriptive propositions, or more widely, models that outline the structural features of the concept of love, and attempt to say things regarding what love is, in the philosophy of Kant, for example. We can observe reality and use our reason to criticise the proposition sets we have suggested, and through the critical process we may replace our old propositions with better ones. Or we may be able to formulate propositions that *endure*, that come to appear as sustainable within the critical process, the process through which our fallible knowledge of reality grows and becomes more refined. But this is not something for us to decide as authors of propositions, but a matter of later critical scrutiny. In practice, learning love is slow. It is not a sprint but a never-ending walk towards what is better. A climb, if you will. While a given proposition can perhaps be theoretically understood relatively quickly – it can be analysed and given an interpretation within its model or a confined semantic universe – this is not so when it comes to incorporating the concept of love into one's life or one's moral behaviour. The normative requirements of the model must be embraced in a deeper way. That is the difficult part, and that is where the real work of practical philosophy happens. What is comforting is that, due to the very slow acquisition process of the concept of love, the love thus obtained is not a mere chimera but instead becomes an integral part of one's life experience. One must become so immersed in the practical concepts one studies that the concepts become dynamic forms of life that are communicated both rationally and emotionally on various levels of interaction with others. Love is real. It is not a dream one wakes up from in the morning, so that then it's gone. It is here, in this reality and on this planet, and it can be studied. If we persevere and work diligently to understand love better, we are entitled to the rational hope that gradually, over the course of time, reality will become more loving.

Appendix: Explanatory Note on Fig. 8

It is quite possible that after reading the whole study, fig. 8 (see Conclusion) will appear self-explanatory. However, despite their illustrative power, diagrams necessarily lose so much information that I think a brief explanatory note on the *pictorial image* of the ascent model is in order, if for no other reason than to preserve some of the ambiguity that interpretative positions within the exegetical study of Kant necessarily involve. There are also some philosophical commitments made in fig. 8 that should not appear necessary based on the propositional results of the chapters, and I wish to clarify these points of emphasis, which are prevalent in the image but may seem to contrast or be ambiguous in relation to what I say about a particular aspect of love in my actual discussion.

I note that love of God and love for the law are bracketed as idealisations, and they depict rational conditions and endpoints of moral striving. It should be transparent that arational animal mechanical self-love lies completely on the side of nature and consists of the impulses of love of life, narrow sexual love and parenting, and instinctive sociality. The self-love for which reason is required can be viewed in terms of nature through the general division, so that love of benevolence is wanting things to go well for oneself and to be loved by others and love of delight is taking pleasure in those maxims. As an inclination, love of honour belongs taxonomically to this level of self-love, whereas 'true' love of honour is a function of respect. In the study I argued that in certain moral contexts it is possible to speak of a moral self-love, which would have to be love of delight, but I feel the need to emphasise that for most purposes it suffices to say more robustly that there is nothing moral about self-love as such. The model should never be read as saying that just any kind of delight in oneself counts as moral self-love. Based on textual evidence, broad sexual love unites the animal impulse especially with love of benevolence, but as I don't see anything to prevent pathological delight, inclination-based benevolence, and intellectual delight from entering the picture, I present the general division on both sides of the nature-freedom distinction. We can hardly avoid being physically delighted by another's physical perfections when such perfections appear, and moral benevolent love will bring about feelings of love (as inclinations to beneficence). Moreover, we take intellectual delight in the humanity and moral perfection of all human beings. Love of beauty appears to lie somewhere between nature and morality (intellectual delight in other human beings hovers somewhat similarly on both sides of the nature-freedom divide). In the figure, I treat love of neighbour and love in friendship in the same lenient way as sexual love. Even though only rational benevolence is commanded, and the predisposition of love of neighbour is (perhaps intellectual) love of delight, I allow inclination-based benevolence and pathological delight to figure in the framework, as these loves, too, will at least occasionally appear when one strives to love others morally. With friendship, published evidence only allows for talk of moral love of benevolence, but the same considerations apply (the lectures further emphasise intellectual love of delight).

In life, all the loves are intermingled, and the higher, actual (non-ideal) aspects in fig. 8 reflect that view. Supposing one strives to become more moral, I see no need to restrict the operation of the general division of love with regard to the highest loves, as long as feelings of love are conditioned by respect, which is the phenomenal foundation of morality. I realise that for a hard-boiled exegete, my treatment of the loves in sexual love, love of neighbour, and love in friendship in fig. 8 may appear too unrestricted or permissive, and if this is the case, I recommend going back to the chapters for my exact positions with reference to given aspects. Fig. 8 is merely a skeleton for understanding love in Kant, and *meaning* has to be sought elsewhere. What I do wish to portray with the figure, in addition to the basic conceptual structure of the ascent model, is that while the general division of love will figure differently and with varying emphases with respect to different aspects of love, we will experience both moral and natural benevolence and delight in loving relationships, and this (as long as respect is in place) is as such nothing to be worried about. The loves are beautiful, and it is a wonderful feature of life that they are there. Finally, the inclusive attitude of fig. 8 with respect to the loves related to other persons is also meant to depict the insight of the mature Kant, according to whom the frame of mind connected to love is *liberal*.

Bibliography

Source

Kant, I. Gesammelte Schriften Hrsg.: Bd. 1–22 Preussische Akademie der Wissenschaften, Bd. 23 Deutsche Akademie der Wissenschaften zu Berlin, ab Bd. 24 Akademie der Wissenschaften zu Göttingen. Berlin 1900 ff.

References to Kant's works are by the volume, page and line in the Academy Edition. Citations in the Critique of Pure Reason follow the A/B standard. The below abbreviations are used:

(LE) 1997 (1762–1794). *Lectures on Ethics.* Heath, Peter (Tr.). Heath, Peter/Schneewind, J.B. (Eds.). Cambridge: Cambridge University Press.
(LA) 2013 (1772–1789). *Lectures on Anthropology.* Louden, Robert et al. (Tr.). Louden, Robert/Wood, Allen (Eds.). Cambridge: Cambridge University Press.
(C1) 1996 (1781/1787) *Critique of Pure Reason.* Pluhar, Werner (Tr.). Indianapolis: Hackett.
(GW) 2011 (1786). *Groundwork of the Metaphysics of Morals.* Gregor, Mary/Timmermann, Jens (Tr.). Timmermann, Jens (Ed.). Cambridge: Cambridge University Press.
(C2) 1996 (1788). *Critique of Practical Reason.* In: *Practical Philosophy.* Gregor, Mary (Tr./Ed.). Cambridge: Cambridge University Press.
(C3) 1987 (1790). *Critique of Judgment.* Pluhar, Werner (Tr.). Indianapolis: Hackett.
(R)   1996 (1793). *Religion within the Boundaries of Mere Reason.* In: *Religion and Rational Theology.* Wood, Allen/Di Giovanni, George (Tr./Eds.). Cambridge: Cambridge University Press. / 2009. *Religion within the Bounds of Bare Reason.* Pluhar, Werner (Tr.). Indianapolis: Hackett.
(MM) 1996 (1797). *The Metaphysics of Morals.* In: *Practical Philosophy.* Gregor, Mary (Tr./Ed.). Cambridge: Cambridge University Press.
(AP) 2007 (1798). *Anthropology from a Pragmatic Point of View.* Louden, Robert (Tr.). In: *Anthropology, History and Education.* Gregor, Mary et al. (Tr.). Zöller, Günter/Louden, Robert (Eds.). Cambridge: Cambridge University Press.

Dictionaries, Encyclopaedias and Other Aids:

Adelung, Johann (1811): *Grammatisch-Kritisches Wörterbuch der Hochdeutschen Mundart.* http://woerterbuchnetz.de/Adelung/, visited on 31 August 2016.
Grimm, Jacob/Wilhelm (1852 ff.): *Deutsches Wörterbuch von Jacob Grimm und Wilhelm Grimm.* http://woerterbuchnetz.de/DWB/, visited on 31 August 2016.
Malter, Rudolph/Ruffing, Margit (1999): *Kant-bibliographie 1945–1990.* Begr. von Malter R., Hrsgb. von Ruffing, M. Frankfurt am Main: Klostermann.
Merriam-Webster's (2015): *Dictionary.* http://www.merriam-webster.com/dictionary/, visited on 31 August 2016.
Naragon, Steve (2006): *Kant in the Classroom. Materials to Aid the Study of Kant's Lectures.* http://users.manchester.edu/FacStaff/SSNaragon/Kant/home/index.htm, visited on 31 August 2016.

Willaschek, Marcus et al. (Eds.) (2015): *Kant-Lexikon*. Hrsgb. von Willaschek, Marcus/Stolzenberg, Jürgen/Mohr, Georg/Bacin, Stefano. Berlin: De Gruyter.

Other References

van Ackeren, Marcel/Sticker, Martin (2015): 'Kant and Moral Demandingness'. In: *Ethical Theory and Moral Practice* 18/1, pp. 75–89.
Allison, Henry (2009): 'Teleology and History in Kant: The Critical Foundations of Kant's Philosophy of History'. In: Oksenberg Rorty, Amelie/Schmidt, James (Eds.): *Kant's Idea for a Universal History with a Cosmopolitan Aim. A Critical Guide*. Cambridge: Cambridge University Press, pp. 24–45.
Allison, Henry (2011): *Kant's Groundwork for the Metaphysics of Morals. A Commentary*. Oxford: Oxford University Press.
Aristotle (1984): *The Complete Works of Aristotle. The Revised Oxford Translation*. 2 vols. Barnes, Jonathan (Ed.). Princeton: Princeton University Press.
Vanden Auweele, Dennis (2014): 'For the Love of God: Kant on Grace'. In: *International Philosophical Quarterly* 54/2, pp. 175–190.
Axinn, Sidney (1994): *The Logic of Hope*. Amsterdam: Rodopi.
Baron, Marcia (1995): *Kantian Ethics Almost without Apology*. Ithaca: Cornell University Press.
Baron, Marcia (1997): 'Kantian Ethics and Claims of Detachment'. In: Schott, Robin (Ed.): *Feminist Interpretations of Immanuel Kant*. Pennsylvania: The Pennsylvania State University Press, pp. 145–170.
Baron, Marcia/Fahmy, Melissa (2009): 'Beneficence and Other Duties of Love in *The Metaphysics of Morals*'. In: Hill, Thomas (Ed.): *The Blackwell Guide to Kant's Ethics*. West Sussex: Wiley-Blackwell, pp. 211–228.
Baron, Marcia (2013): 'Friendship, Duties Regarding Specific Conditions of Persons, and the Virtues of Social Intercourse (TL 6:468–474)'. In: Trampota, Andreas/Sensen, Oliver/Timmermann, Jens (Eds.): *Kant's 'Tugendlehre'*. Berlin: De Gruyter, pp. 365–382.
Baxley, Anne Margaret (2005): 'The Practical Significance of Taste in Kant's *Critique of Judgment*: Love of Natural Beauty as a Mark of Moral Character'. In: *The Journal of Aesthetics and Art Criticism* 63/1, pp. 33–45.
Beck, Lewis White (1963): *A Commentary on Kant's Critique of Practical Reason*. Chicago: The University of Chicago Press.
Cassirer, Ernst (1981): *Kant's Life and Thought*. Haden, James (Tr.). New Haven: Yale University Press.
Cohen, Alix (2014): 'The Anthropology of Cognition and Its Pragmatic Implications'. In: Cohen, Alix (Ed.): *Kant's Lectures on Anthropology. A Critical Guide*. Cambridge: Cambridge University Press, pp. 76–93.
Denis, Lara (1999): 'Kant on the Wrongness of "Unnatural" Sex'. In: *History of Philosophy Quarterly* 16/2, pp. 225–248.
Denis, Lara (2001a): *Moral Self-Regard. Duties to Oneself in Kant's Moral Theory*. New York: Garland.
Denis, Lara (2001b): 'From Friendship to Marriage: Revising Kant'. In: *Philosophy and Phenomenological Research* 63/1, pp. 1–28.

Denis, Lara (2014): 'Love of Honor as a Kantian Virtue'. In: Cohen, Alix (Ed.): *Kant on Emotion and Value*. Basingstoke: Palgrave Macmillan, pp. 191–209.
Denis, Lara/Sensen, Oliver (2015): 'Introduction'. In: Denis, Lara/Sensen, Oliver (Eds.): *Kant's Lectures on Ethics. A Critical Guide*. Cambridge: Cambridge University Press, pp. 1–12.
DiCenso, James (2012): *Kant's Religion within the Boundaries of Mere Reason. A Commentary*. Cambridge: Cambridge University Press.
Edwards, Jeffrey (2000): 'Self-Love, Anthropology, and Universal Benevolence in Kant's Metaphysics of Morals'. In: *The Review of Metaphysics* 53/4, pp. 887–914.
Engstrom, Stephen (2010): 'The *Triebfeder* of Pure Practical Reason'. In: Reath, Andrews/Timmermann, Jens (Eds.): *Kant's Critique of Practical Reason. A Critical Guide*. Cambridge: Cambridge University Press, pp. 90–118.
Fahmy, Melissa (2009): 'Active Sympathetic Participation: Reconsidering Kant's Duty of Sympathy'. In: *Kantian Review* 14/1, pp. 31–52.
Fahmy, Melissa (2010): 'Kantian Practical Love'. In: *Pacific Philosophical Quarterly* 91, pp. 313–331.
Filippaki, Eleni (2012): 'Kant on Love, Respect and Friendship'. In: Heidemann, Dietmar (Ed.): *Kant Yearbook 4/2012*. Berlin: De Gruyter, pp. 23–48.
Frierson, Patrick (2011): 'Introduction'. In: Kant, I.: *Observations on the Feeling of the Beautiful and Sublime and Other Writings*. Frierson, Patrick/Guyer, Paul (Eds.). Cambridge: Cambridge University Press, pp. vii–xxxv.
Frierson, Patrick (2014): 'Affects and Passions'. In: Cohen, Alix (Ed.): *Kant's Lectures on Anthropology. A Critical Guide*. Cambridge: Cambridge University Press, pp. 94–113.
Fromm, Erich (1957): *The Art of Loving*. London: Unwin Books.
Goethe, Johann (1970): 'A Letter to C.G. Voigt 19. Dec. 1798'. In: *Goethes Briefe in Drei Bänden* I. Berlin: Aufbau-Verlag, pp. 517–518.
Goy, Ina (2014): 'Über Liebe. Kant's Auseinandersetzung mit den biblischen Geboten der Gottesliebe, der Nächstenliebe und der Selbstliebe'. In: *Philosophical Readings* 6/1, pp. 6–29.
Green, Ronald (1992): 'Kant on Christian Love'. In: Santurri, Edmund/Werpehowski, William (Eds.): *The Love Commandments. Essays in Christian Ethics and Moral Philosophy*. Washington, D.C.: Georgetown University Press, pp. 261–280.
Grenberg, Jeanine (2014): 'All You Need Is Love?'. In: Cohen, Alix (Ed.): *Kant on Emotion and Value*. Basingstoke: Palgrave Macmillan, pp. 210–223.
Grenberg, Jeanine (2015): 'Love'. In: Denis, Lara/Sensen, Oliver (Eds.): *Kant's Lectures on Ethics. A Critical Guide*. Cambridge: Cambridge University Press, pp. 239–255.
Guyer, Paul (2009): 'The Crooked Timber of Mankind'. In: Oksenberg Rorty, Amelie/Schmidt, James (Eds.): *Kant's Idea for a Universal History with a Cosmopolitan Aim. A Critical Guide*. Cambridge: Cambridge University Press, pp. 129–149.
Guyer, Paul (2010): 'Moral feelings in the *Metaphysics of Morals*'. In: Denis, Lara (Ed.): *Kant's Metaphysics of Morals. A Critical Guide*. Cambridge: Cambridge University Press, pp. 130–152.
Herman, Barbara (1993): 'Could It Be Worth Thinking About Kant on Sex and Marriage'. In: Antony, Louise/Witt, Charlotte (Eds.): *A Mind of One's Own. Feminist Essays on Reason and Objectivity*. Boulder: Westview Press, pp. 53–72.
Hill, Thomas (1993): 'Beneficence and Self-Love: A Kantian Perspective'. In: *Social Philosophy & Policy* 10/1, pp. 1–23.

Horn, Christoph (2008): 'The Concept of Love in Kant's Virtue Ethics'. In: Betzler, Monika (Ed.): *Kant's Ethics of Virtue*. Berlin: De Gruyter, pp. 147–173.
Hull, Isabel (1996): *Sexuality, State, and Civil Society in Germany, 1700–1815*. Ithaca: Cornell University Press.
Hutcheson, Francis (1990): *An Inquiry into the Original of our Ideas of Beauty and Virtue*. In: *Collected Works of Francis Hutcheson*. Vol. I. Fabian, Bernhard (Ed.). Hildesheim: Georg Olms Verlag.
Van Impe, Stijn (2011): 'Kant on Friendship'. In: *International Journal of Arts & Sciences* 4/3, pp. 127–139.
Johnson, Robert (1997): 'Love in Vain'. In: *The Southern Journal of Philosophy* 36, pp. 45–50.
Kain, Patrick (2003): 'Prudential Reason in Kant's Anthropology'. In: Jacobs, Brian/Kain, Patrick (Eds.): *Essays on Kant's Anthropology*. Cambridge: Cambridge University Press, pp. 230–265.
Kneller, Jane (2006): 'Kant on Sex and Marriage Right'. In: Guyer, Paul (Ed.): *The Cambridge Companion to Kant and Modern Philosophy*. Cambridge: Cambridge University Press, pp. 447–476.
Kong, Camilla (2012): 'The Normative Source of Kantian Hypothetical Imperatives'. In: *International Journal of Philosophical Studies* 20/5, pp. 661–690.
Korsgaard, Christine (1996): *Creating the Kingdom of Ends*. Cambridge: Cambridge University Press.
Korsgaard, Christine (1997): 'The Normativity of Instrumental Reason'. In: Cullity, Garrett/Gaut, Berys (Eds.): *Ethics and Practical Reason*. Oxford: Clarendon Press, pp. 215–254.
Langton, Rae (2009): *Sexual Solipsism. Philosophical Essays on Pornography and Objectification*. Oxford: Oxford University Press.
de Levie, Dagobert (1963): 'Zum Begriff und Wort "Menschenliebe"'. In: *Monatshefte*, 55/6, pp. 301–311.
Lewis, C.S. (1963): *The Four Loves*. London: Fontana Books.
Marcucci, Silvestro (1999): '"Moral Friendship" in Kant'. In: *Kant-Studien* 90, pp. 434–441.
Marwah, Inder (2013): 'What Nature Makes of Her: Kant's Gendered Metaphysics'. In: *Hypatia* 28/3, pp. 551–567.
Michalson, Gordon (1990): *Fallen Freedom. Kant on Radical Evil and Moral Regeneration*. Cambridge: Cambridge University Press.
Mikkola, Mari (2011): 'Kant On Moral Agency and Women's Nature'. In: *Kantian Review* 16/1, pp. 89–111.
Miller, Robert (1985): *The Law of Love. A Revised Kantian Approach to Morality and Religion*. PhD thesis. Departent of Philosophy, Monash University.
Moors, Martin (2007): 'Kant on: "Love God above all, and your neighbour as yourself"'. In: Boros, Gábor/De Dijn, Herman/Moors, Martin (Eds.): *The Concept of Love in 17th and 18th Century Philosophy*. Leuven: Leuven University Press, pp. 245–269.
Moran, Kate (2012): *Community and Progress in Kant's Moral Philosophy*. Washington, D.C.: The Catholic University of America Press.
Moran, Kate (2014): 'Delusions of Virtue: Kant on Self-Conceit'. In: *Kantian Review* 19/3, pp. 419–447.

Nagl-Docekal, Herta (1997): 'Feminist Ethics: How It Could Benefit from Kant's Moral Philosophy'. In: Schott, Robin (Ed.): *Feminist Interpretations of Immanuel Kant*. Pennsylvania: The Pennsylvania State University Press, pp. 101–124.
O'Regan, Cyril (2011): 'The Trinity in Kant, Hegel, and Schelling'. In: Emery, Gilles/Levering, Matthew (Eds.): *The Oxford Handbook of the Trinity*. Oxford: Oxford University Press, pp. 254–266.
Palmquist, Stephen (2000): *Kant's Critical Religion. Volume Two of Kant's System of Perspectives*. Aldershot: Ashgate.
Palmquist, Stephen (2009): 'Introduction'. In: Kant, I.: *Religion within the Bounds of Bare Reason*. Pluhar, Werner (Tr.). Indianapolis: Hackett, pp. xv–xlix.
Pasternack, Lawrence (2014): *Kant on Religion within the Boundaries of Mere Reason*. New York: Routledge.
Paton, Herbert (1947): *The Categorical Imperative. A Study in Kant's Moral Philosophy*. London: Hutchinson & Co.
Paton, Herbert (1993): 'Kant on Friendship'. In: Badhwar, Neera (Ed.): *Friendship. A Philosophical Reader*. Ithaca, N.Y.: Cornell University Press, pp. 133–154.
Paytas, Tyler (2015): 'Rational Beings with Emotional Needs: The Patient-Centred Grounds of Kant's Duty of Humanity'. In: *History of Philosophy Quarterly* 32/4, pp. 353–374.
Petschauer, Peter (1986): 'Eighteenth-Century German Opinions about Education for Women'. In: *Central European History* 19/3, pp. 262–292.
Plato (2006): *Plato on Love*. Reeve, C.D.C. (Ed.). Indianapolis: Hackett.
Powell, Samuel (2011): 'Nineteenth-Century Protestant Doctrines of the Trinity'. In: Emery, Gilles/Levering, Matthew (Eds.): *The Oxford Handbook of the Trinity*. Oxford: Oxford University Press, pp. 267–280.
Rauscher, Frederick (2012): 'Kant's Social and Political Philosophy'. In: *The Stanford Encyclopedia of Philosophy* (Summer 2012 Edition). Zalta, Edward (Ed.). http://plato.stanford.edu/archives/sum2012/entries/kant-social-political/, visited on 31 August 2016.
Reardon, Bernard (1988): *Kant as Philosophical Theologian*. Houndmills: MacMillan.
Reath, Andrews (2006): 'Kant's Theory of Moral Sensibility: Respect for the Moral Law and the Influence of Inclination'. In: Reath, Andrews: *Agency & Autonomy in Kant's Moral Theory. Selected Essays*. Oxford: Oxford University Press, pp. 8–32.
Rousseau, Jean-Jacques (1974): *Émile*. Foxley, Barbara (Tr.). London: Everyman's.
Rousseau, Jean-Jacques (1997): *The Discourses and Other Early Political Writings*. Gourevitch, Victor (Tr./Ed.). Cambridge: Cambridge University Press.
Russell, Bertrand (1945): *A History of Western Philosophy*. New York: Simon and Schuster.
Schleiermacher, Friedrich (1799): 'Review of Kant's Anthropology'. In: *Athenäum 2.2*. Berlin: Heinrich Frolich, pp. 300–306. https://ia800209.us.archive.org/29/items/athenaeumeineze01schlgoog/athenaeumeineze01schlgoog.pdf, visited on 24 August 2016.
Schneewind, J.B. (1997): 'Introduction'. In: Kant. I.: *Lectures on Ethics*. Heath, Peter (Tr.). Heath, Peter/Schneewind, J.B. (Eds.). Cambridge: Cambridge University Press, pp. xiii–xxvii.
Schneewind, J.B. (2009): 'Good out of Evil: Kant and the Idea of Unsocial Sociability'. In: Oksenberg Rorty, Amelie/Schmidt, James (Eds.): *Kant's Idea for a Universal History with a Cosmopolitan Aim. A Critical Guide*. Cambridge: Cambridge University Press, pp. 94–111.

Schott, Robin (1997) (Ed.): *Feminist Interpretations of Immanuel Kant*. Pennsylvania: The Pennsylvania State University Press.
Schröder, Hannelore (1997): 'Kant's Patriarchal Order'. Gircour, Rita (Tr.). In: Schott, Robin (Ed.): *Feminist Interpretations of Immanuel Kant*. Pennsylvania: The Pennsylvania State University Press, pp. 275–296.
Schönecker, Dieter (2010): 'Kant über Menschenliebe als moralische Gemütsanlage'. In: Archiv für Geschichte der Philosophie 92/2, pp. 133–175.
Schönecker, Dieter (2013): 'Duties to Others From Love (TL 6:448–461)'. In: Trampota, Andreas/Sensen, Oliver/Timmermann, Jens (Eds.): *Kant's 'Tugendlehre'*. Berlin: De Gruyter, pp. 309–341.
Shell, Susan (2015): 'Anlage'. In: Willaschek, Marcus/Stolzenberg, Jürgen/Mohr, Georg/Bacin, Stefano (Eds.): *Kant-Lexikon*. Berlin: De Gruyter, pp. 96–97.
Šimfa, Elvira (2013): 'Being Moral and Loving Oneself. Kant on Morality, Self-Love and Self-Conceit'. In: *Religious–Philosophical Articles (Religiskifilozofiski raksti)* 16, pp. 90–110.
Singer, Irving (2009): *The Nature of Love 2. Courtly and Romantic*. Cambridge, MA: The MIT Press.
Smit, Houston/Timmons, Mark (2011): 'The Moral Significance of Gratitude in Kant's Ethics'. In: *The Southern Journal of Philosophy* 49/4, pp. 295–320.
Smit, Houston/Timmons, Mark (2015): 'Love of Honor, Emulation, and the Psychology of the Devilish Vices'. In: Denis, Lara/Sensen, Oliver (Eds.): *Kant's Lectures on Ethics. A Critical Guide*. Cambridge: Cambridge University Press, pp. 256–276.
Soble, Alan (2003): 'Kant and Sexual Perversion'. In: *The Monist* 86/1, pp. 55–89.
Stevenson, Leslie (2014): 'Kant on Grace'. In: Michalson, Gordon (Ed.): *Kant's Religion within the Boundaries of Mere Reason. A Critical Guide*. Cambridge: Cambridge University Press, pp. 118–136.
Streich, Detlev (1924): *Der Begriff der Liebe bei Kant*. Doctoral Dissertation. Greifswald: Ernst Moritz Arndt Universität. Note: only available copy in the archives of the Berlin Staatsbibliothek.
Sussman, David (2010): 'Something to Love: Kant and the Faith of Reason'. In: Bruxvoort Lipscomb, Benjamin/Krueger, James (Eds.): *Kant's Moral Metaphysics. God, Freedom and Immortality*. Berlin: De Gruyter, pp. 133–148.
von Tevenar, Gudrun (2006): 'Gratitude, Reciprocity, and Need'. In: *American Philosophical Quarterly* 43/2, pp. 181–188.
Timmermann, Jens (2007): *Kant's Groundwork of the Metaphysics of Morals. A Commentary*. Cambridge: Cambridge University Press.
Timmermann, Jens (2009): 'Acting from Duty: Inclination, Reason and Moral Worth'. In: Timmermann, Jens (Ed.): *Kant's 'Groundwork of the Metaphysics of Morals': A Critical Guide*. Cambridge: Cambridge University Press, pp. 45–62.
Timmermann, Jens (2011): 'Introductory Note'. In: Kant, I.: *Groundwork of the Metaphysics of Morals*. Gregor, Mary/Timmermann, Jens (Tr.). Timmermann, Jens (Ed.). Cambridge: Cambridge University Press, pp. ix–xiv.
Timmermann, Jens (2013): 'Kantian Dilemmas? Moral Conflict in Kant's Ethical Theory'. In: *Archiv für Geschichte der Philosophie* 95, pp. 36–64.

Timmermann, Jens (2016a): 'Kant's Journey from the Canon to the *Groundwork*'. In: Bacin, Stefano/Sensen, Oliver (Eds.): *The Emergence of Autonomy*. Cambridge: Cambridge University Press (forthcoming).

Timmermann, Jens (2016b): 'Kant Über Mitleidenschaft'. In: *Kant-Studien* 107/4, pp. 729–732.

Tomasi, Gabriele (2015): 'Kant on Beauty and Love'. In: The Proceedings of the 12th International Kant Conference. Berlin: De Gruyter (forthcoming).

La Vopa, Anthony (2005): 'Thinking about Marriage: Kant's Liberalism and the Peculiar Morality of Conjugal Union'. In: *The Journal of Modern History* 77/1, pp. 1–34.

Wike, Victoria (2014): 'Kantian Friendship: Duty and Idea'. In: *Diametros* 39, pp. 140–153.

Wood, Allen (1970): *Kant's Moral Religion*. Ithaca: Cornell University Press.

Wood, Allen (1991): 'Unsociable Sociability: The Anthropological Basis of Kant's Ethics'. In: *Philosophical Topics* 19/1, pp. 325–351.

Wood, Allen (1996): 'Self-love, Self-benevolence, and Self-conceit'. In: Engstrom, Stephen/Whiting, Jennifer (Eds.): *Aristotle, Kant, and the Stoics: Rethinking Happiness and Duty*. Cambridge: Cambridge University Press, pp. 141–161.

Wood, Allen (1999): *Kant's Ethical Thought*. Cambridge: Cambridge University Press.

Wood, Allen (2007): 'Translator's Introduction to Conjectural Beginning of Human History'. In: Kant, I.: *Anthropology, History and Education*. Gregor, Mary et al. (Tr.). Zöller, Günter/Louden, Robert (Eds.). Cambridge: Cambridge University Press, pp. 160–162.

Wood, Allen (2008): *Kantian Ethics*. Cambridge: Cambridge University Press.

Wood, Allen (2009): 'Kant's Fourth Proposition: the Unsociable Sociability of Human Nature'. In: Oksenberg Rorty, Amelie/Schmidt, James (Eds.): *Kant's Idea for a Universal History with a Cosmopolitan Aim. A Critical Guide*. Cambridge: Cambridge University Press, pp. 112–128.

Wood, Allen (2015): 'Kant on Friendship'. In: Sensen, Oliver/Bacin, Stefano (Eds.): *Kant's Ethics in Context*. Cambridge: Cambridge University Press (forthcoming).

Index of Persons

van Ackeren, Marcel   132
Allison, Henry   25 f.
Aquinas, St. Thomas   3, 9
Aristotle   3, 9, 32
Vanden Auweele, Dennis   4, 85, 99
Axinn, Sidney   84, 91 f.

Baron, Marcia   4, 51, 58, 62, 110, 121, 134 f., 141, 145, 147, 163
Baxley, Anne Margaret   16, 66
Beck, Lewis White   53

Cassirer, Ernst   13
Cohen, Alix   31, 80

Denis, Lara   8, 16, 25, 31–33, 59, 82 f., 145, 150, 156
DiCenso, James   22, 26 f., 91
Diotima   10, 65

Edwards, Jeffrey   18
Empedocles   3, 169
Engstrom, Stephen   18, 41, 43

Fahmy, Melissa   4, 110, 130, 132–135, 137–140
Filippaki, Eleni   145, 154
Frierson, Patrick   24, 61 f.
Fromm, Erich   5

Goethe, Johann   58
Goy, Ina   84 f., 87, 104, 110
Green, Ronald   143
Grenberg, Jeanine   5, 12, 112
Guyer, Paul   27, 124, 128

Herman, Barbara   58, 72, 75
Hill, Thomas   18
Horn, Christoph   110, 141 f.
Hull, Isabel   58
Hume, David   121
Hutcheson, Francis   3, 9, 18, 121

Van Impe, Stijn   145, 153, 158, 160–162

Jesus   3, 84, 89, 96, 115 f., 118, 120, 128, 142 f.
Johnson, Robert   133

Kain, Patrick   38
Kneller, Jane   75 f.
Kong, Camilla   40
Korsgaard, Christine   25, 40, 59, 72, 75, 82, 148, 152, 156

Langton, Rae   25, 58, 61, 69, 72, 82 f., 99, 148, 165
de Levie, Dagobert   125
Lewis, C.S.   5

Marcucci, Silvestro   145, 153, 158–160, 162
Marwah, Inder   58, 80 f.
Michalson, Gordon   26 f.
Mikkola, Mari   58, 74–77
Miller, Robert   4
Moors, Martin   5, 12, 84 f., 103, 107, 126
Moran, Kate   43, 145 f., 153, 162, 165

Nagl-Docekal, Herta   58

O'Regan, Cyril   98

Palmquist, Stephen   22, 26, 84, 91 f., 98
Pasternack, Lawrence   22, 26
Paton, Herbert   18, 25, 37, 145
Paytas, Tyler   139
Petschauer, Peter   62
Plato   3, 10 f., 23, 65, 170
Powell, Samuel   98

Rauscher, Frederick   75
Reardon, Bernard   84, 91 f.
Reath, Andrews   18, 43
Rousseau, Jean-Jacques   22 f., 30, 112
Russell, Bertrand   106

Schleiermacher, Friedrich   58
Schneewind, J.B.   22, 31, 112
Schott, Robin   58

Index of Persons

Schröder, Hannelore 58, 62, 71, 74, 76, 81
Schönecker, Dieter 4f., 12f., 52, 106, 110, 124f., 127–129, 142f., 154
Shell, Susan 26
Šimfa, Elvira 18
Singer, Irving 73
Smit, Houston 16, 31f., 135f.
Soble, Alan 25, 59
Socrates 10, 23
Stevenson, Leslie 99
Sticker, Martin 81, 132, 136
Streich, Detlev 5, 11, 142
Sussman, David 167

von Tevenar, Gudrun 135
Timmermann, Jens 25, 36f., 39f., 48, 51, 81, 86f., 92, 94, 104, 113, 116–118, 132, 134, 137–139, 174
Timmons, Mark 16, 31f., 135f.
Tomasi, Gabriele 16, 57, 66

La Vopa, Anthony 71, 75f.

Wike, Victoria 147
Wood, Allen 18, 22, 25–27, 31, 39, 49, 58, 64, 69, 71, 84, 104, 117–119, 137f., 145f., 152f., 155–157, 161, 165, 174

Subject Index

affects 60, 157
agape 115
amor benevolentiae 9, 12, 127, 131
amor complacentiae 9, 12, 107
amour de soi-même 23
amour propre 23, 30
animality 8, 10, 21, 24, 26, 28f., 33, 172
– animal nature 25, 31, 33, 48f.
appetite 69, 71
approximation 6, 14, 20, 53–55, 78
arrogance (see also self-conceit) 46–48, 55
ascent model of love 10f., 13, 15, 19, 21, 165, 168, 172
aspects of love 1, 6, 9f., 13, 15, 105, 149, 168, 170, 182
attraction and repulsion 154
autonomy 40, 42, 76, 87, 149, 167

beautiful and the sublime (see also love of beauty) 61f., 65
beneficence
– and benevolence 131
– delight taken in 114
– from duty 114, 117, 128
– from inclination 63
– will produce love 127
benevolence (see also maxim)
– active 132, 138, 140
– and beneficence 131–133
– divine 103
– from inclination 113f.
– in wishes 12, 131
– practical 132
– rational 15, 51, 64, 68, 73f., 89, 132, 138, 141, 155, 158, 162, 168, 181
– sympathetic 119f.
– towards oneself (see also self-benevolence) 42
– towards others 52, 56
– universal 132

change of heart 50, 98f.
Christianity 3, 84, 86, 122, 125f., 168

commandment 12, 88–90, 94, 101, 103, 108, 110, 115f., 118, 120, 126–128, 132, 142
– to love 84, 87–90, 104, 115, 120, 126
compassion 116f., 139
concubinage 74f.
cultivation 8, 10, 15, 51, 79f., 88, 108, 110–112, 119, 121, 124, 131–136, 138–141, 143f., 147, 164f.

delight (see love of delight)
– intellectual 11, 15, 114, 151, 181
– moral 15, 47, 53f., 96f., 99f., 103f., 109
– pathological 149, 181f.
– sensuous 114f., 151
desire 17, 20f., 23–26, 30, 32f., 36, 50, 55, 63f., 68–70, 72, 79, 132, 152, 167, 172
– faculty of 23f., 32, 40
– sexual 22, 25, 60, 63f., 67, 69, 71–73
determining ground of the will 38–40, 43, 49–51, 119
discipline 29
dominance 31, 76, 82
drive (see also impulse; instinct) 21–23, 30–32
– sexual 22, 62, 70
– social 22, 70
duties (see duty of love)
– as divine commands 86f., 90, 103
– to God 88
– to others 113, 130, 168
duty of love 12, 16, 46, 85, 103, 122, 126, 130f., 134, 136, 150, 154–156, 159, 161
– duties of love 12, 52, 110, 130, 133f.

emulation 31, 33
equality 32f., 57f., 75f., 147, 150, 153, 155, 160, 164f.
eros 3, 10, 22, 172

fear 36, 79, 93, 108
feeling
– finer 61, 80f.
– moral 48, 124f., 135, 141f.

– natural 8, 133, 140, 143
– of love 2f., 8, 11, 63, 110f., 116, 118–120, 128–130, 134, 141–143, 145, 154–158, 160, 181f.
– of sympathy (see also sympathy) 61
– sexual 60
feminism 58
friend of human beings 12, 15, 160, 162–166
friendship
– aesthetic 157
– cosmopolitan 10f., 162, 165, 169
– idea of 147f., 150
– moral 145, 153, 157–160
– of disposition 148, 153, 157
– of need 147, 149, 157
– of taste 147, 157
– pragmatic 157
– universal 163

general division of love (see love of benevolence; love of delight) 1, 6–10, 13–16
genuine love (see also true love) 69f., 83
gladness 87, 89f., 95, 107f., 121
God (see love of God; Christianity; trinity)
– attributes of 97, 100
– concept of 106
– idea of 85, 99f., 107, 109, 168, 171
godliness 92f.
good
– approximation to the highest 20, 54
– highest 3, 10f., 14f., 20, 27, 29, 48, 52–56, 81, 86f., 99, 102, 106f., 109, 121f., 146, 162, 165, 167f., 170–172
– moral 26–29, 66, 77, 79, 90
– physical 10, 28f., 77f., 169
good will 7, 116f., 121
grace 85, 99
gratification (see also satisfaction) 24, 60, 116, 138
gratitude 15f., 130, 133–137, 139, 144, 160

happiness 5, 18–20, 35–41, 43f., 48f., 51–56, 59f., 62f., 74, 77f., 81, 83, 95, 100f., 103, 106, 115–117, 122, 131, 137, 147, 152, 162, 165–168, 172
– analogue of 53

– morally deserved 1, 10, 20, 27, 29, 55, 87
– my own 51
– of others 12, 18, 51, 53, 55, 60, 95, 114, 117, 132f., 150, 163
– of women 81f.
– perfect 54, 122, 167
homosexuality 59
humanitas aesthetica 138, 141, 151
humanitas practica 138–140, 151
humanity 10, 12, 15, 19, 21, 23, 26, 29, 31, 45, 49, 52, 72f., 80f., 95–97, 99, 115, 118, 129, 137, 141, 146, 149–153, 162f., 165, 168, 181
– love of 163
– of the other 72f., 152, 161
– sexual end of 73
husband 59, 74–76, 79, 81f., 150, 161

ideal 15, 27, 29, 64, 84, 86, 90, 92–95, 121, 146f., 149–152, 154, 157, 162, 165, 168, 171f., 182
– highest 1, 172
– moral 16, 99
– of friendship 149, 156f.
– rational 90, 97, 172
– regulative 10, 14, 78, 87, 92, 97, 147
– unattainable 84, 90
immortality 54
imperative 37, 108
– categorical 25, 37, 71, 118
– hypothetical 37, 41
impulse 7, 10, 13f., 16, 19, 21–24, 28–30, 32f., 45, 55, 57–61, 64f., 68, 70, 72f., 77, 88f., 94, 116, 165, 169, 172, 181
– impulses of human nature 1, 9, 14, 19, 21, 29, 33, 55
– sexual 25, 57, 59–73, 77, 154
incentive 18, 25, 41, 44, 49, 51, 54, 87, 89, 100, 119f., 136
inclination 8f., 12, 15, 30–33, 35f., 39–42, 44–47, 49–60, 63, 67, 72, 79, 88–90, 93–95, 114–118, 120f., 123, 128, 133, 141, 143, 149, 151f., 154, 156f., 163f., 181f.
– benevolent (see benevolence, from inclination) 51, 115
– contra-moral 11, 14, 18, 95, 121

Subject Index — 187

– inclination-based love   7f., 88–90, 114, 118, 141, 143, 151, 156
– sexual   51, 57, 60, 62, 68–74, 83, 114, 151
– to beneficence; to benefit others   95, 127f., 181
instinct   10, 24f., 36, 57f., 64, 68, 72, 83, 112, 118
interest   6, 36, 61, 66f., 76, 116f., 163f.

kindness   101–103, 113f., 135, 168

liking   7, 17, 50, 63, 65, 88, 91, 93f., 108, 119, 151
love and respect   46, 82, 133, 140, 145f., 153f., 158, 160–162, 165
love as desire   9, 23, 172
love for the law (see also love for the moral law)   12, 16, 49–51, 85–87, 89–96, 98, 121f., 168, 172, 181
love for the moral law (see also love for the law)   11f., 84f., 88, 90, 108
love of beauty (see also taste for beauty)   6, 10, 12–16, 57–62, 64–68, 81, 181
love of benevolence (see benevolence)
– active   112f., 118
– God's   9, 15, 96, 101, 104, 108
– moral   14, 57, 115, 156f., 182
– rational   43f., 73, 143, 151, 156, 158
– wishful   112
love of delight (see delight)
– God's   15, 99f., 104
– in oneself   46, 48, 55
– intellectual   74, 114, 124, 143, 149, 151f., 158, 161, 182
– moral   44, 47, 49, 53, 108, 152, 154
– pathological   7, 89, 123, 129, 164
love of God (see also love for the law; love of benevolence, God's; love of delight, God's)
– actuality of love for God   93–95, 108
– ascent model of love of God   14, 86, 104f., 109
– God is love   84, 91f., 96–98, 100f., 103
– God's perfect love   100
– perfect love for God   93, 95
– scale of love for God   93, 95
– two-directionality of love of God   103

love of honour   16, 19, 31–33, 181
– true   33, 181
love of human beings   16, 73, 118f., 125f., 136
– system of   112
love of life   9, 12, 14, 19, 22, 28f., 36, 55, 70, 73, 78, 181
– and sexual love   13, 28f., 70, 78
love of neighbour (see feeling of love; love of benevolence; love of delight; practical love)
– feeling-action-cultivation account of   15, 111, 124, 131, 141–144
– taxonomy of   142–144
love of science   170, 172
love of truth   17
love of wisdom   169–172

marital love (see also sexual love, broad)   81f.
marriage (see also husband; marital love; wife)   14, 57–59, 63, 68, 71, 74–76, 82f., 150, 161
– and friendship   82, 150
– morganatic   74f.
– right   58, 68, 71, 75
maxim   24, 33, 35, 40f., 43–46, 50–52, 55, 91, 94, 107f., 118f., 130–132, 150, 157, 167, 181
– moral   119
– of benevolence   126, 130
– of one's own happiness (see also self-love, maxim of)   35, 38, 51f., 91, 108
– of practical love   52
mechanism   23, 72
merit   32, 47f., 55, 84, 98
morality   3, 8, 18, 20f., 27, 31–33, 35–37, 44, 47, 49, 52, 57f., 61, 65, 68, 79f., 83, 86–90, 95, 98, 103, 106f., 119, 121–125, 128, 133, 142, 147f., 167, 181f.
– end of   20, 123, 152
– ground of   95, 121–123, 137
– leads to religion   14, 99
– principle of   39, 121
– pure   36
moral law (see love for the moral law; respect for the moral law)

moral love   32f., 57, 59, 63, 66, 68, 71, 74, 77, 102f., 154, 161
motivation   36, 40, 87f.
mutual love (see also reciprocal love)   87, 147f., 150, 152–155, 160f., 164f.

objectification (see also sexual object)   58, 61

parental love   16f.
passion   12, 60f.
pathological love   89, 111, 117f., 120, 122f., 158, 167
– and practical love   110, 117, 120, 123, 129, 143
perfection   10, 15, 83, 86, 90, 94, 96, 99, 114, 130, 133, 141, 151f., 154, 181
– moral   6, 19, 49, 52, 90, 97, 99, 107, 121f., 129, 152, 157, 164, 181
– one's own   133
– physical   149, 151, 181
personality   21, 26, 75
personhood   25, 72, 74–76, 162
philanthropist   116, 118f.
philautia   42, 46f.
philosophy (see love of wisdom)
– moral philosophy (see philosophy, practical)   2, 8, 13, 18f., 24f., 32–34, 51, 58, 74, 88, 101, 110, 125, 133, 141f., 161, 171
– of history   29f., 33, 58, 66, 68, 78
– practical (see philosophy, moral)   1, 171, 173f.
– theoretical   13, 171
pleasure   2, 6–8, 24, 27, 29, 38–41, 43, 47f., 54f., 60, 63, 65f., 70, 73, 96f., 113f., 127–130, 138, 141, 147, 151f., 156, 160, 181
– displeasure   24, 39, 48, 138
– intellectual   153, 162
– moral   47f.
– sensible   71, 74, 77, 95
– sexual   60
polygamy   74f.
postulate   29, 54, 102, 106
practical love (see benevolence, active; love of benevolence, active; maxim, of practical love)

– of benevolence   7, 54, 59, 74, 120, 127, 142, 155f.
predisposition   11f., 15, 21–23, 26f., 29–31, 45, 57, 66, 70, 77, 110, 124f., 127, 129, 158, 181
– aesthetic   119, 124f., 127–129, 143, 154, 156, 158, 161
– natural   26f., 31, 48, 110, 124, 126, 141, 149, 154
– of humanity   30
– original   21f., 26f.
– to animality   26
– to the good   19, 21f., 26f., 33, 55, 59
principle   18, 24, 29, 35–39, 44f., 52f., 55, 60f., 79–81, 83, 87, 89, 91, 96, 101, 113f., 117f., 125, 148, 154f., 159, 164
– moral   139–141, 150
– objective   18, 37
– of love   125, 140, 155f.
– practical   19, 31, 37, 39, 42, 45, 116
progress   12, 19, 28f., 65, 78f., 93–95, 113, 119, 162, 165, 168
– cultural   78
– moral   11, 20, 28f., 33, 50, 54f., 59, 77, 79, 81, 95, 104, 150, 162
prudence   8, 20, 38, 43, 51
purpose (see also purposiveness)   27, 29, 36–38, 59, 62, 66f., 72, 79f., 99–101, 106, 109, 167
purposiveness (see also purpose)   66f.

quasi-induction   6, 17

rationality   7, 14, 19, 26, 38, 42, 44, 55
– instrumental   44
rational love (see also self-love, rational)   8, 35, 44f.
reason, pure practical   2f., 8, 23, 26, 33, 40f., 50, 68, 89, 119, 141, 170
reciprocal love (see also mutual love)   150, 152f., 160
reciprocity (see also mutual love; reciprocal love)   59, 82, 139, 164f.
respect for the moral law   3, 8, 16, 18, 32, 36, 45, 47, 53, 87, 90, 95, 108, 135, 140, 149
reward   47, 87, 121

satisfaction (see also gratification)   7, 24, 35 f., 40 f., 45, 53, 60 f., 63 f., 71, 73, 108, 116, 131 f., 147, 152
self-benevolence   20, 41, 52, 126
self-conceit (see also arrogance)   18 f., 31 f., 34, 36, 39, 41–43, 45–49, 55
self-contentment   8, 45, 48, 53, 55
– moral   20, 48, 56
self-esteem   47 f.
self-estimation   47
self-love (see self-benevolence; self-conceit; self-contentment)
– made an unconditional law   46, 48
– maxim of   35, 38, 52, 91, 108
– of humanity   19, 26, 30 f., 33, 35, 55
– persistence of   14, 20, 55 f.
– rational   19, 35, 41, 43–45
self-preservation   9 f., 12, 14, 19 f., 22 f., 28 f., 36, 55, 70, 73, 78
sexuality   5, 9, 19 f., 22 f., 25, 54, 57–61, 64–68, 73, 77, 79, 83
sexual love (see also love of life, and sexual love)
– and friendship   69, 82
– broad   14, 57–59, 68 f., 71, 74, 77, 81–83, 181
– narrow   14, 57, 61, 68–71, 77, 79, 82, 181
sexual object (see also objectification)   63 f.
sexual organs   74
sociality   14, 19, 22, 29 f., 33, 54 f., 165, 181
– animal   31, 33

solipsism   25, 46, 58, 61, 82
striving   8–10, 15, 18, 30, 50–52, 78, 83, 87, 90, 92, 96, 98–100, 102, 104, 108, 121 f., 133, 166, 168, 172, 181
sympathetic participation (see sympathy)   61, 130, 133 f., 136, 139–141, 159
sympathy (see sympathetic participation)   15, 39, 48, 116 f., 134, 137, 139–141, 144, 164

taste for beauty (see also love of beauty)   65
teleology   13, 29, 33, 55, 57 f., 67 f., 77, 80 f.
– natural   79
– sexual   59, 79–81
tenderheartedness   61
trinity   96, 98
true love (see also genuine love)   26, 33, 161, 167

universal love (see also benevolence, universal)   17, 126
unsociable sociability   30–32

well-being   6, 10, 27, 30, 35, 37 f., 43, 66, 102 f., 115, 131 f., 150, 152 f., 163 f.
wife   63, 74–76, 79, 81 f., 150, 161
wisdom (see also love of wisdom; philosophy)   79, 97, 171 f.
– doctrine of   170 f.
worth   19, 30, 33, 36, 50 f., 63, 80, 116–119

www.ingramcontent.com/pod-product-compliance
Lightning Source LLC
Chambersburg PA
CBHW031432150426
43191CB00006B/479